Praise for

Our Moment of Choice

"*Our Moment of Choice* has come at the perfect time, a testament to the great work that all the Evolutionary Leaders are doing in the world. We are primed for an evolutionary leap. This book will definitely inspire you!"

—Jack Canfield, coauthor of the #1 *New York Times* bestselling series *Chicken Soup for the Soul*

"*Our Moment of Choice* is a soul-restorative salve of compassionate healing wisdom for our world, and a most timely and stirring visionary contribution to the Great Work. This lived understanding—our human capacity to cooperatively galvanize consciousness in service of beneficent species-wide planetary evolution, infuses each of the thirty-seven stellar chapters comprising this remarkable book. I gratefully anticipate the depth of visionary wisdom, cutting-edge scientific discovery, socially progressive economic and educational direction, and regenerative environmental and climate-change strategies, so brilliantly expressed by the authors and editors of *Our Moment of Choice*, shall be enthusiastically welcomed as a life-beautifying gift of Gaian medicine for our seven generations, and beyond."

—Oscar Miro-Quesada, founder of The Heart of the Healer

"This innovative and revolutionary message of hope and wisdom from many of the greatest visionaries and evolutionary leaders of our times is creating a global movement that will lead us to growth and transformation as we usher in a new Earth. I highly recommend this book."

—Anita Moorjani, *New York Times* bestselling author of
Dying to Be Me and *What if This Is Heaven*

"Important medicine for a time of rapid change!"

—Stephen Dinan, CEO of The Shift Network

"Our Moment of Choice is a magnificent affirmation of choice, care, and compassion. It is a song of love."

—Gary Zukav, author of *The Seat of the Soul*
and *The Dancing Wu Li Masters*

"This is a book writ large—a beautiful, symphonic composition from different eminent authors who discern the confluence of the great evolutionary flow of human consciousness that is ushering us into the higher realms of global transformation. A moving, astounding work that expresses the underlying unity that exists in the pluralistic and diverse external world and lovingly, thoughtfully guides us into transcendence. The multi-perspectival approaches expressed consistently point to the truth of our wholeness that will lead us to a planetary wholesomeness built on the foundation of love, compassion, and selfless service to humanity. A revelatory map that charts the course to our collective awakening."

—Audrey Kitagawa, chair of the Parliament of the World's Religions

"Thanks to the evolutionary leaders, forty-three brilliant minds who share their views of humanity's greatest challenges, their personal visions of the future, and their solutions to unlock and enlighten our multidimensional global crisis. In an alignment of consciousness, these wise elders articulate a worldview for the sur-THRIVAL of a planetary civilization."

—Alex Grey and Allyson Grey, visionary artists,
cofounders of CoSM, Chapel of Sacred Mirrors

"In *Our Moment of Choice*, a remarkable community of wisdom teachers share their profound reflections, and call each of us to a journey of discovery. Each chapter invites us to awaken the potential within to make the choices that will nurture wholeness and connectedness in self, other, and world. Together these authors are midwives of a movement for an expanded human consciousness, ancient and new, offering hope and pathways to renewed life at a time of human and planetary reckoning."

—The Reverend Victor H. Kazanjian Jr., executive director,
United Religions Initiative

"Our entire species, including your soul and mine, is about to make a decision that will be its most important ever. We are about to answer the question, *who am I, and who do I choose to be?* This is not just about the improvement of life on Earth, but the evolution of the spirit as well. The words in this remarkable book, from these remarkable people, can make a remarkable difference in your life and on the planet, that you bequeath with love to those who have trusted you to do your best to help make things better. Thank you for deeply considering them. Time is of the essence."

—Neale Donald Walsch, *New York Times* bestselling author
of nine books on spirituality, including *Conversations with God*

Our Moment of Choice

EVOLUTIONARY VISIONS AND HOPE FOR THE FUTURE

Edited by Robert Atkinson, Kurt Johnson, and Deborah Moldow

ATRIA PAPERBACK
New York London Toronto Sydney New Delhi

BEYOND WORDS
Portland, Oregon

ATRIA PAPERBACK
An Imprint of Simon & Schuster, Inc.
1230 Avenue of the Americas
New York, NY 10020

BEYOND WORDS
1750 S.W. Skyline Blvd., Suite 20
Portland, OR 97221-2543
503-531-8700 / 503-531-8773 fax
www.beyondword.com

Managing Editor: Lindsay S. Easterbrooks-Brown
Copyeditor: Jenefer Angell
Proofreader: Kristin Thiel
Design: Sara Blum
Composition: William H. Brunson Typography Services
First Beyond Words/Atria paperback edition May 2022

ATRIA PAPERBACK and colophon are trademarks of Simon & Schuster, Inc.
BEYOND WORDS PUBLISHING and colophon are registered trademarks of Beyond Words Publishing. Beyond Words is an imprint of Simon & Schuster, Inc.

For information about special discounts for bulk purchases, please contact Simon & Schuster Special Sales at 1-866-506-1949 or business@simonandschuster.com.

The Simon & Schuster Speakers Bureau can bring authors to your live event. For more information or to book an event, contact Simon & Schuster Speakers Bureau at 1-866-248-3049 or visit our website at www.simonspeakers.com.

Manufactured in the United States of America

10   9   8   7   6   5   4   3   2   1

The Library of Congress has cataloged the hardcover edition as follows:

Names: Atkinson, Robert, editor. | Johnson, Kurt, editor. | Moldow, Deborah, editor.
Title: Our moment of choice : conscious evolution and hope for the future /
    edited by Robert Atkinson, Kurt Johnson, and Deborah Moldow.
Description: New York : Atria Books [2020] | Includes bibliographical references. |
    Summary: "This timely and compelling anthology is a rousing call to action for all of us
    to help transform the world into a just, peaceful, and thriving one—featuring creative and
    practical solutions to the many crises facing humanity today. Featuring entries by forty-three
    cutting-edge thinkers, such as Deepak Chopra™, Lynne McTaggart, and more."
    —Provided by publisher
Identifiers: LCCN 2020014011 (print) | LCCN 2020014012 (ebook) | ISBN
    9781582707624 (hardcover) | ISBN 9781982154233 (ebook)
Subjects: LCSH: Humanity. | Social evolution.
Classification: LCC BJ1533.H9 O97 2020 (print) | LCC BJ1533.H9 (ebook) |
    DDC 170/.44—dc23
LC record available at https://lccn.loc.gov/2020014011
LC ebook record available at https://lccn.loc.gov/2020014012

ISBN 9781582708638 (pbk)

The corporate mission of Beyond Words Publishing, Inc.: *Inspire to Integrity*

Our deepest gratitude to all of those at the leading edge of the evolution of human consciousness and in loving appreciation for all beings on planet Earth.

Contents

Circle One
Bridge-Building

*Together, we can build a global community
and create a culture of peace.*

Circle Two
Restoring Ecological Balance

We regard the universe as alive and conscious;
we are planetary stewards.

Circle Three
Conscious Enterprise and Social Change

We are ethical stewards of the earth's economic
and communications integrity.

Circle Four
Healing Ourselves and the Planet

*Working with the mind-body-spirit connection,
we can heal the whole system.*

Circle Five
Integrating Science and Spirituality

*We utilize research and education to awaken, elevate,
and evolve consciousness.*

Circle Six
New Frontiers Beyond Space and Time

*From outer space to inner space, we view the cosmos
as a fully integrated whole.*

Circle Seven
The Big Picture

*We envision the whole to support sustainability,
prosperity, and global transformation.*

Preface

EVOLUTIONARY VISIONS AT THE
DAWN OF A NEW ERA

Reverend Deborah Moldow and Diane Marie Williams

O ur moment of choice is at hand. There has never been a more urgent moment than today for humankind to come together and prepare for the task ahead by taking on a new kind of evolutionary leadership grounded in the principle of synergy.

This book is about hope. It's about action. It's about innovation. It's about a synergistic convergence of the worldwide network of interconnected humanity ushering in the next level of human consciousness.

The future is fast approaching. Yet despite images of fast-flowing melting glaciers and cataclysmic natural disasters on our screens and the politics of division tearing at our collective soul, we are in the midst of the greatest evolutionary leap in consciousness in human history.

The Source of Synergy Foundation supports the release of synergistic energy that exponentially expands and creates global ripples in planetary consciousness. When individuals, organizations, communities, and nations unite in a shared sense of responsibility for the common good, their collective efforts have a far greater effect on the whole. The Evolutionary Leaders Circle emerged from such synergistic momentum.

The Source of Synergy Foundation teamed up with Deepak Chopra™ and the Chopra Foundation in 2006 to unite visionary authors, educators, and social activists who are forging a conscious evolutionary movement for global transformation. In 2008, the Source of Synergy Foundation and the Chopra Foundation joined with the Association for Global New Thought in California to convene thirty-five evolutionary leaders who put forth "A Call to Conscious Evolution" that asks the question: *What can we do together to accelerate the shift in consciousness?* The Call, which has received support from close to fifty thousand members of the evolutionary community, continues to unify those who are inspiring, supporting, and serving humanity's conscious evolution. (You are warmly invited to sign the call at evolutionaryleaders.net/acallto consciousevolution.)

Today, the Evolutionary Leaders Circle is comprised of 186 individuals united by a shared commitment to strategically engage their collective field of potential and synergize with the evolutionary community around the globe, to reverse the current course we are on, and to support a shift to our next level of collective evolution. All the contributors to this book are members of this Evolutionary Leaders Circle, who have donated their chapters to cocreate a synergistic whole greater than the sum of its parts.

Our intention with this unique book, *Our Moment of Choice: Evolutionary Visions and Hope for the Future*, is to offer tools, insights, and inspiration that will support us as we each respond in our own way to the powerful call of our time. We believe that the evolution of consciousness happens when we make a commitment to lead our lives consciously, intentionally unleashing our greatest potential. We make this choice from moment to moment to drive evolution forward for the benefit of the whole.

The book's seven areas explore where we are heading as we evolve toward a society dedicated to the collective good. Each section demonstrates the power of synergy as a key to building a coherent field and accelerating an evolutionary leap in consciousness.

You are reading this book because you are part of this evolutionary community leading the conscious evolutionary movement for global transformation. You are an integral part of the collective field of love and healing that will generate a heart-centered future based on co-creation, caring, compassion, appreciation, and cooperation.

We hope that this book will serve the evolutionary process by creating waves of momentum to help our fullest evolutionary potential transform today's challenges—and to help us to fully live in a whole new operating frequency that will show us the way forward to flourish on our beautiful Earth.

Let us dive into the new paradigm by activating the greatest vision of who we can become and what we can do together. The choice is ours.

For more information, please visit sourceofsynergyfoundation.org, evolutionaryleaders.net, and ourmomentofchoice.com or contact info@sourceofsynergyfoundation.org.

Introduction

THE NEW HUMAN STORY: THE POWER TO THRIVE IN OUR TIME OF EXTREMES

Gregg Braden

A single question lurks at the very core of our existence: It's the unspoken question lying beneath every choice we'll ever make; it lives within every challenge that will ever test us, and it's the foundation for every decision we'll ever face. The question at the root of all questions—one asked countless times by countless individuals during our estimated two hundred thousand or so years on Earth—is simply, *Who are we?*

Our Story Matters

While the question itself is simple and brief, the story we tell ourselves about ourselves has implications that we simply cannot escape. It tears directly into the heart of each moment of our lives. Our story—what we believe about our past, our origin, our destiny, and our potential—defines the way we see ourselves, other people, and the choices we make. It determines who we invite into our lives as friends, partners and life-mates, what careers we choose, and how we heal our bodies. The implications of our story are woven into the very fabric of our society. They show up in everything from how we choose to nourish our bodies, to the way we care for ourselves, our children, and our aging parents.

The implications of our story go even deeper. They inform the thinking at the foundation of civilization itself. Our story influences how we share the vital resources of food, water, medicine, and the basic necessities of life. It determines why, when, and how we go to war, as well as when we choose to accept peace. What we believe about ourselves even justifies our thinking for when we save a human life and when we choose to end one.

In what may be the greatest irony of our existence—at the dawn of the twenty-first century, following more than five thousand years of recorded history—we have still not clearly answered this most basic question about ourselves. And while at any time discovering the truth of our existence would be worth the needed energy and resources, faced with the greatest crises of life and survival in our species' memory, it's especially critical.

Navigating a Time of Extremes

We're living in a time of extremes—*extreme* shifts in the world and *extreme* changes in our lives. To be clear, the extremes I'm talking about aren't all bad: extreme shifts in technology and the internet, for example, now provide the broadest levels of human connection and information sharing in recorded history. It's the extremes in unsustainable thinking and living that are the problems. The best minds of our time acknowledge that when it comes to factors such as climate, energy, poverty, and environment, if unchecked, our current trajectory of unsustainable practices places us on multiple collision courses that threaten local communities, global society, and ultimately, civilization itself.

In *Our Moment of Choice*, we explore the reasons for the extremes and how to embrace them in a healthy way. Their emergence presents a rare window of opportunity—*our moment of choice*. Will we choose to replace today's broken and failed systems with the sustainable technologies and practices of healing, peace, and cooperation that are at our doorstep? Or will we ignore our window? Will we choose to cling to the familiar habits of ego, money, power, and competition that keep us locked in the turmoil polarizing our world today? Our success hinges upon us and the way we respond to two key factors—our willingness to (1) acknowledge the extremes and (2) embrace new ways of thinking and living that reflect the uniqueness of our time.

Although we face many unknown factors in our moment of choice, one thing we can know with absolute certainty: our lives are changing in ways that we haven't been prepared for, and it's happening at a speed that we've never known.

Creating the World We Know Is Possible

We're being asked to embrace new discoveries revealing who we are— the new human story—and through that new story to radically, and quickly, shift the thinking of the past when it comes to us and our relationship to the world.

I'm an optimist by nature. I see real reasons for optimism in our lives. At the same time, I'm also a realist. I am under no illusion when it comes to the effort—the work—that it takes to make such a shift. In his 1923 classic book *The Prophet*, philosopher and writer Kahlil Gibran described work as love made visible. This perspective reminds us that the tremendous effort required to thrive and transcend our time of extremes is the visible expression of our love for ourselves, one another, and the world. The world that we leave for our children, and theirs, will be our legacy to our love made visible.

Fortunately for us, we already have the solutions to the big problems of the world—the physical ones, that is. The scientific principles are already understood. The technology is already available. They exist right here, right now, at our fingertips. What stands between us and the world we know is possible—where clean, abundant, and sustainable energy is accessible to every member of our global family; where live, healthy food and clean water is plentiful and accessible to every mouth on the planet; where every human is able to obtain the basic necessities of life and the support to live a healthy and meaningful life—is something that we can't build, touch, or measure. The elusive link that's missing in the equation that brings this world to life is the *thinking* that makes room in our world for what already exists in our minds.

Are we willing to embrace the vision that makes such possibilities a priority? Will we allow the discoveries that reveal the deepest truths of our relationships to ourselves, one another, and the earth to become the passport to the emerging world? Will we embrace the work it takes to expand our thinking—our love made visible for ourselves and our planet? This is where *Our Moment of Choice: Evolutionary Visions and Hope for the Future* comes in.

While there is certainly no shortage of books that identify the extraordinary conditions of change we face today, they typically fall short of addressing the single element at the heart of how we deal with the conditions. How can we possibly know what technology to choose, what policies to enact, what laws to pass, or how to build sustainable economies, share life-saving technologies, and bridge the issues tearing the fabric of our relationships and society, until we've answered that most fundamental question of our existence: *who are we?* As individuals, as families, as nations, and as a civilization, this most basic understanding becomes the cornerstone for the priorities in our choices and policies.

Without the answer to this question, making life-altering decisions is like trying to get into a house without knowing where the door is. While it's possible to break in through a window or knock down a wall, we'd damage the home in the process. And maybe this is a perfect metaphor for the quandary we find ourselves in. For our human family—which has more than quadrupled in a little over a century, from 1.6 billion in 1900 to about 7.7 billion in 2019—can use the key of understanding who we are to move through the door of successful solutions, or we can continue to respond to crises with the knee-jerk reactions and false assumptions based in incomplete, or obsolete, science until we damage our home, both Earth and ourselves.

This book identifies seven areas of discovery that will radically change the way we've been led to think about our world and ourselves, as we open new horizons of hope and possibility. In the pages that follow, you will discover the keys to

- building a global community as a culture of peace,

- revisioning the universe as alive, conscious, and intelligent,

- renewing an ethic of deep integrity in conscious business, media, and entrepreneurship,

- healing the whole body as a way of living, rather than as a response to illness,

- awakening the power of a spiritually based science,

- understanding new scientific discoveries that reveal the cosmos as a deeply connected and fully integrated system, and

- knowing sustainable living and prosperity as a foundation for global transformation.

Taking a Personal Journey

Our Moment of Choice is written with one purpose in mind: to empower us with an honest, truthful, and factual understanding of our relationship with the earth, one another, and perhaps most importantly, ourselves. In doing so, we develop new insights and discover new answers to the ancient and timeless question: *who are we?*

The key to our moment of choice is simply this: the better we answer this question, the better we know ourselves and the less we fear change in the world. In the absence of fear, we are better equipped to make conscious and informed choices.

I invite you to take the discoveries in these pages and explore what they mean to you. Talk them over with the people in your life; discover if, and how, they change your story and the story that is shared in your family. New discoveries regarding our origin, our past, and the most deeply held ideas about our existence give us reasons to rethink the traditional beliefs that define our lives. When we do, the solutions to life's challenges become clear and the choices become obvious. This book is dedicated to revealing the discoveries that have yet to show up in our textbooks and classrooms; they hold the key to awakening our new human story.

Circle One
Bridge-Building

*Together, we can build a global community and
create a culture of peace.*

1

The Great Map of Peace

James O'Dea

Peace may seem an elusive concept in a world with horrific violence, brutal conflict, and exploitation, yet never in humanity's history has such a comprehensive map of peace emerged as is now evident to individuals, communities, activists, spiritual practitioners, educators, health professionals, researchers, and academics alike.

What we call a culture of peace comes from a whole-systems perspective, which sees all things as interconnected and influencing each other. We can map whole societal shifts and transformations from ancient cycles of violent division and conflict to demonstrated strategies for conflict resolution, social healing, and reconciliation. We are increasingly aware of our interconnection and interdependence, and we act accordingly. We can embody a visionary activism as conscious evolutionaries, integrating previously separate fields of knowledge.

Accountability and the Law

A foundational building block for creating a global culture of peace is the contribution of the rule of law and its protections. In 1945, as the world

3

was recovering from a cataclysmic world war, the trials in Nuremberg laid out a pivotal new framework that defined crimes against humanity: flagrant violations of basic human rights by genocidal, ethnocentric, and totalitarian regimes. In 1948, the fledging United Nations proposed a comprehensive vision for the creation and protection of every person on planet Earth, the Universal Declaration of Human Rights, a binding legal covenant to be signed by all the world's governments. Many believed, and still do, that this sounded the call for the new global story for humanity.

Instead, this covenant was never adopted; ideological differences split it into two covenants. One, the Covenant on Civil and Political Rights, was signed by the governments of the West, while the other—the Covenant of Economic, Social and Cultural Rights—was signed by the Communist bloc and the governments of the Global South. These differences have kept most governments from fulfilling the vision contained in both.[1]

Despite this regrettable fracture, the last decades of the twentieth century saw a profound contribution to a global culture of peace with legislation, international treaties, and a new level of consensus on the rights of refugees, minorities, women, and children. Civil rights, political rights to organize and express dissent, labor rights, humane treatment in conflict zones, freedom from torture, and freedom of the press were also part of this stream of international law in which we see an evolutionary trend of greater and greater inclusivity, which now also includes support in the areas of sexual orientation, health, and environmental protections.

We also see that law as a driver of evolutionary progress and cultural transformation has its limitations. In Nuremberg, for example, we saw the issue of selective application of law—one law for the victor and another law for the vanquished. (Do not the Allied bombings of Dresden, Hiroshima, and Nagasaki also fall into the category of war crimes?) We can find many other examples of governments selectively applying human rights and peace treaties they have ratified while lacking a full commitment to their enforcement. In response, human rights movements all over the globe continue to mobilize, pressing for account-ability and transparency in violations of law.

Restoring Justice

The legal paradigm is also limited by the worldview of the accompanying punishment. Laws violated require violators to be punished and regimes to be sanctioned. The punitive worldview often includes lengthy prison sentences with little effort made to rehabilitate prisoners, leading to high recidivism. The punitive worldview does not deal with underlying narratives of trauma and wounding, which often erupt as cyclical patterns of violence and revenge, so it becomes self-perpetuating. Fortunately, the punitive worldview is not the only one we have.

A potent configuration of elements has been converging to open up worldviews that are more transformational and healing. One of those elements was a shift in psychology away from a focus on pathology to positive strategies that bring about change. As positive psychology gained momentum by the end of the twentieth century across the planet, people began to engage in democratic change. Participation became a central theme, and people's movements began to flourish. The Berlin Wall was torn down, apartheid ended, and many dictatorships were brought to an end, as the positive psychology principle of creating the change you want to see in your life was also expressed on the political stage in the notion that we not only have rights but also responsibilities to create the culture we wish to live in.

There was a blossoming of citizen activism on strengthening civil rights, confronting racism, exposing gender bias, promoting fair trade, and establishing environmental protections. A guiding vision for this call to assume responsibility for deep cultural transformation, for many NGOs (nongovernmental organizations), was expressed in *The Earth Charter*, drafted through an international consultative process in the late 1990s.

While people continue to be imprisoned and tortured and to give their lives for social justice, a sea change occurred in the fifty years from Nuremberg to the Truth and Reconciliation Commission (TRC) in South Africa in 1995. The most important change there was not just making apartheid illegal or punishing those responsible for maintaining its systemic abuses but rather demonstrating an extensive effort toward restoring justice. The goal of the TRC was to address accountability while also examining the roots of the nation's deep trauma and creating a context to help heal its wounds. The TRC's restorative approach to post-conflict justice environments moved beyond a retributive or punitive justice. It also created a benchmark in honoring not only the truth as reflected in factual narratives but the truth as reflected in traumatic experience. During the TRC process, tears were welcomed and the subjective experience was primary in the restorative approach.

While restorative justice has been gaining interest and serious attention on the global political stage, it is by no means a new approach. Restorative justice, built on victim/offender interaction and accountability, has strong roots in a variety of indigenous practices. It can be found, for example, in Bedouin, Polynesian, Native American, and several African societies. I was personally privileged to be given permission to observe a Gacaca trial in Rwanda dealing with the aftermath of the genocide there. I was so impressed with the degree of active and energetic participation by so many villagers connected to the case and their inspiring commitment to get to the whole truth and to forgive when real contrition was expressed.

Forgiveness, and its role in personal and societal healing, has seen a surge of interest in recent years. Forgiveness moves the victim beyond the trauma of violation and the trap of wound-attachment syndrome. Without forgiveness, victims are often left with unresolved resentment and even hatred. Forgiveness does not have to be unconditional; the restorative justice process highlights the benefits of reparation and atonement that reinforce the sense of genuine remorse by the perpetrator. Forgiveness offers a path of redemption for the perpetrator and a path to healing for the victim. Forgiveness work contributes to the map of peace, the connection between inner healing and outer relational repair at individual and community levels. This concept of integral mapping of the inner and outer is a key driver of evolving peace paradigms.

Practicing Peace

The accelerating contribution of two previously distinct areas—neuroscience and mindfulness practices—has also strengthened an integral approach to building a global culture of peace. Neuroscience has revealed, through neuroplasticity and other concepts, that we are designed for adaptability and fresh insight. Even long-established neural pathways that convey reactivity and prejudice can be rewired to become more open to empathy, connection, and commitment to others. This creates new opportunities that help us integrate new meaning, by softening fight-flight-freeze triggers and allowing us to relate more deeply to others.

Research on meditation and mindfulness suggests regular meditative practices, including loving-kindness meditations, significantly reduce anxiety, stress, and emotional reactivity. In addition, a variety of breathwork and heart-centering techniques help support peaceful communication, peaceful heart resonance, and compassionate listening.

New, more intentional, nonviolent communication approaches that are more skilled in diplomacy and conflict resolution are also propelling the evolution of a culture of peace. Effective heart-centered communication builds environments where people listen deeply and feel seen and heard while expressing their truth. Dialogue of this type can be profoundly healing when it allows us to experience a deep sense of unity in diversity. These skills are especially needed culture-wide—in the home, at school, at work, in our communities, and in our political discourse—as they create fields where people feel nourished and even loved despite their differences.

This heart-centered communication leads us to the door of spiritual growth where we can explore the terrain of inner peace. As we evolve in the outer world, we also ascend an inner pathway to unconditional and lasting peace. Meditation and mindfulness are one facet of creating inner peace, but as progress on the path is made, a self-reflective consciousness emerges that helps surface blind spots and conditioning. This spiritual work has a transformative effect on how we view and do peace work. More people now, especially activists, are seeing how ego, personal agendas, and the projection of unresolved issues sustain polarities and breed a sense of superiority and self-righteousness. We realize that we ourselves must be the change we seek in the world. We know we can no longer channel our own unresolved hostility, anger, and frustration in the name of peace. We know that being against is not the same as cultivating an openness to working together.

In the last decade, this integrated form of activism embodied by the great peacemakers Mahatma Gandhi and Martin Luther King Jr. has started to be known as sacred activism, mystical activism, conscious activism, evolutionary activism, and visionary activism. This type of activism calls for cultivation of wisdom and passion for engaging the whole person and the whole truth; it is deeply dialogic and informed by the integration of new science and spirituality. It expresses deep ecological and environmental awareness, mobilized by new forms of conscious organizing. It envisions the birth of a new humanity.

Our vision of a culture of peace includes the following:

- School classrooms where teachers know how to set the field of heart coherence so emotional intelligence can flourish and support optimal learning

- Whole educational systems committed to teaching and practicing nonviolent communication

- Communities where restorative justice gathers momentum

- More governments framing policies that honor multicultural values and appreciate that ecology and economy can be designed to sustain the interconnection and interdependence of all life

○ Spiritual movements taking people beyond dogmatism and competing religious claims to affirming universal oneness and infinite diversity

○ Societies healing the multiple traumas of the past and ending the intergenerational transmission of wounds

○ A new generation of mindful, compassionate, and ethically evolved political and social leaders who are integrated visionaries

○ An awakening of collective responsibility transforming gross destructive materialism into whole-Earth planetary service

○ The emergence of a cosmology of consciousness evolving and blossoming into sustainable and lasting peace

How will *you* participate in creating this evolutionary culture of peace?

Chapter 1 Spotlight

To bring the story of wholeness and peace into being, our challenge is to build bridges where there are none and strengthen those that already exist. James O'Dea says we are becoming increasingly aware of our interconnection and interdependence, and as we act accordingly, peace will be the culmination of this long and convulsive evolutionary process. Our inner and outer transformations—including many social, scientific, and spiritual advances, such as global efforts of restorative justice, personal and social healing through compassion, accountability, and forgiveness, heart-centered communication, and meditation and mindfulness—are all part of that path, where we eventually live in the understanding that we must be the change we seek in the world.

Call to Action

Each morning, take five minutes to meditate on the evolutionary process leading humanity toward a culture of peace. Then, throughout the day, make a conscious effort to bring your own inner peace outward by being kind to everyone you encounter.

2

Spirituality in the Twenty-First Century: A Quiet Revolution

Reverend Deborah Moldow

We are living in extraordinary times. Almost the moment we learned to feed ourselves abundantly, to live in relative peace and easily communicate across the planet in minutes, we have awakened to the great destruction industrialization has caused to the very Earth that sustains us. So far, we tend to approach this existential crisis through the narrow lens of our individual nationalities and cultures instead of the global family we truly are. Yet the turbulence and chaos of this crisis provide us with the fertile soil in which to plant the dream of a new human civilization blossoming into a worldwide culture of peace. And the light that will help bring it to fruition is inside each and every one of us.

Something different is emerging: a new consciousness that is our best hope for planet Earth to renew her invitation for us to inhabit the only home we know. At this level of consciousness, we see ourselves—for the first time in history—as members of one planetary family sharing one common home. At the same time, decades of interfaith engagement have led us to understand that all religions point to a truth beyond our comprehension. All express, through different languages, cultures, and eras, the need for us to be kind to one another and to tame our natural instinct to act for our own benefit in favor of acting for the greater good.

This realization is now building a sense of community based on shared values that transcend our diverse backgrounds and beliefs. Those on the leading edge of this trend are taking part in a yet-unrecognized movement that is increasingly giving meaning to people's lives and nurturing a growing appreciation of the sacredness of every person and every aspect of the world around us.

This profound spiritual emergence has the power to unify us, at long last, as one humanity. The United Nations was a major attempt to build peace among nation states, but with so many agendas often in conflict with one another, in practice it has rarely been able to act in the common interest of all stakeholders. In contrast, when we unite at the heart level and put our tribal, national, and religious identities aside in service to the whole, we will be able to surmount even the greatest challenges that face us today and threaten our tomorrows.

This quiet revolution extends an open invitation to all people to develop their individual gifts, to manifest their purpose in joyful service to something greater than us all. We are called to live into the next level of our collective evolution and create together a future beyond our imagining, where peace on Earth is only the beginning.

There are three primary factors driving the emergent global culture:

Globalization

This large term encompasses many areas of technology, travel, and communications. But ever since the first cameras penetrated untouched indigenous tribal domains, it's been clear that one day we would reach the point where the entire globe was mapped out and its populations known. This process speeded up during the twentieth century with the rise of jet planes, television, the United Nations, and, finally, the

World Wide Web. At the same time, the technologies of agriculture and commerce have spread a uniformity of production that has seriously undermined the rich biodiversity of our ecosystems and created a culture of disposability that has filled our planetary home with useless trash instead of following the cycle of life that is nature's design.

While great changes are needed to clean up vast amounts of pollution and find healthier ways to live in harmony with the earth, our common bonds around the world are strengthened through sympathy in times of natural disaster and political unrest, drawing us together in spite of the recent spike in nationalistic backlash. Our feeling of sharing one planet cannot be denied.

Climate Change

The crises set in motion by our melting glaciers and rising oceans are already being experienced as harsh weather events across the globe. Our coastlines are changing as we face increasingly powerful hurricanes, typhoons, tornadoes, fires, and floods. And although governments have consistently failed to agree to measures powerful enough to mitigate the effects, it is clear that no nation alone can successfully address what is coming.

Those of us fortunate enough to have been born in the world's richest countries are being called upon to examine the costs of our privilege and to revisit our relationship with the beautiful planet that gives us life.

Spirituality

One hundred years ago, most people practiced the religion into which they were born—and many still do, particularly in less developed areas of the world. But now that educated people everywhere have access to all sorts of religious and indigenous traditions, there is a quietly growing appreciation of value in all spiritual teachings and that all belief systems lead to universal values such as compassion, generosity, and kindness.

The secularism that developed in the West as it embraced the impressive march of science since the Renaissance has proven insufficient to address humankind's deep need for meaning in the face of the vastness of the universe or the suffering of an individual. A new kind of spirituality not tied to a particular dogma is breaking through into everyday life. People in Western countries are seeking healing and strength through practices with Eastern spiritual roots, such as yoga and tai chi. They are seeking stress relief through meditation, and transcendental meditation is even being taught in schools. People of all faiths and no faith may bless their food or participate in a Native American ceremony or take a minute of silence together for world peace.

This evolution stands on the shoulders of the interfaith movement of the late twentieth century, which greatly increased dialogue among leaders of different religions and opened the door to greater mutual understanding. Interfaith services, once a rarity, are now common in response to hate crimes or natural disasters.

In an age of enormous individual empowerment, we hunger for community that cannot be sated by adding more Facebook friends. And we are yearning for a deeper connection to nature, as many of us reawaken to the knowledge long held by indigenous people everywhere that we belong to the natural world as unique expressions of the web of life that we lost touch with while we were busy making ourselves safe and comfortable.

In the past, religious people felt motivated to do good within their own communities. Today's spiritual seekers wish to be of service to all of humanity. This may seem a bit daunting, but it is the way of the future and the momentum is building as the stakes get higher. The will-to-good—the essence of every religion and spiritual tradition—is breaking through the tribal strictures of the past into a planetary impulse to serve that is giving people a highly enhanced sense of meaning and purpose to their lives.

This spiritual revolution, combined with and amplified by the massive waves of immigration caused by globalization and climate change, is melting the previously calcified divisions of nationality, language, culture, tradition, and even that great challenge to human oneness: race. While we are currently experiencing a serious backlash against this rising tide in the form of extreme nationalism and no end to the current militarism in sight, the gentle yet powerful shift in consciousness is actually taking place quite rapidly. The question is: will this new consciousness reach a tipping point in time to allow humanity to thrive for future generations?

It's up to us.

Chapter 2 Spotlight

The process of practicing inner peace while striving for spiritual growth, Deborah Moldow points out, is leading us in the direction of a new consciousness that is enabling us to see ourselves—for the first time in history—as members of one planetary family sharing one common home. This, in turn, after decades of interfaith engagement, is leading us to understand that all religions point to universal truths, allowing us to build a sense of community based on shared values that is melting away previous barriers and divisions that stood in the way of unity.

Call to Action

All wisdom traditions share universal values through different windows. Take the time to learn about a new religious or spiritual worldview that is different from your own. Let this be your call to see the light of the Divine in everyone.

3

Integrating an Evolutionary Vision of the Future with "Hard" Science

David Sloan Wilson, PhD, and Kurt Johnson, PhD

In the spring of 2019, the Mind and Life Institute invited one of us (David) to have a one-on-one conversation with His Holiness, the Dalai Lama at his residence in Dharamsala, India.[1] David's work has helped revolutionize evolutionary biology where, through refinement of science's understanding of natural selection (namely, "group" and "multilevel" selection), the place and role of cooperation and altruism in evolution can now be clearly understood.[2]

David was allowed to bring a guest and immediately extended the invitation to the other of us (Kurt), who had introduced David to the evolutionary leaders. Both of us have doctorate degrees in evolutionary biology and qualify as "hard" scientists. We also share a deep interest in conscious evolution, which would be regarded as "fringe" by many of our evolutionary biology colleagues.[3]

David told His Holiness that when he entered the field of evolutionary biology in the 1970s, it was confined to the study of genetic evolution, leaving the study of cultural and personal evolution to other disciplines. All genes were labeled "selfish," and the evolution of altruism was regarded as highly implausible. Evolution was said to have no purpose, with mutations taking place at random and the effects of natural selection limited to how organisms adapted to their immediate environments.

At face value, that Western vision of evolution shared little common ground with Buddhism, the root tradition of His Holiness, and its abandonment of the self with the goal of ending suffering! But, David continued, hard evolutionary science has expanded to include epigenetic, personal, and cultural change in addition to genetic change. It can explain the evolution of altruism in addition to selfishness. And it is no longer heretical to say that evolution can have a directed component, especially in the case of human cultural evolution. These developments in evolutionary thought are transforming our exploration for common ground with the twenty-five-hundred-year-old tradition of Buddhism, as well as all the religious and spiritual traditions of the world.

David's message to His Holiness is equally relevant to the group of people who call themselves evolutionary leaders, whose vision of evolution is far more expansive than genetic evolution, including personal, cultural, and even cosmic evolution. For them, evolution has a conscious dimension and is even heading toward a global consciousness that the paleontologist and Jesuit priest Pierre Teilhard de Chardin (1881–1955) called the Omega Point.[4] And their vision of ecology tends to be holistic, treating the whole earth as a single organism that deserves to be revered—the metaphorical goddess, Gaia.

In some respects, hard evolutionary science is catching up with the evolutionary leaders' visions. And it has something to give in return. Evolution can become a conscious process, and the whole Earth can become like a single organism, but the particular conditions to enable this will not self-organize. Specific conditions must be met, and they must be socially constructed. When this happens, cultural evolution will have become a fully conscious process.

In the meantime, here's how hard evolutionary science can affirm and contribute to the vision of evolutionary leadership.

Beyond Genetic Evolution

Darwin knew nothing about genes. He defined natural selection in terms of variation, selection, and replication, or the tendency of off-spring to resemble their parents. Darwin was also convinced that his theory could explain the length and breadth of humanity, not just the natural world.

With the advent of the science of genetics in the early twentieth century, however, the study of evolution quickly became restricted to genetic evolution, as if the only way for offspring to resemble parents is by sharing genes. Disciplines such as anthropology, sociology, history, and psychology studied cultural and personal change largely in isolation from and sometimes in perceived opposition to evolutionary theory. They also developed largely in isolation from each other, resulting in an archipelago of knowledge—many islands of thought with little communication among them.

More recently, evolutionary biologists are going back to the basics, defining evolution as any process that combines the three ingredients of variation, selection, and replication. In addition to genetic replication, other mechanisms of replication include epigenetics (changes in gene expression rather than gene frequency), forms of social learning found in many species, and forms of distinctively human symbolic thought.[5] Also, in addition to being transgenerational, evolutionary processes can take place during the lifetime of a single organism, such as the adaptive component of the immune system, the kind of trial-and-error learning made famous by B. F. Skinner, and the rapid evolution of symbolic meaning systems. In short, a theory that has proven itself within the biological sciences can now be extended to cover all of the fast-paced changes swirling around us (cultural evolution) and within us (our personal evolution).

This "extended evolutionary synthesis"[6] does not *replace* current disciplinary knowledge but does promise to *integrate* it, just as it integrated all branches of biological knowledge during the twentieth century.

Evolution Is the Problem and the Solution

Evolution doesn't make everything nice. It frequently results in adaptations that benefit some beings at the expense of other beings, some groups at the expense of other groups, or short-term welfare at the expense of long-term welfare. This is true for human cultural and personal evolution as well as genetic evolution. In fact, most social pathologies are actually adaptive in the evolutionary sense of the word. Self-preservation is a good thing—until it results in self-dealing. Helping your kin is a good thing—until it results in nepotism. Helping your friends is a good thing—until it results in cronyism. Nations growing their economies is a good thing—until it results in a global race to unsustainably plunder resources and overheat the earth.

Other pathologies, both individual and social, are the maladaptive result of evolutionary mismatches and are maladaptive in every sense of the word.[7] An evolutionary mismatch occurs when adaptations to past environments misfire in current environments. For example, aeons of genetic evolution have adapted baby sea turtles that hatch on beaches at night to quickly make their way to the sea. The cue that they evolved to rely upon is light, because the sea reliably reflects more light than the inland—until humans arrived with their beach houses and streetlamps. Adapted only to their past environments, the baby sea turtles tragically head inland to their deaths. Only subsequent genetic evolution or human intervention can prevent their extinction.[8]

Mismatches are an inevitable consequence of evolution in changing environments for all evolutionary processes—cultural and personal in addition to genetic. When we consider adaptations in the evolutionary sense that are socially pathological, along with maladaptive evolutionary mismatches, then the conclusion is obvious: work is required to align evolutionary processes with our normative goals. Otherwise, evolution becomes the problem rather than the solution. Fortunately, conscious evolution makes such an alignment possible.

Conscious Evolution

The idea that evolution has no purpose, that mutations are arbitrary, and that organisms only adapt to their immediate environments were the main tenets of the so-called modern synthesis that emerged in the 1940s. These claims have proven to be too simple in a number of ways, even for genetic evolution. For example, artificial selection, whereby humans consciously select for traits in their domestic plants and animals: this is a form of genetic evolution with a conscious component supplied by humans. But animals select traits in each other all the time, and self-domestication has become a hot topic in the study of human evolution.[9] If organisms qualify as conscious and their choices influence genetic evolution, then genetic evolution acquires a conscious component. This kind of directed evolution was proposed in the early twentieth century but only now is receiving the attention it deserves.[10]

Human cultural evolution clearly has a conscious component. The outdated dogma helps explain why it has taken so long for this realization to emerge in science, even though it has always seemed obvious for the world's spiritually directed communities. However, it is important to realize that human cultural evolution also has a large undirected component, based on the collisions and unforeseen consequences of our intentions. In many respects, life consists of many inadvertent social experiments, a few that hang together compared with many that fall apart. What works evolves largely without anyone knowing how or why. Also, as mentioned, what works at a small scale—such as an agricultural practice or new military technology—can become part of the problem at a larger scale. In the future, human cultural evolution must become more intentional and directed toward the global good than ever before.

Steering toward the Omega Point

Hard evolutionary science today is far more supportive of the vision of evolutionary leaders than when we entered the field in the 1970s. It is like sailing with rather than against the wind. However, even with the evolutionary wind at our backs, a lot of scientific know-how will be required to steer cultural evolution in a direction that provides the solutions rather than causing the problems. We look forward to more communication between evolutionary leaders and hard evolutionary scientists in the future.

Chapter 3 Spotlight

Bridging science and spirituality, David Sloan Wilson and Kurt Johnson report a revolution in mainstream science leading to the multilevel understanding of natural selection. The old view of post-Darwinian science was that natural selection always selects for the best competitor—and this view of survival of the fittest (social Darwinism) came to dominate global economics, business, and politics. Mainstream science now holds that selection in nature for the best competitor happens only at the lower levels of complexity. Among groups or hierarchies, natural selection selects the best cooperator. This timely sea change aligns science's view of evolutionary process with the heart of the wisdom traditions.

Call to Action

Consider the spiritual law of cooperation, how this guides humanity's collective evolution, and how this is reflected in the natural world, as well. Seek out people in your business, school, or community with whom you can work collectively for the benefit of all.

4

Jamming: Cultivating Connection, Community, Collaboration, and Co-liberation

Shilpa Jain

These days, my husband, Austin, and I have taken to saying, "I am and we are 100 percent blessed." It is partly a recognition of all the gifts, privileges, and support we have been given in our lives: our families and friends, our respective educations, work and travel opportunities, our home and community in the Bay Area. "One hundred percent blessed" is also about taking a stand. We are choosing to see the challenges in our lives and in this world as blessings too. They open us up to our tenderness and awaken our creativity and imaginations. We see them as invitations to go further and deeper and use all that we are, all that we have, on behalf of all that we love.

I have the honor of serving as the executive director of YES!, a thirty-year-old nonprofit organization, which connects, inspires, and collaborates with young and multigenerational changemakers at the meeting point of personal, interpersonal, and systemic transformation (see yesworld.org). Our flagship programs, called Jams, bring together about thirty people at a time, all dedicated to contributing toward healing, love, justice, and connection in the world. Modeled in the spirit of a musical jam, each person is invited to bring forward their questions, struggles, wisdoms, hopes, fears, talents, and resources and listen to one another deeply to cocreate new, unique synergies. With vulnerability, integrity, and honesty, Jam participants take off masks and stretch together to learn, unlearn, and uplearn—about themselves, about each other, about the earth, about how to build the world we want to see. Jams are powerful greenhouses for body, heart, and soul wisdom, and these wisdoms guide our paths forward.

I have been Jamming for over eighteen years now, and I have seen over and over that community is at the center of every solution we need for our world. Actually, every solution we need is already here. They exist, both fully and sometimes like puzzle pieces to be put together through relationships and shared knowledge. All we need in these times is to bring diverse people together to tune in to their deeper wisdom, to listen to each other, to align and collaborate. Through this attunement, they will co-liberate themselves and access the solutions that already reside within.

That's a small order in its simplicity and a big order in its complexity, at the same time. Each of the parts—the coming together, the diversity, and the listening—has its difficulties. Many changemakers are internally challenged, unpracticed at tuning in to their own wisdom instead of being governed by their inner critics. That voice of self-doubt, not-enoughness, comparison, imposter syndrome, fear, anxiety, shame, etc., can block the divine genius that flows through every being. On the internal level, for many reasons, people do not freely trust or relate to one another, especially across social identities of race, class, gender, sexuality, nationality, religion, and age. Usually, in moments of conflict, relationships and communication break down and people wind up further apart. Most of us haven't come across, much less practiced, the tools to shift conflicts from breakdowns to breakthroughs. On the systemic level, institutions of education, politics, economics, and society have often generated even more scarcity, violence, and isolation, so there have been few practice grounds for slowing down together and feeling the abundance of possibilities.

Indeed, between the political divisiveness, social breakdowns, economic insecurity, and environmental upheaval, I often feel like I am walking the line between emergence and emergency. It takes energy, dedication, and fortitude for me to stay present, to be with what is coming, and to walk a clear path forward that reflects my values. And I can't do it alone. When the going gets tough, I need beloved community to show me that we move forward by turning to each other instead of turning on each other.

Nurturing a Conscious Community

Culture eats strategy for breakfast, so the saying goes. Change doesn't come about simply with getting better ideas or generating positive actions. These are important, and yet, without being held in holistic environments, they will soon be taken down by inner or outer conflicts. Instead, we need to cocreate positive cultures, which invite, then nurture and sustain, transformations for the long haul so that the beautiful seeds we plant can turn into saplings, then to flowering plants, then to trees, into forests, into the new normal for our world.

My friend Roni Krouzman (founder of The People Piece) talks about culture as a combination of structures, skill sets, and mindsets. That is to say, all of these elements need to be addressed if we want to cocreate cultures rooted in abundance, connection, and well-being for all. In that kind of culture, our souls and our solutions can flourish.

I have come to see YES! Jams as powerful culture-making and culture-changing platforms. The Jams use particular structures that value inclusion and wholeness of self and of all, such as check-in circles, community teams, and flow between collective and self-organization. They develop vital skill sets, like practicing self-awareness; listening without taking on and without judging, interpreting, or fixing; sharing from the heart; slowing down during conflict; and participating in appreciative inquiry. Embedded through and bolstered by these structures and skilled practices are life- and world-changing mindsets, such as presence, compassion, generosity, spaciousness, and love. Jams counter the dominating culture of separation, of divide and rule, and instead call forth a culture of interconnection, wholeness and shared, dynamic leadership.

Each participant gives to and receives from Jam culture, as we weave together powerful webs of meaning, learning, and support, embodying the world we want to see. Jam culture also supports changemakers, so they learn to dig deep during difficult conflicts. By learning to identify and slow down our fight-flight-freeze reactions, we experience opportunities for growth and connection. Jams provide space for both inner and outer healing so that we can choose a generative path in challenging moments. The culture encourages each of us to reshape our interactions with existing systems, to find the spaces within them that transform polarization and separation into understanding and relationship.

After Jammers individually and collectively dig deep and live out their responses to these questions, they "spread the Jam," with their families, friends, colleagues, movement-builders, neighbors, and strangers. They integrate practices and shift structures and operate with transformative mindsets, still rooted in the value of and respect of each person they encounter. It's not theoretical change; it's practically lived through ways of doing and ways of being. Step by step, breath by breath, Jammers shorten the distance between Jam life and daily life; they transform the rest of the "real" world into one of true authenticity: calling, connection, commitment, and community.

An Invitation to Jam

Jams invite each of us to consider and practice: How can our work, play, and lives increase connectivity in our world? How can each of us learn to respect and "re-spect"—to look again, past our first judgments and reactions, and be willing to listen, share our truths, and recognize the complex and whole picture of our shared humanity? How can each of us celebrate the divine presence of each being, uplift heart, soul and body wisdom, and move beyond right and wrong? How can each of us be in service, generate common ground, and build visionary futures together?

Every single person plays a role in shaping the collective container, and the depth and breadth of that container are what give way to higher-order solutions and previously unimagined outcomes. Just as every solution we need is already here, so is every person on the planet here with a genius and purpose. Sometimes, all that is missing are the loving mirrors from one another to help us see ourselves more clearly and the companionship to move ourselves forward.

Of course, I would love for you to one day experience a Jam, but I realize that may not be possible for you. So, I invite you to take Jamming—as a set of practices and principles—into your own lives, workplaces, and communities:

Practice listening without taking on, judging, interpreting, or fixing. At the heart of Jamming is a different form of listening— one that leaves plenty of room for the speaker and plenty of room for yourself. Try listening to others in your context without thinking about what you're going to say or how you're going to respond. That kind of spacious listening creates powerful connections and allows creativity and awareness to come forth.

Bring in play wherever you can. Instead of working to build the world you want, can you play your way toward it? A sense of play and practices of play—such as games, improvisation, and humor— transforms the field of what is possible. When you come together with others, infuse play and watch the energy expand and the intimacy grow.

Make space for all the feelings that arise. We can support more healing and freedom in the world by allowing for all of our and others' feelings: love, grief, satisfaction, anger, joy, frustration, and so on. Again, by not trying to fix or change these feelings— in yourself or others—they can flow through us and offer us the medicine we need in the moment. On the other side of our expressions are opportunities for unlearning and co-learning.

When things get hot, slow down. So many times our misunderstandings are just that: missed understandings. Rather than letting them spiral into judgments, assumptions, and stuck stories, take some time to slow down, breathe, and see if you can become curious about the person or situation. Follow that spark as a guide and use your wonder to regenerate a connection together.

Value the person over the plan (agenda/outcomes/goals). To counter the dehumanization of modern institutions and systems, we need to do things differently. As human *beings*, not human *doings*, making the shift to prioritize people's experiences, with love and truth, over "getting things done" will help us embody to the world we want to see.

Chapter 4 Spotlight

Shilpa Jain shares another form of bridge-building with us: the YES! Jams, developed for multigenerational changemakers who come together to connect, inspire each other, and collaborate for personal, interpersonal, and systemic transformation toward healing, love, justice, and connection in the world. Putting community at the center of everything, she and her Jammers know the power of a beloved community—we move forward by turning *to* each other, not *on* each other. This model contains at least five practices and principles that can be applied in any community setting for coming together as one.

Call to Action

Look at someone in your life, even someone with whom you seem to have little in common. Bring curiosity and listen for their truths, seeing deeply into their struggles, gifts, and purpose; then share your own vulnerably with them as well. Catalyze a connection that reflects your heart's values and deepens community.

5

Is World Peace Possible?

Reverend Michael Bernard Beckwith

Peace, a timeless and universal vision, is the pre-eminent equal-
izer, belonging to all and dependent upon the efforts of all. Peace
isn't something that only a group of world leaders will achieve, no
matter how good their intentions. When peace erupts on Earth, it will
come from individuals everywhere who have entered a new state of
consciousness.

The peace that's inherent in our species is even now exerting itself on
an increasingly global scale. It's the people who know they are facing a
daunting task and work at it anyway who are making a significant difference. And it has been that way throughout history.

There have always been people who—when faced with a problem
that seems intractable—find a way around it instead of resigning themselves to it. People have always brought about change of this magnitude,
whether it was fighting the challenges of various seemingly incurable
diseases, working toward education for the masses, or creating the freedom to pursue our own economic pursuits. Those who won against the
odds were inspired to operate out of a new paradigm—one that, often,
the vast majority simply hadn't caught up with. We too can bring about a
state of global peace our species hasn't yet experienced.

What Is Peace?

When we talk about peace, we have to define it. People tend to think that peace as an absence of conflict or negativity, but that's not really what peace is about. As I describe it, peace is the dynamic of harmonizing good. It is a quality within us.

Peace is a certain quality. For instance, you walk into a room that on the surface looks peaceful. People aren't fighting or even arguing, but the energy in the room tells you that there's no peace there, that they're at odds with each other, that they don't like each other. Peace would not be evident in that consciousness, even though there's no conflict.

You walk into another room and notice people disagreeing on a particular point, but the atmosphere is full of peace because the people are mature enough to converse even when they don't necessarily agree, and peace, love, patience, kindness, and compassion are still active within their consciousnesses.

So, when we talk of peace, we're speaking about a quality that is as real as love, harmony, and beauty. When it comes to world peace, we're talking about a consciousness of people who are no longer suppressing peace—because peace is everywhere and it has been there all along, like the presence of God, except when being suppressed by a limited point of view.

Human beings share an aspect of our brains with animals, reacting with our animalistic nature to whatever comes along. A part of the human brain is like this. But human beings also have a higher aspect of the brain capable of a consciousness that flows from Spirit. This part of our brain doesn't just react but expresses its loving nature.

Tapping into Peace Consciousness

The consciousness to tap into this peace is only now in our generation beginning to make its presence known on the world stage. Whether we are talking about nuclear disarmament, global warming, environmental

issues, water shortages, poverty, famine, or a lack of adequate housing—
all potential triggers for future wars—only today is the part of the brain
capable of addressing these issues through mutual cooperation coming
to the fore.

Even for those who disagree so violently on entrenched issues, such
as the Israelis and Palestinians, peace is still achievable. They may seem
to have little in common, but the truth is that they agree on most things.
They come from the same religious roots; they eat a similar diet. They
want protection and peace for their families and the freedom to pursue
an education for their kids, work they enjoy, and time to relax with their
families. They agree on most things.

The issue is the land. This is where we have to separate the government from the people. Riddled with self-centered politicians voted in
by fearful people, governments get in the way of peace. Coming from a
myopic position, they use the media to get the masses to buy into their
self-serving policies. If it weren't for governments, Israelis and Palestinians would get along just fine, as many already do.

Throughout the land, you don't find a lot of individuals who are filled
with hatred. You find people who have been hurt. The healing begins
with forgiveness. Place a number of Palestinians in a circle and invite
them to talk to each other concerning their heartbreaks, the death of
people close to them, and their children being killed in Gaza. Surround
them with Israelis who just listen to them without interrupting. Then
reverse the situation, with Israelis sharing their experiences. Let each
group witness the tears and sadness of the other group.

Seeing something from the other person's point of view leads to the
birth of compassion. With compassion, there is understanding; from
understanding comes dialogue. When dialogue emerges, then a way
out of no way emerges. With empathy, compassion, understanding, and
dialogue, people can see a solution that wasn't there before; a shift in
consciousness happens to enable a new insight.

But the people who sing and dance together and the thousands who
are in school together don't make the headlines. Where the media is
concerned, *if it bleeds, it leads*. News is projected from an old paradigm

of fear. And even though corporate news isn't interested in conveying it, the old paradigm is still being replaced. A vision of how peaceful the world could be is taking form.

War is part of our dysfunction; it's not a reflection of who we are in our highest form. Wars emerge over resources and when myopic leaders enforce the idea that their nation is "number one." However, the idea of being number one isn't reality. It represents a pseudo form of patriotism. A new paradigm is now emerging in which we want to rise up and be one with the One, meaning, recognize that the human race is one whole. The real news, which the headlines haven't caught up with yet, is that individuals are embracing peace in increasing numbers across the globe. Emerging peaceful markets, like the green markets, with solar panels, and the holistic medicine markets, are starting to outstrip traditional markets. These are all clear signs that we are in the midst of a great transformation toward a peaceful world.

Many levels of this transformation exist at the same time. On an individual level, the peace I have in mind is deep within us. It emerges as a result of taking time each day to connect with the universal Presence that's at the heart of our being. In a regular spiritual practice, where we become really still, the "peace that passes understanding" progressively infuses every aspect of our day so that it becomes realer than anything that may happen to us. This is the kind of peace that breaks in upon people in the worst of circumstances, as it did in a prison cell for Nelson Mandela. This is a level of spiritual maturity that happens either through pain or insight; it is a peace that never leaves us.

This type of peace naturally extends to a community level. If we become activists, the mental vision of how the world could be springs from our essence, maintaining our energy and commitment. This peace doesn't have to be put aside, waiting for the world to change before we can enjoy it. We become the instrument of that change, this peace already within us.

You can hear it in Dr. Martin Luther King Jr.'s words: when he spoke about all brothers and sisters being one, in the midst of a time of tremendous bigotry and racism, he tapped into that love and peace even while that wasn't necessarily a fact in the world. All of us have access to that love and peace—we just have to find our way to it, to tap into that kind of vision and that kind of spiritual sustenance, even while working for peace, or ecology, or justice.

In other words, peace isn't the end goal. Peace is in the journey, with every step we take. We carry it with us, and its impact is felt on a much wider scale. We all have to find our own neighborhood, in our own community, where we're willing to share our gift. It might mean joining a neighborhood watch or a community group or volunteering in a way that brings hope and joy to others.

On the national level, different states of consciousness exist within the local, state, and national scene. You don't opt out of that, but you participate in it without attachment, without hate of the so-called other side. You get into a great discovery as to who most represents your particular point of view, that point of view that's going to bring about a greater sense of oneness on the planet, and you support that. When we get involved with others in a way that aligns with our particular gifts, we seed society with possibilities.

Many people don't realize that small groups of people around the world doing things with compassion have an impact on the mental and emotional atmosphere of the entire world. That's how all the levels of building peace are interconnected.

By having peace within, we build peace all around us. We seed all levels of society with possibilities at the same time. Great change happens when we seed what we want. I agree with Victor Hugo that this process would create an idea whose time has come. We all need to continue to cast a vision, bring that into focus, step up, and walk in that direction. In the words of the hymn, I say to you, "Let there be peace on earth, and let it begin with me."[1]

Chapter 5 Spotlight

World peace will be possible when enough people everywhere enter a new state of consciousness. Fortunately, Michael Bernard Beckwith points out, this is already happening on a global scale. We are in the midst of a great transformation in which more and more people carry within them a vision of a peaceful world. We are embracing a new paradigm with wholeness at its center in increasing numbers across the globe. This is a peace that starts within, a quality that inspires us to harmonize good by expressing an energy of love, patience, and compassion in whatever situation we find ourselves in. This is a peace that comes from our highest aspect of consciousness, that flows from Spirit and helps us rise up and be one with the One, that expands through all the levels of our connections and impacts the entire world. Living by this peace within us, we are each instruments of this change.

Call to Action

Begin to recognize that you carry the seed of peace within you at every moment. How can you share that peace in your world? What community group do you care about most? Now is a perfect time to volunteer.

Circle Two
Restoring Ecological Balance

We regard the universe as alive and conscious;
we are planetary stewards.

6

Evolutionary Wisdom for a World in Great Transition

Duane Elgin, MBA, MA

Humanity has faced challenges throughout history, but this time is unique in one respect, and this makes all the difference: The circle has closed. There is nowhere to escape the consequences of climate disruption, unsustainable population, water scarcity, the mass extinction of plant and animal species. Humanity has created an unprecedented systems crisis that is placing the entire human journey in peril. Where are we to find the evolutionary wisdom for moving into a sustainable and thriving future? Following, I share some key insights from wisdom traditions, the frontiers of science, and people's direct experiences. This includes philosophies from indigenous elders like Luther Standing Bear; guidance from spiritual leaders as diverse as Sir Nisargadatta and Meister Eckhart; scientific support of a living Universe; and the experiences of people from all walks of life, speaking about unity. Together, they offer us a road map for envisioning a promising future.

Indigenous Wisdom: The Living World

How did our ancestors experience life and the world? Here are quotes from several indigenous cultures that reveal a subtle and refined understanding of reality that has existed for millenia.

Luther Standing Bear, Lakota elder: "There was no such thing as emptiness in the world. Even in the sky there were no vacant places. Everywhere there was life, visible and invisible, and every object gave us great interest in life. The world teemed with life and wisdom; there was no complete solitude for the Lakota."[1]

The Ohlone lived from the San Francisco Bay Area to Monterey, California: For the Ohlone, religion was pervasive, "like the air." Nature was seen to be alive and shimmering with energy. Because everything was filled with life, power was everywhere and in everything. Every act was a spiritual act because it engaged the worlds of power. All tasks were done with a feeling for the surrounding world of life and power.[2]

The Koyukon of north-central Alaska: The Koyukon live "in a world that watches, in a forest of eyes." They believe that wherever we are, we are never truly alone because the surroundings, no matter how remote, are aware of our presence and must be treated with respect.[3]

Sarayaku Kichwa of the Ecuadorean Amazon jungle: Believe "everything in the jungle is alive and has a spirit."

We find a common intuition in indigenous wisdom around the world: our life exists within a larger aliveness. A living presence permeates the world and naturally includes consciousness—a "forest of eyes," according to the Koyukon—aware of our presence, no matter who or where we are; a life force, or "sacred wind," blows through the Universe and brings the capacity for awareness and communion with all of life.

Spiritual Traditions: The Regenerative Now

Consistent with indigenous views, many traditions share the understanding that the Universe is continuously arising anew at every moment. A regenerative flow cuts through notions of solidity and permanence to reveal the Universe as emerging as an undivided whole in an unutterably vast process of awesome precision and power:

Christian: "God is creating the entire Universe, fully and totally, in this present now. Everything God created. . . . God creates now all at once."—Meister Eckhart, Christian mystic[4]

Islam: "You have a death and a return in every moment. . . . Every moment the world is renewed but we, in seeing its continuity of appearance, are unaware of its being renewed."—Rumi, thirteenth-century Sufi teacher and poet[5]

Buddhism: "My solemn proclamation is that a new universe is created every moment."—D. T. Suzuki, Zen teacher and scholar[6]

Hindu: "The entire Universe contributes incessantly to your existence. Hence the entire universe is your body."—Sri Nisargadatta, Hindu teacher[7]

Taoism: "The Tao is the sustaining life-force and the mother of all things; from it, all things rise and fall without cease."—*Tao Te Ching*[8]

Beneath differences of language, we see a common understanding revealed: the Universe is continuously emerging as a fresh creation at every moment. And we are an inseparable part of that process—paradoxical beings both entirely unique and completely connected within the generative Universe.

Scientific Discoveries: The World as Superorganism

Until recently, suggesting the Universe might be a unified, living system would have been regarded as fantasy by mainstream science. Now, the findings of quantum physics and other disciplines have led to a fresh reconsideration of the ancient intuition of a living Universe as science cuts away superstition to reveal the cosmos as a place of unexpected wonder, depth, dynamism, and subtlety. In a stunning challenge to materialism, scientists have recently discovered that the overwhelming majority of the Universe is invisible and *not material*! Scientists estimate that 96 percent of the known Universe is invisible to our physical senses.[9]

A new picture of our Universe is coming into focus: a living, cosmic hologram—a unified, "superorganism"—who is continuously regenerated at each moment and whose essential nature includes consciousness, or a knowing capacity, that enables systems at every scale of existence to center themselves and exercise some measure of freedom. We are completely immersed within this regenerative, holographic Universe.

Direct Experience: Feeling the Presence of Aliveness

How widespread is the experience of a permeating aliveness and deep unity in everyday life? How often do people feel aliveness that connects them with the larger world? Here are the results of scientific surveys from the Search Institute to Pew, from young people to elders, on these questions taken in different parts of the world:

○ A global survey from 2008, involving seven thousand youth in seventeen countries, found that 75 percent believe in a "higher power." A majority claimed to have had a transcendent experience, believe in life after death, and think it is "probably true" that all living things are connected.[10]

○ In 1962, a survey of the adult population in the US found that 22 percent reported having a profound experience of communion with the universe. By 2009, the percentage of the population reporting a "mystical experience" had grown dramatically to 49 percent.[11]

○ In a national survey of the US in 2014, nearly 60 percent of adults reported they regularly feel a deep sense of "spiritual peace and well-being," and 46 percent say they experience a deep sense of "wonder about the universe" at least once a week.[12]

A powerful conclusion emerges from these surveys: our species is measurably waking up! More than half of humanity appears to have regular experiences of connecting with the aliveness of the universe and our deep unity within it.

A Fresh View of the Evolutionary Journey

If we are being realistic, the human community seems unlikely to turn away from our current path of overconsumption and deep injury to the earth—*unless* we are called by a pathway into the future that is so remarkable, transformative, and welcoming that we are drawn together by the astonishing promise of its invitation. Integrating insights from people's direct experience, discoveries in science, and shared understandings across the world's wisdom traditions reveal the path. We are discovering that, instead of struggling for meaning and a miracle of survival in a dead universe, we are being invited to learn and grow forever in the deep ecologies of a living Universe. We are being called to gather the wisdom of the past so that we might transcend the wounds of history and begin a process of reconciliation and healing to realize a remarkable future we can only attain together.

To step into the invitation of learning to live consciously in a living Universe is to begin a new chapter in humanity's evolution.

Chapter 6 Spotlight

To re-envision the universe as alive and us becoming its stewards, Duane Elgin finds enduring wisdom from indigenous traditions that share with us that life and Spirit are everywhere and in everything and that this consciousness brings with it the capacity for communion with all of life. This understanding of the nature of the universe is also found in the mystic traditions of the world's spiritual and religious traditions, and together with new scientific discoveries, we are seeing a new picture of a living, unified universe come into focus.

Call to Action

Remembering that the entire universe surrounding you is alive, strive each moment to draw upon the ageless wisdom encouraging you to become its tireless steward. Throughout the day, remember that your thoughts, words, and actions have power. Use that power for good in everything you do.

Regenerating Earth and Her People

Daniel Christian Wahl, PhD

We are living in times of breakdown and breakthrough, which makes them perilous but also an evolutionary opportunity. Our survival now depends on humanity's collective ability to come together as one. Our deep love and need to care for the entire family of life is the higher ground that can unite us in all our magnificent diversity. To heal Earth, we have to heal humanity. To heal humanity, we have to reperceive and remember our intimate relationship with each other and all life as coinhabitants of this planet.

As we wake up to this reality, it becomes evident that everything is an intervention, and conscious participation literally matters. To regenerate Earth and her people, all our designs will have to contribute to the health and wholeness of the nested complexity in which we participate. We are all designers: cocreators manifesting the future potential of the present moment. This is done through how we show up and what we activate through our attention and intention today—now.

It is time for an evolutionary leap, for our species to become healers with a regenerative impact on the wider community of life and each other. It is time for unprecedented cooperation and deep care for all life, where we reconnect, charting the humble path of geotherapy—rather than hubristic geo-engineering—as we come to embody our intimacy with the living Earth.

Facing the Extent of Our Ecological Crisis

Humanity has become an existential threat to its own existence. In the last five thousand years, we have cut down more than half of the world's forests. In the last fifty years alone, human activity has contributed to the loss of nearly two-thirds of the world's mammals, birds, fish, and reptiles.[1] We are decimating the biodiversity that humans, ecosystems, and planetary health depend upon.

It can't be overstated that the window of opportunity to avoid cataclysmic climate change is closing fast. Science-based predictions look bleak. The International Panel on Climate Change (IPCC) suggested in 2018 that we have twelve years left to respond before these processes take us beyond a point of no return. Failure to act with urgency is now deeply irresponsible.[2]

Planetary Healing: Addressing Causes Rather than Symptoms

In the face of unprecedented biodiversity loss, climate change, unacceptable levels of global inequality, and imminent societal, economic, and ecological breakdown around the world, we have to think in terms of evolutionary opportunity. And to address the underlying causes of our unsustainable worldview by changing our hearts and minds to become humble stewards and careful healers cocreating conditions conducive to life.

Life Is about Cooperative Abundance (Not Competitive Scarcity)

Life's evolution follows a pattern of diversification and subsequent integration of diversity at higher levels of complexity. Throughout evolution, this integration has predominantly been achieved through new forms of cooperation and symbiosis. It is time to reperceive life as a planetary process of cooperation in which a unified whole expressing itself on nested temporal and spatial scales of complexity evolves in intimate reciprocity as a living planet. Life is a regenerative community rooted in patterns of symbiosis and cooperation that creates shared abundance and conditions conducive to life.

Competition clearly does exist but in far smaller proportions than our myopic focus on scarcity as the driver of evolution has led us to believe. To offer an analogy, one could say that the role of competition in life's evolution is proportional to the waves and ripples at the surface of a vast symbiotic and cooperative ocean. Evolution is coevolution! Throughout its evolution, life itself has continued to create the conditions conducive for more diverse and complex life to evolve.

To list just a few of the many pronounced leaps of evolution marked by new forms of cooperative complexity:

1. The merging of two non-nucleated cells to form the first eukaryotic cells that made more complex life possible

2. Such cells coming together into multicellular organisms

3. The cooperative differentiation of cell types and functions that enabled complex organisms such as vertebrates

4. The complex patterns that create collaborative advantage in social mammals such as whales, elephants, wolves, apes, and humans

5. Our human systems of governance and conviviality at the scale of neighborhood, city, bioregion, nation, and the United Nations

6. Recent discoveries about the role of the human microbiome in maintaining health and regulating gene expression, which reveal that our bodies are actually highly diverse and cooperative walking ecosystems with more nonhuman than human cells in and on them

In the face of converging crises, our relatively young species is now poised for an unprecedented evolutionary development. Facing the possibility of premature extinction is pushing us into a global rite of passage as our species comes of age. It is time to grow up and become mature and responsible members of the community of life.

The only appropriate response to life being in crisis on the planet is to aim to be of service in Earth's healing and regeneration. In doing so, we will begin to heal our disconnected and fractured selves as we re-indigenize, reconnect, and reinhabit what the poet Mary Oliver called "our place in the family of things."[3]

Embracing New Ways of Doing

Yes, we need to rapidly engage in the more than a hundred existing and proven technological and policy pathways that would help us to draw carbon dioxide from the atmosphere. (To get involved, look up organizations such as Project Drawdown, the Carbon Underground, Zero Carbon Britain, and the Rapid Transition Alliance.)

Yes, we will have to come together at the bioregional scale to regenerate healthy ecosystem functions by planting diverse and locally appropriate forests and restoring grasslands, mangroves, salt marshes, and freshwater wetlands. And likewise restoring coral reefs and seagrass meadows in the oceans. (To get involved, look up organizations such as Commonland, Regeneration International, Rewilding Europe, Global Forest Generation, and the Global Coral Reef Alliance.)

Yes, we have to nurture planetary and ecosystem health to improve human health while regenerating bioregions and creating community climate resilience as we prepare for a turbulent three or four decades ahead. During that time we will have to maintain our regenerative efforts to restabilize climate patterns and heal the earth, even if the lag in the climate systems will initially see conditions worsening despite our best efforts. (To get involved, look up organizations such as Planetary Health Alliance, C40 Cities, Regenerative Communities Network, Global Ecovillage Network, Common Earth, Resilience Brokers, and Global Resilience System.)

Yes, we need a more equitable and just world where qualities of relationships and experiences matter more deeply than material accumulation and financial wealth. We need to create the social foundations for diverse regenerative cultures to live well within planetary boundaries. This will require a redesign of how we feed, house, move, dress, power, educate, and govern ourselves along with transforming our structurally dysfunctional economic and monetary system to enable such change. (To get involved, look up organizations such as the Doughnut Economics Action Lab, the Capital Institute, the Common Earth Alliance, Wellbeing Economy Alliance, P2P Foundation, Biomimicry Institute, and Regenesis Group.)

Embracing New Ways of Being

Yet we need to do more than that to draw on a new kind of wisdom: We need genuine transformation if we are to chart our course into this uncertain, uncontrollable, and unknowable future. A caterpillar turns into a butterfly only when its old identity dies. This unleashes its inherent potential to push through the process of transformation.

We are now witnessing a rapid shift in human awareness toward a deeper understanding of our fundamental interdependence with the wider community of life. People all over the world—young and old—are stepping up to defend ecosystems against further destruction, lobbying for the rights of nature, working to rewild, or at least restore them to a healthier state. We are waking up from centuries of sleepwalking toward catastrophe, unaware of the deeply destructive influence our mistaken worldview had on our behavior. Life is first and foremost a planetary process, and as life, we human beings are not separate but intimately tied to all other life on Earth.

For too long have we separated self from world, culture from nature, mind from matter and lived within this illusion of separation that made us behave like masters rather than stewards of life on Earth. Our role now is to create conditions conducive to life.

To heal the earth, we have to heal our way of being, both in and through relationships. We can start by loving what is right in front of us, being with and appreciating the everyday beauty of life in the midst of a dying system and patterns that no longer serve. How we show up today is important. As systems thinker and dharma teacher Joanna Macy reminds us, we are now playing dual roles: hospice workers to a dying world (including our own outdated patterns) and midwives of a regenerative future.[4]

We will not know for decades—well into the second half of this century—whether we will make it through the eye of the needle and come out the other end having cocreated a regenerative human civilization worthy of that name. The journey toward diverse regenerative cultures is not one of guarantee but one of healing and service.

Uncertainty and not-knowing will keep us humble and able to learn. We have to embrace the paradox of knowing that all our actions and inactions—our way of being—matter and yet accept the limits of our knowing and release our obsession with prediction and control. We have to individually and collectively live into the question: how can we become mature and humble healers of the planet—by *being* life consciously creating conditions conducive to life?

Chapter 7 Spotlight

Calling for new ways of doing and being that will regenerate healthy ecosystems, create community climate resilience, and rebuild an equitable and just world that prioritizes qualities of relationship, Daniel Christian Wahl advocates addressing causes, rather than symptoms, and shifting our focus from competitive scarcity toward collaborative abundance as an enabler of planetary healing. This means reconnecting and embodying our intimacy with an animate Earth, requiring unprecedented cooperation and deep care for all life. In other words, seeing that act of serving the health and well-being of all as the most enlightened pathway to serving ourselves.

Call to Action

Today, take one specific action to regenerate the environment and care for all life deeply. You could plant a tree, join a community garden, donate blood, or pick up the garbage you see on the sidewalk.

8

One Good Person

Constance Buffalo

*T*here was a time when the people had forgotten how to be kind to the earth, to her creatures, and to each other. The Great Council in the Spirit World had finally given up on humans. Mankind had been given so many gifts and opportunities to become part of the family of life, and yet they continued to think only of their own welfare and disrespect the world around them. They were taking more than they required and neglecting the elders and those in need. They had forgotten their sacred kinship and interdependence with the world in which they lived.

The council concluded that the next day this young species would be eliminated. The great eagle heard their words on the night winds. She had flown above the villages and loved the promise she saw in so many hearts. She knew she had to travel into the dawn light between night and day and speak with the council.

She said, "I have heard the prayers and seen the hearts of those who seek to live in balance and respect. I have smelled the smoke of the sage burning as they begin each day with these prayers in their hearts. I know that they carry love for their world and ask for mercy and help so that the relationship with creation can grow."

57

> *It was decided that day that as long as one good person remained,*
> *humanity would have a place in the circle of life.*
>
> —*Traditional Chippewa story*

For years it was my job to figure out how to destroy the earth and her people. I was then CEO of a chemical and biological decontamination company. By understanding the threats, we could create the antidotes. Between this background and my being a member of the Chippewa, the preceding story has particular significance to me. You may also know my tribe as the Ojibwa. I come from a northern woodlands tribe of Chippewa located on the great Lake Superior in Wisconsin. Our nation is the fourth largest in the United States and the second largest in Canada.

I made it through those years of corporate Armageddon speculations by returning to my Anishinaabe teachings and traditions that taught us the value of life as a sacred gift.

One day, when I was living in Denver, Colorado, I had a profound experience that carried me back 156 years.

I was traveling in the Colorado Mountains and stopped in the small village of Kremmling for the night. At the registration desk of Bob's Western Motel, I felt an intense sense of unease. I mentioned it to the receptionist, who surmised it must be from the animal trophies hanging on the wall in the small office. But I felt something much sadder.

I finally saw an old Indian quiver and bow on the wall. Sorrow welled up inside me as she pointed out the scalps hung over one end of the bow. "From somewhere around Sand Creek," she said. I left, overwhelmed by memories from the past.

Sand Creek was the site of one of the most horrendous Indian massacres of the West. While Black Kettle's tribe waited to sign new treaty papers, the men went out to hunt for food, leaving mostly women and children at camp. They felt safe with an American flag hanging in the center of the village and a white flag to show they were peaceful. Unbeknownst to them, Colonel John Chivington and 675 soldiers surrounded the encampment the night of November 28, 1864, and opened fire in a dawn attack. His orders were "Kill and scalp all [Indians], big and little; nits make lice."[1]

Kill and scalp and mutilate they did, leaving between 130 to 150 Cheyenne and Arapaho dead, about two-thirds of whom were women and children. The desecrated body parts were brought to Denver, hung up across the Apollo Theater stage, and traded, one scalp for one pair of boots.

This barbarity against a peaceful camp ignited Indian retaliations across the West and destroyed peaceful prospects advocated by many who sought peace. It won both Governor Evans, who ordered the attack, and Colonel Chivington honors, at least in the short term. Later, investigations by the military and one by the Joint Committee on the Conduct of the War led to this excerpt from the panel's findings:

As to Colonel Chivington. . . . He deliberately planned and executed a foul and dastardly massacre which would have disgraced the veriest savage along those who were the victims of his cruelty. Having full knowledge of their friendly character, having himself been instrumental to some extent in placing them in their position of fancied security, he took advantage of their in-apprehension and defenseless condition to gratify the worst passions that ever cursed the heart of man.[2]

Colonel Chivington retired from the military before he could face charges. John Evans lost his federal appointment as governor of Colorado.[3]

The traffic on the highway brought me back to what I had seen in the registration office. Since this was the night for my annual reconsecration of my life and spirit, I had gotten in my car and headed to I-didn't-know-where. Beside me appeared an older Indian man wrapped in a blanket. It was an apparition; I knew that, but he spoke softly, telling me where to go for ceremony. Up the mountain, off the road, into the black of the forest we climbed. He directed my turns since all I could see was the narrow pathway illuminated in the beams of my headlights. Suddenly, he told me to stop. I found myself on the edge of an outcropping overlooking an expansive lake.

I took out my pipe to pray and was told not to smoke it. The black lake in front of me was smooth as glass and reflected the light of a million stars. I actually couldn't tell where the lake ended and the sky began. Awed by its magnificence, I once again heard the voice in my mind: "You and others are more vast than all the stars you see tonight. You have just forgotten, but it's time to remember. Take the scalps back to Sand Creek and give them an honorable burial. Pray for those who killed them as well as for those who were killed. You can work your pipe when all of this is completed."

I sat for a long time that night looking into the star field in front of me and reflecting on the words. My spirit companion had left, and somehow I found my way back down the mountain trail.

In the morning, I went to the office and found Bob, who owned the hotel, at the front desk. Bob was a large man with a plaid shirt, red suspenders, a generous belly, and well-worn jeans. I asked about the scalps, and he told me his great-grandfather had fought in the battle.

I said quietly, "My friend, it was not a battle but a massacre."

He told me he had been offered an RV for the scalps, but he turned it down. As he fingered the fringe on the old quiver, he spoke almost to himself of how he had to repair it someday.

I listened to him, softly touched his arm, and said, "It's time for them to go back now, Bob."

He slowly turned to me, tears in his eyes. "I never believed in this killing. If I could come back again, I'd be an Indian, riding free and long before the white people ever came." He put the scalps in my hands and walked away.

There were two of them, each about twelve inches long, sewed together with fine pink stitches. I stood with the scalps and felt them with my soul. The tears just came.

I wrapped them in red cloth and tied the bundle with ribbons the colors of the four directions. As soon as I got back to Denver, I called the leader of my Native American church, and he in turn contacted a Lakota woman elder to help me prepare for what was to come. We also reached out to Cheyenne and Arapaho tribal members to invite their participation but did not hear back from them.

We held a sweat lodge for purification, obtained permissions for the burial at Sand Creek, and invited other Indians to join us for the ceremony. The giveaways (offerings for the participants) were chosen and tobacco ties prepared. Each night, with the sacred bundle of scalps on my altar, I would sing to them. I didn't know any Cheyenne or Arapahoe songs, but I sang every song I knew and hoped they would feel my intentions.

As we set up camp at Sand Creek for the burial, some of the men went to walk around—and quickly returned, reporting they heard camp noises, as if the village were still alive. At dawn, as we began the ceremony, two birds flew above our group of twelve. They didn't fly in circles but just hovered for the whole ceremony. When the songs had been sung, the prayers made, and the traditional foods offered, they flew away. It was all done in the best way we knew how.

I tell this story because we are once again at a point where so many have forgotten the kindness, dignity, and respect that all our relations deserve.

One of my people's greatest values is bravery, which is defined as integrity in the face of the foe. Have we come full circle now? Now, one good person can easily combine with others through the internet and other media to share ideas, offer solutions, listen to adversaries, and find solutions as new as the challenging situations we encounter.

My experience has taught me that the spirit world and the physical world are not just concepts but a reality. The spirit world is there to assist us and help when we pray with pure hearts. All the spirits—those of the victims *and* the perpetrators—can use our prayers. Prayer doesn't abdicate wrong; the perpetrators are still accountable for their deeds. But we pray with love and faith for all who are on this life walk.

We know from our earliest teachings that we humans are of the Fourth World. The First World was the creation of the elements (wind, water, air, and fire) and the star nations. The Second World brought the lands and oceans, mountains, and all that covered the earth. The Third World was all the animals, the crawlers, swimmers, fliers, and all the more-than-human creatures of this world. And, lastly, in the Fourth World came the new ones, the humans.

All of those of the worlds before us are our ancestors and our family. We don't see the tree or river as an object but as a relation. To the standing ones, we say Grandfather, and to the moon, we say Grandmother. In this way, we aren't separate but belong, and in that belonging, we love and care for our family. We don't try to protect the earth as if it were separate from us, for we are of the earth.

What Chief Seattle (1786–1866) once said over 160 years ago remains true:

All things are connected. What befalls the earth befalls the sons of the earth. This we know: the earth does not belong to man; man belongs to the earth. All things are connected like the blood that unites us all. Man does not weave this web of life. He is merely a strand of it. Whatever he does to the web, he does to himself.[4]

This kinship helps us to remember that each being is a meaningful thread in the web of life in both the seen and the unseen worlds and that we belong to a reality far greater than ourselves. A reality that gives us our visions, inspires our actions, and endures beyond time as we know it.

Perhaps that's what changed the Great Council's decision in the Spirit World, when the eagle came to ask on our behalf for another chance. If there are some good people, then there can be more. And more can become many, and the many who have reverence for life can become a powerful tribe and—like millions of stars reflected on a mountain lake—bring light to the darkest night.

A last note: Bob from Bob's Western Motel walked on peacefully six months after returning the young men's scalps for burial. We hope that he has found his tribe.

Chapter 8 Spotlight

Indigenous wisdom teaches us how to live in harmony with—and be kind to—the earth, her creatures, and each other. Connie Buffalo's beautiful and touching Chippewa story about how, as long as one good person remains, humanity will have a place in the circle of life is interwoven with her own very personal, powerful, and moving story. How, even when kindness and respect for all our relations seems forgotten, the reality of the kinship between the Spirit World and the physical world was confirmed before her eyes, reminding us that each being is a meaningful thread in the web of life in both the seen and the unseen worlds.

Call to Action

Do an anonymous good deed today—and don't give in to the temptation to tell anyone!

9

Prophecies, Dynamic Change, and a New Global Civilization

Hereditary Chief Phil Lane Jr.

A growing global storm is sweeping the face of Mother Earth, and no place is protected from its cleansing, healing, and unifying power. Even with the current widespread paralysis of will that subordinates national and personal self-interests to concerted global manipulation, a world is emerging in which all members of our human family can live in peace, harmony, and prosperity. Our primary concern right now is how to make the changes needed to transform our world, so cooperation prevails and leads to the establishment of a peaceful global civilization.

Reaching a Turning Point

Many people saw the powerful image of a young Hunkpapa Lakota woman from the Standing Rock Reservation that drew attention to the prayerful and peaceful gathering to stop the Dakota Access Pipeline (DAPL), inspiring a global movement to protect the Sacred.

These unprecedented, unified actions at Standing Rock—and all around Mother Earth—to protect and restore the Sacred, highlight the growing involvement of young people, who now represent more than 50 percent of the world's population. And their return to the Sacred was anticipated in the prophecies about the Seventh Generation following European settlement of the American continent, as described by White Feather (Hopi), among many others whom I discuss more later.

Young people are emerging as leaders in every dimension of human and community transformation; this has been long prophesied by indigenous elders. According to these prophesies, their work also signals a global rise of indigenous leadership while we face the growing threat of runaway climate change, loss of biodiversity, and ecosystemic collapse.

We have now entered the long-promised spiritual springtime, and there is the emergence of the Seventh Generation, and young people from everywhere on Mother Earth are mobilizing to address climate change and biodiversity loss. One such example are those working with Our Children's Trust who have filed several lawsuits on behalf of youth plaintiffs.

Across the Americas and around Mother Earth, the Seventh Generation is resonating with a call for a political, social, and spiritual transformation to address an ineffective and unacceptable political and economic system, everywhere all at once. No matter the challenges, we will eventually awaken to the spiritual and biological reality that we are all one human family, intimately related to all life.

Creating a New Global Civilization

The vision of a new global civilization is a promise found in spiritual and prophetic wisdom, including indigenous sources (such as Black Elk Speaks), the major prophets, the Call to the Nations, the Universal House of Justice, and many elders, spiritual teachers, and faith traditions everywhere. This new global civilization that indigenous peoples and related prophecies speak of is not to be confused—even remotely—with the various new world orders fearfully alluded to by various contending sources. It is not a new world order where the extremely wealthy or a secret elite enslave most of humanity for their own selfish and greedy purposes. Or where everyone is forced to look, act, and think the same or where any one nation-state dominates all others.

To build this new way of life that leads to an equitable, balanced, new global civilization, which is already unfolding, our primary prerequisite is our full commitment to our personal, unfettered, and independent investigation of the truth. The obligation of each human being to acquire knowledge and understanding through their own eyes, and not through the eyes of others, requires our very careful, in-depth reflection, consideration, and investigation of the sources from which we receive our "news."

When we discover this knowledge for ourselves, we will change the way we feel, speak, and act and how we coexist and live together, as we gain an ever-deepening spiritual understanding and purpose in our lives. This new global civilization, long foretold by our indigenous prophecies—including "The Eighth Council Fire," "The Return of the White Buffalo," "The Peacemaker," "Quetzalcoatl," and "Sweet Medicine"—is founded on the unshakable understanding of the oneness of the human family and all life. From this consciousness naturally unfolds the realization that we need

- equality between men and women,

- balance between the extremes of wealth and poverty,

- to eliminate all prejudices,

- to unify science and spirituality,

- universal education,

○ independent investigation of truth, and

○ unity in diversity.

Practicing these unifying principles will bring about a new global civilization where the voices, the wisdom, and the vision of indigenous peoples are justly and respectfully represented, and whose ancient wisdom is listened to and acted upon.

All the human sciences confirm there is only one human race, though it is infinitely varied in the secondary aspects of life. This is why the full recognition of this fundamental truth requires the abandonment of all prejudice—prejudice of every kind: race, class, sexual orientation, color, creed, nationality, gender, degree of material wealth, everything that enables people to consider themselves superior or inferior to others. Abandoning all prejudice is a great spiritual challenge and requirement for all of us at this time.

As we prepare for fundamental changes in the systemic structures of our unfolding global society, the spiritual and physical reality of the oneness of the human family should be taught in every school and affirmed in every nation. World peace will only be fully achieved when this spiritual reality of the Oneness of all Life is realized.

In the meantime, as prophesied, organizations like the United Religions Initiative (URI) and the Parliament of the World's Religions, among others are promoting interfaith and interspiritual understanding and awareness and increasing the momentum of unprecedented, unified actions toward global harmony. The URI preamble, purpose, and principles, organizational framework, and integrative scheme of thought are clearly supporting the fulfillment of the prophecies and helping to build this global movement.

In promoting enduring, daily interfaith cooperation to end religiously motivated violence and to create cultures of peace, justice, and healing for Earth and all living beings, both the Parliament of the World's Religions and URI welcome indigenous faith traditions as coequals in uniting and moving us toward world peace and a new global civilization.

The recognition of the oneness of humankind calls for the reconstruction and the demilitarization of the whole world, one that is naturally unified in all the essential aspects of its life—its political machinery, its spiritual aspiration, its trade and finance, its script and language—and yet infinite in the diversity of the unique characteristics of each culture and bioregion. This promised future will take faith, vision, patience, time, and unified action, well beyond 2030, 2040, even 2050.

Forming a "Global Commons"

These prophecies share that a time will come when a global assembly will be needed to actualize world peace. Representatives of all cultural and spiritual traditions will come together to consult on the ways and means of laying the foundation for lasting world peace. Indigenous women from every part of the world will be an important part of this global leadership.

Prophecies like Black Elk's "Hoop of Many Hoops" clearly outline a "global commons," which will be manifested when there is a shared commitment to place the common good ahead of any national, ethnic, religious, and selfish interests. Uniting all nations, races, creeds, and classes closely and permanently into one human family will also require a new global governing system, rooted locally, organized and scaled bioregionally, and synergized globally, with nonpartisan members elected in a principle-centered manner.

This governing system will steward the sustainable and harmonious development of our global resources and cultures, enacting such laws as needed to regulate and satisfy the needs and relationships of all members of the human family, including balancing the extremes of wealth and poverty and upholding all fundamental human rights, such as universal education, free expression, and individual sovereignty. Indeed, its primary function will be to safeguard the unity and harmony of the whole.

A world language will evolve from our human family's existing languages that will be taught in the schools of all the nations in addition to their mother tongue. Science and spirituality, the two most potent forces in human life, will reconcile, cooperate, and harmoniously develop. The economic resources of the world will be organized for the welfare of all members of the human family to ensure that the distribution of its products and services is equitably regulated. National rivalries and prejudice will be replaced by racial amity, understanding, and cooperation.

The enormous resources freed up by ending war will be dedicated to developing new scientific inventions and technology, increasing productivity, exterminating disease, raising the standard of health systems, ecologically sustaining the resources of Mother Earth, and furthering the intellectual, moral, cultural, artistic, and spiritual life of all her children.

These prophecies foretell a global oneness embracing the entire human family in a respectful, sustainable, and harmonious relationship characterized by the understanding that "the hurt of one is the hurt of all, and the honor of one is the honor of all."[1] This is the day that shall not be followed by night!

Though our work will be long and arduous, the Great Spirit has chosen to confer a prize upon us so precious that neither tongue nor pen can fittingly praise it. Fulfilling this ultimate vision and the prophecies of our indigenous peoples and the Ancient of Days is assured!

Chapter 9 Spotlight

Connecting the long and deep thread of indigenous wisdom with the needs of our time, Phil Lane Jr. shares indigenous prophecies that foretell of the turning point we are now facing. A long-promised spiritual springtime leads to the emergence of the Seventh Generation. This growing global movement of young people addressing climate change, as well as social and spiritual transformation, is leading to a new global civilization: one that is built upon the unfettered investigation of truth, characterized by principles designed to bring about a consciousness of the oneness of the human family, and governed by a global assembly, free from all prejudice and sharing a common language, with strong leadership from all cultures, guided by ancient indigenous wisdom of stewardship and harmony.

Call to Action

Contemplate your own indigenous roots, no matter how far back in history they may be. How does this impact your vision for the future? If you don't know your roots, study other cultures and learn from them. Use that wisdom to reshape your worldview and see all people, animals, and plants as your relations.

10

Reasons for Optimism: Transitioning to a Life Economy

John Perkins

Traveling around the world during this pivotal time in history, speaking at various venues, and meeting people who range from world leaders to subsistence farmers, I have witnessed an amazing awakening, a true consciousness revolution, an understanding that we are the navigators of a beautiful and fragile space station—and that we are currently steering her toward disaster. The COVID-19 pandemic is just one more strong message we've received along with the hurricanes, fires, and other "once-in-a-hundred-years events" that are suddenly happening every year or so. In the virus's case, it shows that the totally unexpected can hit us at any time. It's time to reboot our navigational system.

For at least three thousand of the two-hundred-thousand-plus years that humans, as we know ourselves, have existed, we've developed civilizations based on the exploitation of other people and nature. We've moved from hunter-gathers, through the agrarian and industrial revolutions, and into the current age of technology and information. Yet for these past three millennia, we've continued to build our social, economic, and political structures around hierarchies.

What we have today is a world that is the direct descendant of the classical empires, such as those of China, Persia, Greece, Rome; medieval fiefdoms; European colonizers of Africa, America, Asia, and the Middle East; slave-owning plantation systems; and nineteenth-century factories where women and children worked under horrible conditions.

People employed today by short-term, profit-driven corporations may live less squalid lives than the slaves, serfs, and indentured workers of former times, but they too are subject to the greed-driven, often brutal, policies of their corporate masters. They are bought and sold in the labor markets, sent off to fight wars that profit Big Business, and paid wages that are hundreds or even thousands of times lower than those of their bosses. Billions of people around the world labor long, hard hours, often under insufferable conditions, for wages that are insufficient to support their families, their health, and their own retirements. When the coronavirus hit, many found themselves in the terrible position of having to choose between going to work sick (and probably infecting others) and not providing food for their families. Others were forced out of a job, laid off or furloughed, left wondering where rent money would come from, if not that first month but the one after that. Meanwhile, fortunes that boggle the imagination are piled into the treasure chests of a handful of billionaires, the latest version of global potentates.

We have witnessed major changes since the beginning of the Industrial Revolution. We humans have created miracles in science, technology, medicine, and the arts. Many countries have efficient systems for handling sewage, providing potable water, and illuminating our darkest alleys. The infant mortality and poverty rates have decreased in many places. Our wondrous modern engineering has enabled many cities to cover old cities and cesspools and build skyscrapers, bridges, and governments to produce vehicles that probe the limits of our solar system. Most countries have writers, artists, and philosophers who expose the follies of war and tell the truth about what our hearts, minds, and souls demand of us.

However, inequality and suffering still are rampant. Many of us in the wealthy countries—and the prosperous citizens of poorer ones—insulate ourselves from the desperate people who make up more than half the world's population.

We exploit cheap labor and commandeer resources. We build legal walls—as well as ones of brick and mortar. In the process, we have created a global economic system that is based on war or the threat of war and the destruction of the very resources upon which war depends. This system threatens irreversible climatic changes and a nuclear holocaust. It is a death economy, consuming itself into extinction.

And yet we've already started the transition into what economists refer to as a life economy: a system that rewards businesses that clean up pollution, regenerate devastated environments, recycle, and develop new technologies for energy, transportation, communications, and many other sectors. This transition can be made much more easily than the one from agrarian to industrial societies.

Many individuals and organizations today are working to inspire and motivate people, corporations, and institutions to take the actions necessary to transition out of the death economy. Every day more people from all walks of life—consumers, investors, workers, CEOs, and government officials—are awakening and committing themselves to replacing that old worn-out system with a new one. They realize that the future lies in businesses that pay returns to investors who invest in an economy that is itself a renewable resource. They understand that this new definition of "success"—along with the accompanying values and actions—reinforces democratic decision-making processes and management styles—both in business and government. The coronavirus pandemic has had the positive effect of forcing us to understand that we simply must change; we must become more adaptable; and we must focus our economies and our actions on things that bring us together—people of all nationalities, cultures, and races—to foster a more sustainable and egalitarian human presence on the planet. Following is a comparison of the key characteristics of death and life economies and our responsibilities to make the transition.

Identifying a Death Economy

Here are some key characteristics of the death economy:

○ Its goal is to maximize short-term profits for a relative few.

○ It uses fear and debt to gain market share and political control.

○ It promotes the idea that for someone to win, another must lose.

○ It is predatory, encouraging businesses to prey on each other, people, and the environment.

○ It destroys resources needed for its own long-term survival.

○ It values extracted and materialistic goods and services above those that enhance quality of life.

○ It is heavily influenced by nonproductive financial deals (stock manipulation and financialization/"gambling").

○ It ignores externalities in measuring profits, gross domestic product, and other yardsticks.

○ It invests heavily in militarization, in killing, or threatening to kill, people and other life-forms and destroying infrastructure.

○ It causes pollution, environmental collapse, and drastic income and social inequality, and may lead to political instability.

○ It vilifies taxes, rather than defining them as investments in infrastructure, social services, healthcare, and so on.

- It is undemocratic, encouraging the growth of large corporations controlled by a few individuals whose money has a strong influence on politics (monopolies that lead to oligarchies).

- Business and government organizations are based on top-down, authoritarian chains of command that support autocratic management styles.

- It places higher values on jobs that promote competition (venture capitalists, lawyers) than on those that enrich life (teachers, musicians).

- It keeps billions of people in poverty.

- It classifies plants, animals, and the entire natural world as resources to be used for human benefit, while failing to respect and protect nature, thereby causing massive extinctions and other irreversible problems.

- It has become the predominant form of capitalism around the world.

Identifying a Life Economy

Here are some key characteristics of the life economy:

- Its goal is to serve a public interest and maximize long-term benefits for all.

- Its laws support level playing fields that encourage healthy non-monopolistic competition, innovative ideas, and sustainable products.

○ It embraces a sense of cooperation, the idea that we all can win when we set our goals on long-term benefits for all.

○ It values quality-of-life goods, services, and activities above materialism and extraction.

○ It is based on beneficially productive activities (for example, education, healthcare, the arts versus stock manipulation and financialization/"gambling").

○ It cleans up pollution and regenerates devastated environments.

○ It is driven by compassion, fair resource allocation, and debt-avoidance.

○ It helps hungry people feed themselves, those without shelter to secure it, those who are sick to access treatment, and those without resources to find some—or even to create their own.

○ It includes externalities in its financial and economic measurements.

○ It innovates—develops and embraces new, regenerative, sustainable technologies.

○ It recycles.

○ It regards taxes as investments in a mutually beneficial infrastructure, social services, healthcare, and so on.

○ It is democratic, encouraging locally based commerce and employee- or community-owned businesses (for example, cooperatives, benefit corporations, etc.).

○ In business and government, it reinforces democratic decision-making processes and management styles.

○ It places a high value on jobs that enrich life (for example, artists, volunteers).

○ It rewards investors who support these characteristics.

○ It is based on a foundational knowledge that humans are in a symbiotic relationship with our planet, that we must respect, honor, and protect the natural world.

○ It was the predominant form of economic evolution for much of human history.

The last point—that the life economy is part of an age-old human tradition—offers both perspective and hope. We all come from ancestors who understood the importance of long-term sustainability, a life economy. Our heritage as human beings includes a belief that we have a responsibility to pass on to future generations a world that is as resource-rich as—or richer than—the one we inherited. The traditional lifestyles of indigenous people are examples of life economies that have been successful for millennia.

It is up to each of us to facilitate the transition. Even relatively small groups of consumers, employees, and investors accepting the values of a life economy, taking actions to support businesses that promote these values, and pressuring governments to codify them into laws will eventually transform our obsolete economic system into a successful one.

Chapter 10 Spotlight

Adding to the many reasons for optimism about our future, John Perkins describes how we have already begun to make the transition from a long dying economic system to a successful economy that will not only sustain all life but also help it to thrive and prosper. Knowing that humans are in a symbiotic relationship with our planet will help us supplant our death economy with a life economy. This will transform our markets by rewarding businesses that clean up and regenerate the environment; develop new, innovative, and sustainable technologies; serve the public interest; create a level playing field; and encourage cooperation and compassion.

Call to Action

What pattern in your own thoughts or behavior is worn out and needs to be replaced with a new, life-sustaining approach? Make a list of these old patterns of behavior and then make a new list of ways you can change them to live a more positive, optimistic life. Take the actions necessary to manifest this new life. Know that living such a life will help future generations of all species, and it will bring you a greater feeling of satisfaction.

Circle Three
Conscious Enterprise and Social Change

We are ethical stewards of the earth's economic and
communications integrity.

11

The Dawn of a Conscious Business Movement

Steve Farrell

U rgent action is needed to reverse the effects of unconscious business. Unbridled capitalism, such as global economy addicted to growth at any cost, is the primary example of the damage unconscious business is doing to our communities and the global environment.

But we don't need just a business movement. If we are to create effective change, business must come to the front and lead. Businesses becoming conscious will only bring about lasting change if humanity as a whole becomes more conscious. Most of the challenges and chaos being experienced on Earth today are a result of unconscious living. Everyone on the planet is part of this and/or affected by it. So for a real business revolution, we first need a revolution in humanity's conscious evolution.

Business may be the primary contributor to unconscious living, but this call to action—and message of hope—is for everyone. We all have the opportunity—and responsibility—to heal discord by embracing conscious living. This is the change we are being invited to make, individually and collectively.

A recent program for spiritual activists, the Crestone Convergence in Colorado, with about fifty leaders present, addressed the hot topic of global capitalism. An emotional discussion surfaced with people sharing grave concerns about the direction of global business. This was a powerful affirmation that real change is on the horizon, that an evolutionary tornado has landed. The civil rights movement in the United States and the movement for independence in India are two examples of evolutionary tornadoes. Evolutionary tornadoes beckon change; they are disruptive and stubbornly resist premature closure. They always take civil society to a new destination, though the course may be halting, and right and left, more than straight ahead.

Less than a decade ago, with dysfunctional business on our minds, Humanity's Team (awakening the world to Oneness through education programs) studied progressive business models such as B Corps, conscious capitalism, natural capitalism, and other models to understand what role we might play in curbing business abuse and creating conscious business systems that support a flourishing world. We determined that while these business models were valuable and pointed business in healthier directions, they ignored real conscious business or stopped short of defining conscious business in a manner that can be uniformly and sustainably manifested worldwide.

Exploring the Essence of Conscious Business

Chris Laszlo, of Case Western Reserve University, says that conscious business must include both inner transformation and outer transformation dimensions.[1] B Lab and other progressive organizations often focus just on outer transformation—people, planet, and profit, for example. Laszlo shares that business must focus on the welfare of people and planet, not just profit. In Humanity's Team, we agree, and, as Chris points out, inner transformation is also critically important to feed a flourishing business while at the same time honoring the whole which makes it all possible.

Inner transformation focuses on practices like mindfulness but goes beyond to a deeper place where we commune with Source energy. People may individually find any number of equally valid and compelling ways to commune with this energy, from spiritual beliefs and practices rooted in a belief in the Divine to a deep resonance with the principles of quantum physics, which unambiguously establish that life is interrelated, interconnected, and interdependent. Everything is part of a single reality. We are all emanations of one thing.

One year, during Global Oneness Day on October 24, we coined the concept of the 4P model: people, planet, presence, and profit. Presence brings in wholeness, unity, and awakened consciousness. It looks out at the world and sees a deeply spiritual or interconnected ecology. When we become conscious, everything changes. Many then see the likeness and image of God in ourselves, each other, and the world around us. Others experience a resonant connection with Source in less spiritual terms, perhaps as an undeniable, uplifting energy that threads through all things, connecting all life forms.

Business models focusing just on outer transformation help businesses to do less harm, but one definition of a flourishing business also requires inner transformation, where interior process comes into play. The inner journey is a soulful experience of love, beauty, goodness, and truth. It shapes how we see ourselves and what we see when we look out on the world. We become anchored in this new reality. Life is sacred, and we place our lives in service to the sacred.

It is only a matter of time before these perspectives find their way into the workplace. Mindfulness, for instance, is already coming in strong. And it's critically important that leaders facilitate the business dialogue in a wholly inclusive manner, avoiding prescriptive statements about a singular ideology or path. The great religions of the world honor Divine inspiration and connection with Source. Science is also increasingly confirming that all the cosmos is connected. We are part of a natural and social web of life that nurtures and sustains us.

Spirituality, religion, and leading scientific thought likewise all have a stake in supporting people's inner transformation. If the core values and culture of the company are open and inclusive, honoring diverse spiritual, religious, and scientific perspectives, things will fall together beautifully. (See Humanity's Team as a case study.) Conscious business creates the opportunity for integration of deeply held values into work life, which in turn includes quality of life and markers of success other than profit when assessing an organization's value and quality. Unconscious business focuses almost exclusively on financial gain. This is precisely why we stand in a social and economic quagmire today.

Ken Wilber, one of the most important philosophers of our time, identified one of the most challenging and pressing problems in the world today: overfocusing on the outer world, which creates a "flatland" where consciousness is caught in a mundane experience of routines and day-to-day living that don't nourish or inspire the whole person or organization.[2]

Creating the Conscious Business Alliance

The enormity of the problem caused Humanity's Team and three other NGOs (nongovernmental organizations) to come together and create a Conscious Business Alliance. We were joined by the Club of Budapest (Hungary), the Goi Peace Foundation (Japan), and the Fowler Center for Business as an Agent for Public Benefit (Case Western Reserve University). Our first task was to create a brief, yet global and comprehensive, Conscious Business Declaration that describes the role conscious business can play in creating a flourishing world. Our presentation had to be one businesses could easily grasp so we could conform business models across intercontinental operations.

As part of a global community, we are committed to developing the awareness and skills needed to consciously evolve our organizations in alignment with these principles:

1. "We Are One" with humanity and all of life. Business and all institutions of the human community are integral parts of a single reality—interrelated, interconnected, and interdependent.

2. In line with this reality, the purpose of business is to increase economic prosperity while contributing to a healthy environment and improving human well-being.

3. Business must go beyond sustainability and the philosophy of "do no harm" to restoring the self-renewing integrity of the earth.

4. Business must operate with economic, social, and ecological transparency.

5. Business must behave as a positive and proactive member of the local and global communities in which it operates.

6. When business sees, honors, and celebrates the essential interconnected nature of all human beings and all life, it maximizes human potential and helps create a world that works for all.

7. When aligned with Oneness, business is the most powerful engine on Earth for creating prosperity and flourishing for all.

These are also principles that can be seen as catalysts to inspire any individual to align themselves with the principles and actions of conscious evolution. Try replacing *business* with *I* and see how this feels to you personally. Each one of these principles could then become the basis for action steps in the world.

If you are in the business world, envision how these might apply to your every action as a businessperson. Imagine how it fits your business as a whole. If the declaration does resonate with you, we invite you to sign it at consciousbusinessdeclaration.org.

We believe that the declaration brings the fullness of consciousness to business. A conscious business determines how it can meaningfully contribute first and then focuses on financial gain. As Michael Bernard Beckwith puts it, a conscious business is a mission with a business, not a business with a mission.

Fostering Conscious Business Activation

Recognizing a declaration needs an activation vehicle, such as a vision for training, consulting, and certification services to globally manifest conscious business, we created a program to teach people how to become Conscious Business Change Agents with a structured process leading to certification with the tools needed to transform a business.

Having signed the declaration, attended the training, and joined a vibrant community of business transformation practitioners, they all promote conscious activism in business by participating in specialized forums to share knowledge, forming partnerships, and gaining access to exclusive training programs with leading experts in business transformation.

Are you willing to join the emerging conscious business movement so we may course-correct and create a world that works for humankind, for the planet Earth, and for future generations?

As consumers, we each have the power to impact how businesses carry out their enterprise for the good of the whole. For example:

○ Becoming a conscious consumer

○ Becoming more discerning about the brands you place into your shopping carts

○ Choosing recyclable or compostable products with a goal of zero waste

○ Buying from companies that use regenerative practices

○ Choosing suppliers that respect human rights

○ Choosing products from companies that honor, respect, and pay their employees fairly

○ Buying from companies that prioritize sustainable practices and transparently share accounting, social, and ecological information

It will take time to interrupt old buying patterns—but let's get started! Let's align our values with our buying decisions. Let's reward conscious consumer brands and with our families become an expression of our values through the products and services we choose.

This is a purposeful journey. It involves creating new behaviors, so it will be challenging at times. But we can create a conscious world if we practice, stretch, gain new understanding, and express our values through our choices. Imagine a world with only conscious businesses and where conscious practices support (and are supported by) our families and communities. Let's devote ourselves to manifesting this dream together. Let's focus on this as though our lives depend on it.

Because, indeed, they do.

Chapter 11 Spotlight

Being ethical stewards by infusing a deep integrity, with a consciousness of the whole, into business, entrepreneurship, and media is a vital part of our global challenge. Steve Farrell, at the vanguard of the Evolutionary Leaders Synergy Circle for Conscious Business and as the copublisher of *Conscious Business* magazine, calls for urgent action to reverse the effects of unconscious business, to heed the evolutionary tornado that has landed beckoning change. Only *both* inner and outer transformation connecting us to a deeper place of communion with the one reality will create prosperity for all.

Call to Action

Become a conscious consumer. Choose what you purchase according to your values. Make a positive contribution to the businesses in your community that are ethical and sustainable. Ask yourself how you can be more conscious in all that you do.

12

Youth-Led Social Enterprise Projects

Gino Pastori-Ng

Transforming the global, exploitation-based economy into an equitable and life-affirming system for collective well-being is the greatest challenge humanity has ever faced. We can map every current societal problem to our economic model, which treats life itself as a commodity. The financial sustainability of this model depends on externalized costs, especially the pollution of our land, air, and water and the exploitation of human labor. As long as civilization's success is defined by production (the gross domestic product), the earth will be ravaged to the point of ecosystem collapse and the majority of human beings will live in abject poverty, consumed by the struggle to meet their most basic needs while others hoard more than they can use in a hundred lifetimes.

In the midst of this unprecedented challenge, the young people inheriting a world in crisis are still being encouraged to channel their talent and energy toward the maintenance of a destructive status quo. Young climate and peace activists are even criticized for joining together to demand desperately belated action.

Given the urgency of this problem, every school classroom should be transformed into an innovation laboratory where young people can experiment with ideas to solve social and environmental problems. But the majority of the educational system still operates under the industrial revolution model, preparing students for repetitive tasks in administrative and service-based careers that will soon be obsolete and failing to nurture their innate creativity. Students are pressured to assimilate into the exploitation economy and are rarely given the opportunity to manifest their own ideas in a meaningful way.

As growing numbers of young people enter adulthood already in debt, struggling to secure meaningful employment, the illusion that going to school and getting a stable job will result in a prosperous life has come crashing down. Faced with the increasingly unattainable goal of becoming economically independent and the prospect of an uninhabitable earth on the near horizon, young people around the world are rising up to demand a swift transition toward a life-affirming economy.

Although there has been a recent increase in media coverage of youth activism, from the Parkland students' gun law reform efforts to Greta Thunberg's climate advocacy, meaningful policy change and significant financial investment in the visions of young people have been nearly nonexistent. For planet Earth to remain livable, we must cultivate the brilliance and creativity of youth, encouraging and meeting them with real financial investment.

The new story already emerging is local, circular economies that recognize the interconnectedness of all life. A reclamation is underway, in which the word *economy* is returning to its etymological roots, meaning "to take care of the home." The old story of business as a vehicle for individual enrichment is no longer defensible, with a 2019 report from the United Nations estimating that 1 million plant and animal species are facing extinction, many within decades, due to human activity.[1] In order to diverge from what many are referring to as the sixth mass extinction, a new economy is manifesting, and its primary goal is to take care of our home, the earth.

Envisioning the New Economy

I envision a global network of hyperlocalized economies led by those who have been most marginalized by the exploitation economy. They are the ones who have become the most creative, resilient, and evolutionary just to survive under our current circumstances. They are the best equipped to create meaningful, lasting solutions if given access to the proper resources and opportunities. Imagine a world where everyone's basic needs are met, where every being has the opportunity to share their gifts, and where human existence actually improves the health of our ecosystems and increases biodiversity.

What is needed to achieve this vision is a global movement, in which diverse innovators are supported by a massive influx of resources from those who have inherited the wealth of the exploitation economy. Those who have reaped the financial rewards of the status quo have a historic opportunity and moral obligation to turn the tides of climate collapse and social inequity by divesting from extractive, exploitative industries and investing in the birth of a life-affirming economy.

Organizations like Resource Generation have led the way, but we need the proliferation of more that actively engage young people with wealth privilege to redistribute resources toward social, racial, economic, and environmental justice. It is estimated that in the US, baby boomers will transfer around $30 trillion in inheritance to their children. In order to rapidly accelerate the transition to a life-affirming economy, a significant portion of these resources must be directed toward manifesting the visions of those who have been suffering under the current paradigm.

What gives me hope is a surge of innovative, locally based solutions in my hometown of Oakland, California, where I have witnessed the emergence of a new story. As cofounder and codirector of Youth Impact Hub, Oakland, I have supported the launch of over seventy-five youth-led social enterprise projects created by resilient young people who have been marginalized by the exploitation economy and are rising up to take action. We have cultivated an intergenerational community of support fueled by a generous network of volunteer mentors and investors who are united in elevating and showcasing young people's innovative ideas in service to an economy that cares for the people and the planet.

The framework is simple, yet radically different than what most young people experience in school. We find participants who have personally experienced problems in their community and ask them how they want to address them. We create a collaborative atmosphere that provides resources to anyone prepared to use them, an active departure from the competition that defines most classrooms and business incubation programs.

Results have been absolutely phenomenal. For example:

Desire Johnson-Forte watched her community get decimated by a range of diet-related illnesses, like obesity and diabetes, due to living in a "food swamp": an area characterized by a lack of access to healthy food with abundant access to fast food. In response, she founded Damn Good Teas, which uses local, sustainably grown herbs to create healthy, nourishing beverages.

Trang Tran knew from personal experience that queer Vietnamese youth are often persecuted by their families and lack the social support they need to feel a sense of belonging. Trang responded by cofounding QTViệt Cafe, which uses the power of food to facilitate dialogue between queer and trans Vietnamese youth and their elders. Supportive elders share their family recipes with the youth and then offer dishes to the community at interactive events that create deep healing and connection for all involved.

Jasmine Curtis noticed her hair was falling out in college as a result of using toxic products. In response, she founded Avocurl, a natural hair care product made using edible ingredients, a much-needed alternative in the beauty supply industry that all too often pollutes the earth and increases cancer rates, particularly in the black community.

Typically, participants report that this is the first time they have been part of a community where their creativity and innovation is fully embraced. Many have been pushed out of schools or shunned by their families for breaking from the status quo. The fact that they continue to walk their own unique path and follow their dreams in spite of extreme adversity fills me with a tremendous sense of hope for the future.

These young people have experienced the worst of the exploitation economy, and they are using their unprecedented access to online information and lived experience to inform solutions that are socially equitable and environmentally sustainable. Most importantly, they are doing so collaboratively. Instead of competing for limited resources, they barter their skills and leverage their social networks to expand their collective impact. This depth of collaboration is fueled by a sophisticated analysis of our political and social context, as well as an advanced degree of spiritual understanding. Young people join our community filled with inspiration ranging from the Black Panthers, to Afrobeat music, to the healing properties of crystals. Each January, when a new cohort creates group agreements, they reference concepts like *Ubuntu* (a Zulu word that means "I am because we are") and *In Lak'ech* (which means "You are my other me" in Mayan). The social enterprise projects they create directly reflect their deep awareness of the interconnectedness of all life.

The young people coming of age in this extraordinary moment were born with innate gifts that are tailor-made for these times. Every organization on earth needs to engage them in meaningful ways and approach them as valuable thought partners. They are ready to solve problems, not sometime in the future, but *now*. When young people have ideas to improve the world around them, we must invest as many resources as possible toward their vision in order to birth a new global economy that reveres all life as sacred.

Chapter 12 Spotlight

Youth will always have a critical role in social benefit enterprise, as Gino Pastori-Ng describes so poignantly. His vision of a global movement of hyperlocalized economies that actively engage the brilliance and creativity of young people is already being cultivated in Oakland. Having launched over seventy-five youth-led collaborative social enterprise projects, he is helping to cultivate an intergenerational community of support, rooted in their deep awareness of the interconnectedness of all life.

Call to Action

Identify a youth group or organization in your area and discern how you can cultivate collaborative intergenerational support. Can you volunteer your time? Can you donate money to support their efforts? Find tangible ways to encourage, inspire, and collaborate with the young people in your community.

13

A New Consciousness of Money

Sarah McCrum

Picture a large gold coin representing our current financial systems. On one side is an image of apathy, disenchantment, and disempowerment. It represents people who live in scarcity and believe they never have enough to live a fulfilling life. On the other side is an image of force, competition, and exploitation. It represents people who pursue wealth and believe fulfillment depends on a lot of sacrifice and extremely hard work.

These two sides of the same coin represent the prevalent view of money as limited, corrupting, possibly evil, and only rewarding to a few at the expense of many. Consequently, few of us, whether wealthy, poor, or in-between, have a comfortable relationship with money.

People are often afraid to make money by doing something good for the world. If someone believes that money corrupts, it becomes virtually impossible to grow the amount of good they do. We can't live without it, and we can't easily live with it either. And yet money as a tool for our economy, our sharing of resources, is deeply rooted in our society and being—so something has to change.

A decade ago, shortly after my business failed and closed down, someone gave me a book called *How to Become a Money Magnet*, by Marie-Claire Carlyle. Sitting down one day with my notebook, I looked at the exercises at the end of each chapter. One of the questions asked, "What does money want to say to you?" As I placed my pen on my notebook, it started to write automatically. I saw words flowing out that were not my own. The first thing it wrote was, "I would like to tell you to love me." It continued, "Smile at me. Collect me. Enjoy me. Feel my power. Spend me. Invest me. Give me. Pay with me. Take me. I am an energy. I am very powerful and beautiful." It carried on for two pages, ending with the words, "I will love you."

It brought me to tears when I read it back. I had never conceived of money in the way it portrayed itself, as an energy of love and generosity that supports human creativity and connectedness.

In the following months I wrote another sixty-eight messages from money, which I published as a book called *Love Money, Money Loves You*. Since then I have been exploring the transformational implications for individuals and society, for business and personal life, if our relationship with money aligns with the information I received.

Recognizing the Deep Nature of Money

It is time to recognize the deeper truth about money. Our current understanding has created conflict on our planet. Our belief in scarcity of resources, personal limitations, and social constraints is reducing our creativity and ability to solve problems.

We now face issues as a species that are new for us. We've faced huge challenges in the past, including war, famine, disease, and natural disasters, but in our recorded memory, we haven't yet had to solve the combined problems of climate change, pollution, and inequality at the scale they exist today.

When money spoke through my pen, it revealed itself as an energy that is a part of all of our lives and lies behind the financial systems we use every day. Its true role is to enable us to create what we want so we may experience in life and share our unique contribution with society, in a perpetual process of giving and receiving.

Money shared that it is always available and has never been the devil or in any way harmful. It acknowledged that human beings do harmful things with money but that this has nothing to do with the true nature of money itself. It said repeatedly that anyone can be as wealthy as they wish if they learn how this energy really works. But our fundamental misunderstandings about money gives us a society where some people live in poverty and some pursue wealth in a way that hurts others.

The most surprising thing that emerged is the connection between money and love. It expressed love throughout its communication. Its tone was sweet, generous, and beautiful. A profound contrast to everything we have come to believe about money in modern Western culture.

This is hard to understand if we only see money as something we have to work for so we can pay our bills. To grasp the depth and power of this message, we need to suspend our current ideas about money and open to a new perception of it.

When we face this simple shift in consciousness about money, we shift the deepest source of conflict, both inner and outer, on our planet at the current time. This is the conflict between our material desire for a financially abundant life and our deeper spiritual aspirations for joy, inner peace, love, beauty, and freedom.

If we suspect that money is evil, a corrupting influence, or a risk to our virtue and integrity—and at the same time we desperately need or want more of it—we experience confusion and pain. This has to be buried deep inside ourselves so we can keep working, making money, and paying our bills.

Equally, if we believe we can only experience joy, freedom, and peace if we give up material desire and become spiritually pure, which we learn from both Eastern and Western teachings, we experience a disconnect from our natural inner abundance.

Then we experience a constant daily need and desire for more money accompanied by fear, distaste, or even disgust at ourselves for having to fulfill this need. In our desire to avoid feeling such a level of confusion and disconnect, we work harder and harder, or find other ways to obliterate our feelings, hoping it will take away the pain and atone for our wish for material satisfaction.

We're willing to make ourselves exhausted and sick, completely ignoring our own needs, so we can make more money. We often ignore our family's need for deeper connection and love as we search for material success. But true abundance remains elusive as long as we are caught in the trap of believing money is bad or responsible for suffering.

It's time to wake up and resolve this misunderstanding once and for all. Money is an energy, or a presence, of love and generosity that flows through our world, connecting us all together in vast threads of exchange and service. It is an energy that tracks every human wish or desire. It responds by fulfilling our wishes as directly as we allow. It travels freely on lines of relaxation, enjoyment, and openness to those who love its presence in their life. To those who deny its value and refuse its gift, it remains constantly open and available, as if waiting to be recognized for what it really is.

We have not known this in the past. We've been taught that money corrupts, and we've feared its power because we never realized that it connects with love.

It is only when we come to understand that the powerful energy behind our financial systems is intended to be supportive, generous, unlimited, available to all, and loving that we can relax in its presence, delight in sharing our gifts and creativity, and freely accept its financial and other rewards.

It then becomes impossible to continue to make decisions that cause harm to our own or other species; or to make the place where we live so dirty we no longer thrive here; or to deny access to education about wealth to the vast majority of the population in every country across the world.

In turn, this understanding will allow us to create businesses that truly serve in a spirit of generosity and love. It enables us to be rewarded well for doing significant work and growing our impact. It causes us to value the contributions of so many people who are barely recognized in today's economy—the carers, healers, artists, and creators of all forms of beauty and social enhancement.

And perhaps most significantly, it enables us to get in touch with our deepest wishes and learn how they may be fulfilled, simply because that is what money's exquisitely beautiful energy does.

It serves us constantly in a cycle of asking and receiving. It arranges the synchronicities and synergies that make life feel like a magical adventure. It answers our call for beautiful solutions to challenging and disturbing problems.

Everything is possible for the energy that lies behind our financial and economic systems—the same energy that fulfills all our wishes. All it asks is that we truly, deeply understand that it is an energy of love.

Imagine if we could allow ourselves to experience more abundance. Then we could create a healthier, cleaner environment. We could unite across borders to resolve the bigger challenges we're currently facing. We could even dare to ask for our biggest wishes to be fulfilled, for example, money to become a catalyst for good, or the climate to become more livable and more stable across the planet.

This is what money energy does. It fulfills our wishes. It is up to us to learn how it works.

Chapter 13 Spotlight

Reframing our individual and collective relationship with money is much needed in the unfolding process of global transformation, as Sarah McCrum explains. Money's deep nature is an expression of the energy of love, the underlying fabric of life, which is fully available to all. Tuning ourselves to this consciousness of money supports us in making more equitable and just financial decisions, serving others in a spirit of generosity and love, valuing the contributions of all people, and finding solutions to challenging issues that lead to mutual benefit and abundance.

Call to Action

To reframe your relationship to money, take a moment to visualize money as a source of energy expressing love, support, and generosity to enable you to fulfill your highest aspirations.

14

The Core Principles
of a Business
Warrior Monk

Rinaldo S. Brutoco

*In our era, the road to holiness necessarily
passes through the world of action.*

Dag Hammarskjöld, UN Secretary-General (1953–1960)

Addressing the many challenges of our era, from climate change to income inequality, will require our leaders to increasingly embrace a unique combination of traits in a way that I have come to refer to as being a business warrior monk.

This article outlines the four core principles that differentiate a business warrior monk from a traditional leader. These principles have anchored the World Business Academy, an organization I founded as a nonprofit think tank and action incubator that explores the role of business in relation to critical moral, environmental, and social issues of our time. Over the past thirty years, we've successfully built both for-profit (NYSE, NASDAQ, and OTC) and nonprofit (JUST Capital, World Business Academy, Chopra Foundation, Omega Point Institute, Unstoppable Foundation, Gorbachev Foundation, National Peace Academy, etc.) enterprises that strive to "take responsibility for the whole."

Since the formal launch in 1987, the threefold mission statement of the World Business Academy has been

o to shift the consciousness of existing business leadership from predator to steward, because we act differently when we accept we are responsible for the result of our actions;

o to shift the consciousness of young people going into business, particularly at our business schools, to see themselves as entering a noble profession rather than a jungle, because we act differently in the temple than we do in the jungle; and

o to shift the consciousness of the public at large to put its money where its deep values are, because when the public does this, business thrives in response.

The Four Core Principles

Underlying this public mission statement are four core principles that guide the actions and perceptions of a business warrior monk, so those "monks" can share in the noble work of the academy to "take responsibility for the whole" of society. As summarized next, these core principles are orientation to Spirit, clarity of purpose, embracing critical qualities, and redefining success.

Orientation to Spirit
We are not humans having a spiritual experience. Rather, we are spiritual beings having a human experience.[1]

This principle is grounded in the Perennial Philosophy (Aldous Huxley's term), which views all of the world's great religions, despite superficial differences, as sharing many of the same metaphysical truths as manifestations of the "divine reality" (charity, nonattachment, self-knowledge, good and evil, prayer, suffering, faith, etc.). This principle is further amplified by philosophers George Gurdjieff and Pierre Teilhard de Chardin.

Clarity of Purpose

If we accept the conclusion that the universe is benign, then "How can I serve?" will be the transcendental question that defines our life's work.

Einstein concluded that the universe is a friendly place. He famously observed that the only "real choice" was to believe that the universe was inherently threatening or benign: if the former, all was hopeless; if the latter, investigate how you can best harmonize with it. Our ultimate goal is to uncover the clues the universe provides in order to find our respective life's purpose. Integrity means living in harmony with that truth so we can "live the truth we know." An observation I made many years ago and repeat often to this day is "I define personal integrity as living the truth you know—not the truth I know, but the truth you know." And that "pain" as we experience it every day is defined as the distance between living the truth we know and the life we actually live.

Embracing Critical Qualities

Once we understand our life's purpose, we must commit heart and soul to fulfilling it by acting with impeccable discipline, humility, and inspiration.

To achieve our purpose, we must finely hone three essential qualities and employ these in our actions:

1. The *discipline* of a professional athlete, who continually seeks peak performance regardless of changing conditions

2. The *humility* of a Shaolin Buddhist monk, who acts without attachment to results or the need for recognition

3. The *inspiration* of a visionary, who transcends all negative thoughts in order to translate creative ideas into the material world

Redefining Success

If we act in accordance with these principles, we're inevitably led to supreme success, including attracting abundant emotional and material support that enables our work to grow.

Once we are fully committed, as Goethe observed, "Providence moves too. All sorts of things occur to help one that would never otherwise have occurred."[2] By following our purpose and doing what we love, the money follows—more than enough to satisfy our needs. In doing so, we avoid the classic business pitfalls of never having enough money, power, or ego and redefine success to being more than the mere accumulation of wealth. Success means building thriving enterprises that fulfill the academy's fourfold bottom line: people, purpose, profit, and planet.

The Operating Principles

Seeing business as a spiritual enterprise is far from a traditional approach, and we do not ask you to embrace these core principles as a matter of faith. Rather, look at them as an operating manual for the new paradigm of business and judge them on their results.

To this end, we have developed twelve operating principles for successful for-profit and nonprofit enterprises (derived from the core principles).

The twelve operating principles described next can be applied to a variety of enterprises, large and small. They are also applicable to complex domestic and international public policy issues. For-profit enterprises have ranged from cofounding the cable television industry to creating a hydrogen-powered dirigible that has been heralded by multiple high-ranking admirals as the "greatest innovation in flight since Kitty Hawk." Nonprofit enterprises have included developing solutions for climate change, serving Mother Teresa, and providing schooling and clean drinking water for twenty thousand children in Africa.

These are the operating principles:

1. Recognize that, in building highly successful businesses, culture always trumps strategy.

2. Practice "servant leadership," always asking, "How can I serve?"

3. Build disruptive companies, especially companies that disrupt entire industries.

4. Network constantly: if you are not networking, you are not working.

5. Tackle humanity's greatest challenges by "taking responsibility for the whole."

6. Embrace humility: it's amazing how much you can accomplish if you don't have to take credit for it.

7. Think way out of the box to develop innovative solutions for challenging environmental problems.

8. *Change or die!* Follow nature's fundamental law to create game-changing technologies and companies.

9. Apply cutting-edge information technologies to build highly effective marketing campaigns.

10. Pursue radical integrity and transparency: your reputation is your most valuable asset.

11. Beware of out-of-control egos: they destroy people and companies.

12. Trust in the "green energy flow" of the universe. If your idea is true, the capital will follow, abundantly and effortlessly.

The Rise of "Stakeholder Capitalism"

In 2013, the World Business Academy and the Chopra Foundation launched JUST Capital as a paramount extension of the Academy's mission to shift the consciousness of business leadership. By promoting the concept of stakeholder capitalism in forums such as the Business Roundtable and Davos 2020, JUST Capital is already changing the way that the US's leading corporations are doing business by demonstrating that more economically equitable and environmentally sustainable practices are better for the bottom line.

Working closely with JUST Capital further confirmed the wisdom of the Academy's teaching that business is "the most powerful force in the modern world." Accordingly, in order to make positive lasting change, we have to start by conceptualizing business as not simply being about making a profit but as having the moral responsibility for improving the human condition by representing all stakeholders and uplifting all that it touches: employees, customers, shareholders, communities, and the environment.

We launched the nonprofit World Business Academy to show that business could improve quality of life while providing better-than-average profits. In the beginning, we referred to the core principle of Orientation to Spirit as the S-word, fearful that the mere mention of "spirituality" would frighten business executives away.

But the idea of business as a spiritual discipline has come out of the closet. Today it is entering the boardroom wrapped in blue-ribbon concepts—"compassionate capitalism," "the soul of money," "servant leadership"—that express the innovative ideas through which farsighted CEOs, bestselling authors, and business consultants seek to transform companies. It is gratifying to see these new-paradigm business ideas that the Academy has championed for over three decades move from the margins to the mainstream.

In the process of building the Academy, we discovered and implemented—through trial and error, success and failure—the operating principles outlined earlier. We share these principles so that you may consider joining the growing fellowship of business warrior monks who are striving to build successful enterprises, win victories for humanity, and insure a better future for our children's children.

For those who are skeptical, we close with this quote by the English poet Christopher Logue:

"Come to the edge," he said.
"We can't, we're afraid!" they responded.
"Come to the edge," he said.
"We can't. We will fall!" they responded.
"Come to the edge," he said. And so, they came.
And he pushed them.
And they flew.[3]

Chapter 14 Spotlight

Rinaldo S. Brutoco takes serving in a spirit of generosity and love a step further: he and other forward-thinking innovators have worked together for decades to form more conscious business entities based on the innovative concept of stakeholder capitalism. This seminal concept, along with their four core principles and twelve operating principles, allow business to become a spiritual enterprise that takes responsibility for the whole of society. This positive future for business would dramatically reduce both greenhouse gases and income inequality, critical steps toward world peace.

Call to Action

Identify the core principles that guide your life, for example: discipline, compassion, loyalty, generosity, commitment, open-mindedness, honesty, and so on. What are your own core principles, and what can you do to strengthen them?

15

Reinventing the Planet: A Bottom-Up Grand Strategy

David Gershon

I f we wish to change the world, we need to first change the way we
think about change.

At this critical juncture in human evolution, unless our species rapidly
changes its trajectory, our civilization will unravel. The question is, how
do we do that? Many dedicated and heroic changemakers have poured
their hearts and souls into trying to transform the world, but what if the
problem is not the world's unwillingness to change but the approaches
we use? What if our own limiting thoughts about social change and people's abilities are the problem?

Apple anticipated this mindset in its famously provocative "Here's
to the Crazy Ones" ad in the '90s: ". . . The ones who see things differently. They're not fond of rules. And they have no respect for the status
quo. . . . And while some may see them as the crazy ones, we see genius.
Because the people who are crazy enough to think they can change the

world, are the ones who do."[1] These are three questions the crazy ones must keep asking if we want to change the world:

1. How do we reinvent social change?

2. How do we reinvent social activism?

3. How do we reinvent the planet?

Reinventing Social Change

To answer these questions requires us to better understand the nature of social change, how it is currently practiced, and where an opportunity exists for it to evolve.

The world is a composite of many social systems—financial, political, healthcare, educational, etc.—created at a time when the world was much simpler and easier to navigate. They were not designed to meet the stresses of the complexity and discord in the world today.

A deeply stressed social system becomes unstable and starts to oscillate, eventually becoming unmoored from its foundation and breaking down until it is marginally functional or dysfunctional. The US political system is the poster child for a broken social system. But the other social systems are not far behind. The climate change crisis on the planet is the culmination of multiple broken social systems that are forcing humanity to take a hard look at the dysfunction we have created.

When a social system is not tethered to something that keeps it in place, it cannot only break down; it can also break through and evolve to a higher level of performance and social value. In systems theory this is called second-order change or, in this context, transformative social change. The alternative is first-order or incremental social change. I call these two approaches Social Change 1.0 and Social Change 2.0.

Social Change 1.0 consists of the traditional social change tools of passing laws, financial incentives, awareness campaigns, and social protest. At their best, which is certainly not the norm, these tools are able to achieve incremental change. In a business-as-usual world, this is how humanity muddles along. Although necessary, this approach is insufficient in a world that requires fundamental transformation in order to avoid species extinction or the multitude of dehumanizing social problems that seem to be immune to first-order change solutions.

So, if you can't achieve the transformative social change our planet needs by forcing people to change, paying them to change, raising their awareness in hopes that they will change, or shaming them into changing, what is left? Unfortunately for so many, it is despair, apathy, and pessimism.

But what if we could empower people to want to change? What if we could help people tap into their innate desire for a better life, community, and world? What if we could support people to create a vision of these dreams that was so compelling, they were effortlessly pulled toward them? What if we then provided people the tools to attain these dreams? This is empowerment in action! It provides people with the agency that is at the heart of Social Change 2.0.

Reinventing Social Activism

Over the past forty years, I have been considered one of the world's leading experts in empowerment and social change, and I have strived to change the game of change. I have created five second-order change solutions essential to humanity's evolution. I have also written the definitive book on second-order change, *Social Change 2.0: A Blueprint for Reinventing the World*. This book empowers the crazy ones with the five social change superpowers needed to change the world. How to empower, transform, innovate, unify, and mobilize.

What happens when we integrate these five second-order change solutions and five Social Change 2.0 superpowers is an alchemical reaction that changes the game of change. And what emerges is a plan for reinventing the planet!

Reinventing the Planet

1. Climate Goal and Strategy—Cool Block Program

By 2030, empower cities around the world (70 percent of the planet's carbon emissions) and their citizens (70 percent of a city's carbon emissions) with the agency and second-order change knowledge to transform the climate paralysis and create carbon neutral cities and breakthrough solutions.

Our behavior-change and community-engagement programs have empowered millions of people in dozens of countries to adopt low-carbon lifestyles over thirty years. Cool Block, the evolution of these many programs, is a block-based peer support group that helps people become more planet friendly, disaster resilient, and community rich. Participating households reduce their carbon footprint by 25 percent on average, and 56 percent of neighbors invited by a trained block leader participate.

Cool Block is currently operating in four California cities: Los Angeles, Palo Alto, Isla Vista with UC Santa Barbara, and Mountain View. This is the first phase of our larger strategy called Cool California, to create carbon neutral cities statewide.

2. Development Goal and Strategy—Imagine Program

By 2030, empower women in the developing world with the agency and second-order change knowledge to transform the cycle of poverty and create thriving lives and communities.

Johns Hopkins Research indicated women who participated in Imagine were:

o three times more likely to report improved income,

○ ten times more likely to report improved health,

○ fifteen times more likely to report improved relationships.

Imagine is based on the Empowerment Workshop—a four-day training program for disenfranchised women throughout the developing world that helps them envision and create what they want in their lives. So far, twenty-two thousand women in twelve countries have been trained, impacting 5.5 million people. We have plans to scale Imagine to thousands of NGOs (nongovernmental organizations) throughout Africa, South and Central Asia, and the Middle East.

3. Peace Goal and Strategy—Peace on Earth by 2030 Game

By 2030, empower humanity with the agency and second-order change knowledge to transform the paradigm of war and create peace on earth.

In 1986, at the height of the Cold War, a torch of peace was passed around the world, stopping wars and uniting people wherever it went. The First Earth Run directly engaged 25 million people and forty-five heads of state in sixty-two countries and a billion people via the media. Since then, this modern-day mythic story embodying humanity's noblest aspiration for peace on earth has continued to be told all over the world. Now the torch of peace has been reignited to create the Second Earth Run via a Peace on Earth by 2030 game built around the seven strategies that united the world. These strategies have been created into seven actions that are the foundation of the game.

At this critical time when we are becoming more and more divided, the game serves as deep medicine to heal that which separates us. There are so many people of goodwill connected across the planet that with the right spark, we can ignite a global fire that empowers humanity to fulfill its deepest dream. The seven actions for creating peace on earth have proven they can ignite such a global fire.

4. Knowledge Goal and Strategy—Empowerment Institute Centers for Reinventing the Planet

By 2030, empower the world's changemakers with the agency and second-order change knowledge to create transformative solutions that reinvent the planet.

Our pioneering Empowerment Institute, founded in 1981, has created agency and second-order change solutions for a wide variety of social and environmental issues at every level of scale across the planet. Based on our forty years of empowerment and second-order change knowledge, we have established Centers for Reinventing the Planet throughout the US, Africa, India, the Middle East, and Central Asia. Here social entrepreneurs and change agents of all stripes learn the skills to transform the world's most challenging problems.

The mantra of our Centers for Reinventing the Planet is the John Gardener quote: "The world is full of breathtaking opportunities disguised as insoluble problems."[2] With empowerment and second-order change knowledge, the impossible suddenly becomes possible.

5. Money Goal and Strategy—Reinventing the Planet Fund

By 2030, empower the world's social change investors with the agency and second-order change knowledge to invest in transformative solutions that reinvent the planet.

Our Empowerment Institute has raised tens of millions of dollars and recruited thousands of volunteers to deploy its agency and second-order change solutions around the world.

We have created a billion-dollar philanthropic investment fund of top-down and bottom-up investors to implement the five-part "reinventing the planet plan" described in this section. It is our intention to leverage this fund to redirect the trillions of dollars of first-order change investments into second-order change solutions to help this money do good more effectively.

An Idea Whose Time Has Come

We find ourselves at a moment in time when the social and environmental stresses are so pronounced that they have actually become a force to accelerate human evolution. In evolutionary biology, this is called *punctuated equilibrium*—a time when rapid and quantum change suddenly becomes possible.

In 2015, the ambitious UN Sustainable Development Goals for 2030 were launched. Since then, the world has been searching for the means to implement the needed magnitude and speed of transformative social change. This plan to reinvent the planet provides humanity with the means, but it goes beyond that. It allows us to

- O realize our fullest potential as a human species,

- O live in harmony with each other and the earth, and

- O regain control of our destiny, enabling us to experience hope, passion, and excitement about the future.

Please join us for the greatest adventure of our time—reinventing the planet!

Chapter 15 Spotlight

Drawing on his four decades in the trenches working on large-scale societal transformation, David Gershon offers an original and comprehensive road map for bringing about fundamental change in our world. To reverse the accelerating deterioration of so many of our social systems, and to use this circumstance to accelerate human evolution, he provides exactly what is needed to create rapid transformative change. Identifying goals and strategies for second-order social change solutions, he details a bold plan for reinventing our planet that gives us ways to realize our fullest potential as a human species.

Call to Action

Learn the tools of empowerment and second-order change; become one of the crazy ones ready to reinvent the planet. Set the intention to play the role in social change for world peace you were born for. Find organizations in your community already doing this and make time to help in their efforts.

Circle Four
Healing Ourselves and the Planet

*Working with the mind-body-spirit connection,
we can heal the whole system.*

16

Survival, Consciousness, and the One Mind

Larry Dossey, MD, and Barbara Dossey, PhD, RN

The magical, mysterious, sacred revival is already underway, it just isn't paraded by the mainstream yet. But the spores are seeding all over the holy ground of this blessed planet. It will come to pass— it has already been born.

Kingsley L. Dennis, British sociologist

Today we humans confront threats to our existence that many of our forebears never imagined: climate change, polluted air and water; exploding populations; habitat and species loss; water scarcity; deforestation; desertification; murderous ideologies; resource depletion; widespread poverty; long-term wars of choice; ethnic and religious hatreds; lack of decency, love, and kindness toward others—and on and on, all abetted by the materialistic "I've got mine/every man for himself" philosophy that appears to have been adopted by a regrettably large segment of our society, though by no means the majority.

We can succinctly express the origin of the problems like so: Our species has tried to secede from nature, and we have failed. In so doing, we have misconstrued the nature of our own consciousness, our connectedness with one another, and our relationship to all sentient life. Something is missing in modern life. We are starved for vision. We hunger for a culture that transcends the suffocating narrowness and intellectual strangulation caused by prejudice, bigotry, greed, and crass materialism that threaten our future. We yearn for connections, but our yearning does not go far enough. In reality, our connections are not earth-limited; they are infinite.

Poets, Physicists—All of Us—Are of One Mind

Love helps us resacralize our world—make it sacred again. Love is a natural accompaniment of the inherent unity, connectedness, and Oneness that typify human life. If we genuinely sensed our connectedness, we would revise the Golden Rule from the customary "Do unto others as you would have them do unto you" (Luke 6:31) to "Be kind to others because in some sense they *are* you."[1] Love helps us survive.

Sensing our connectedness requires a shift in consciousness so we recalibrate our ethical and moral compass toward planet Earth and one another. It is about changing channels, redialing our attitudes toward the terrestrial crucible that sustains us. Connectedness leads to love, and love leads to caring.

When caring includes all of life, it becomes a vision powerful enough to make a difference in how we approach *all* the challenges we face—not as a mere intellectual concept but as something we feel in the deepest way possible.

Our existence is based on unity, connectedness, and cooperation, not in separation, competition, and rugged individuality, as we've been taught. The act of *caring* arises naturally from these intrinsic relationships.

The unitary, nonlocal nature of consciousness implies that it has no fundamental boundaries and therefore cannot be separated into parts.

In some dimension, individual minds come together as a unitary, collective One Mind. The idea of a universal, collective consciousness has been around for millennia. As Hippocrates stated, "There is one common flow, one common breathing, all things are in sympathy."[2]

The One Mind idea is a core component of perennial wisdom. Modern physicists didn't discover this unity; they reflected and verified what poets and seers across the ages have known. Poet William Butler Yeats wrote of many minds flowing into one another creating a single mind, a single energy[3]; Walt Whitman similarly saw all separations "hook'd and link'd" together[4]; essayist Ralph Waldo Emerson wrote of a universal mind common to all.[5] The great physicists of the twentieth century were likewise strongly aligned with this sense of a single consciousness connecting all things: Nobel Prize winner Erwin Schrödinger wrote that consciousness cannot be divided because "in truth there is only one mind,"[6] while eminent physicist David Bohm agreed, "Deep down, the consciousness of mankind is one."[7]

The One Mind Is Timeless

The One Mind concept envisions a nonlocal unitary consciousness— that is, a consciousness boundless in space, therefore omnipresent, and infinite in time, therefore immortal and eternal. However, science often overlooks the greatest advantage associated with the One Mind concept: as a physician and a nursing scholar, we believe that the terror of physical annihilation has caused more suffering in human history than all the physical diseases combined. The nonlocal One Mind, then, is a potential cure for the greatest of all diseases, the dread of total annihilation with physical death.

Destruction of personhood with physical death is an inescapable part of the materialism package. The cheerleaders of materialism vastly underestimate this enormous cost. Jung viewed it as a vital issue, saying, "The decisive question for man is: Is he related to something infinite or not? That is the telling question of his life."[8] If consciousness is produced by the brain and vanishes with physical death, as materialists insist, then any meaningful relationship to "something infinite" is a chimera. Jung felt so strongly about this issue that he made it a principle in therapy with his patients. "As a doctor," he said, "I make every effort to strengthen the belief in immortality. . . ."[9]

Immortality for the mind was a key feature of physicist Schrödinger's vision: "I venture to call it [the mind] indestructible since it has a peculiar time-table, namely mind is always *now*. There is really no before and after for the mind. There is only now that includes memories and expectations."[10]

Simply put, materialism, mindless consumerism, and environmental debauchery are exacerbated by a denial of immortality. The realization of our essential unity, of a temporally and spatially nonlocal One Mind, is our best hope for our survival on earth. Reaching for our connections with one another at the deepest emotional-psychological level and with the planet itself will enable us to summon the courage necessary to make the tough choices required to stay alive—to save the earth and our own skins.

We are at a hinge point in human history. During the twentieth century, we took the mind apart. Now we must put it back together. We've been taught that our mind is fragmented, that it is divided into the conscious, preconscious, subconscious, unconscious, ego, superego, id, and so on. We are divided not just from within but also from without, from one another.

Looking through the other end of the telescope, the One Mind reveals that our individual minds are part of a greater whole, a dimension of consciousness that encompasses all minds—past, present, and future; human and nonhuman.

A Collective Near-Death Experience Can Transform Us All

Here is one of many scenarios that might play out, as presented by philosopher Michael Grosso in his important book *The Final Choice: Death or Transcendence?* He suggests that, with increasing environmental destruction on the horizon, a planetary version of a near-death experience (NDE) may be coming into being, analogous to the NDE of a person approaching death.[11]

Four features of NDEs underlie Grosso's vision:[12]

1. NDEs can happen to healthy people.

2. NDEs can be experienced by people who do not believe in their validity.

3. NDEs can be experienced simultaneously by groups of people.

4. NDE experiencers are typically transformed dramatically, especially regarding their ethical and moral perspectives, emerging with an intense concern for the future of all living things and the integrity of the earthly environment.

Following an NDE experience, most people find their fear of death vanishes. They become aware of their nonlocal nature and their essential immortality. They typically become more loving, compassionate, forgiving, and intensely aware of their responsibilities in the total global milieu. They often become passionately concerned about environmental issues, the welfare of other living things, and the future of humanity. As Sam Parnia, MD, director of critical care and resuscitation research at NYU Langone School of Medicine in New York City says, "What tends to happen is that people who've had these very profound experiences may come back positively transformed—they become more altruistic, more engaged with helping others. They find a new meaning to life having had an encounter with death."[13]

What we've learned from NDEs opens up new vistas in the human journey. Using the NDE as a portal, we can see how vast numbers of global citizens might make choices in their individual lives that positively influence whether the human species survives and thrives on planet Earth, regardless of their prior beliefs and behaviors. It's not that they newly bypass reason, logic, and evidence; rather, they embrace the evidence they earlier ignored.

The evolutionary leaders who contribute to this book are among those human spores, just as Kingsley Dennis so pointedly stated in this chapter's epigraph. And so are you. Let us together seed the holy ground of this blessed planet.

Chapter 16 Spotlight

Our challenge is healing the whole system, working with all its components as one, as a way of living, in order to maintain its overall harmony and balance. Larry Dossey and Barbara Dossey clearly identify the fallacy we have lived with for too long, not realizing that our consciousness is actually connected to all others, that our individual minds come together as a unity, as One Mind, and that love is what helps us recognize this and helps us survive. This knowledge is timeless—but never more needed than now. A collective near-death experience will transform our collective worldview toward transcendence, compassion, wholeness, and unity.

Call to Action

Meditate on all minds as a great web of interconnected sources of consciousness with you as an integral part, a light among infinite lights. Shine your light!

17

Healing Ourselves, Our Children, and Our World

Lori Leyden, PhD, MBA

Heart-brain-body technology exists to bring about world peace right now. From the Maharishi Effect experiments in the 1960s, we learned that when a small percentage of any population—the square root of 1 percent—achieves inner peace through meditation, that peace is mirrored in the rest of the community in the form of reduced crime, traffic accidents, and emergency room visits.

Follow-up studies have investigated what is needed to achieve a notable shift in consciousness toward peace, most notably the Heart-Math Institute's Global Coherence Initiative (GCI), an international effort that seeks to help activate the heart of humanity and promote peace, harmony, and a shift in global consciousness. GCI conducts groundbreaking research on the power of heart coherence—a state when the heart, mind, and emotions are in energetic alignment and cooperation—to bring about balance, collaboration, and peace in the world.

With the world in such chaos, why aren't we choosing peace now? The answer lies in our unresolved traumas. As a humanitarian and trauma-healing expert working in post-genocide and post-school-shooting communities, I see healing unresolved traumas as one of the greatest challenges—and opportunities—of our time. We all have them to one extent or another, so we can activate and evolve the hidden power of our heart-brain-body to bring about global peace.

Recognizing the Trauma of Loneliness, Separation, and Disconnect

Consider one of the more unrecognized epidemics of our time—a pervasive sense of loneliness, separation, and disconnect that so many of us experience. These feelings are rooted in traumatic experiences—from disconnecting from the Divine to embody our human form to experiencing circumstances and events that disconnect us from our most precious human peace-building gifts of forgiveness, love, and resiliency. In extreme forms, trauma can lead us to acts of violence and terrorism.

Conquering Our Transgenerational Crisis

Now consider how unhealed transgenerational trauma affects our ability to choose peace from the inside out. The trauma of extreme violence, poverty, and oppression—often war or genocide—is transmitted from one generation to subsequent generations. With over 52 percent of our world's population under the age of thirty (3.9 billion) and many people growing up displaced by violence and other disruptions, effectively treating transgenerational trauma is a critical step toward nurturing our young people to become healthy, effective global citizens.

My own personal healing journey and the work I do professionally inspire in me a deep commitment to nurturing our next generation of young people to heal, work, and become heart-centered peace-builders leading us into a peaceful future. I have often reflected on what I yearned for so desperately when I felt so alone and anxiety ridden during my own ongoing childhood traumas. I wanted to be seen, to be heard, to love and be loved, to know that I mattered, to be rescued from the depths of my despair, and to have a meaningful future.

That yearning continues to inspire in me a lifelong adventure to tenaciously investigate, experience, master, and deliver the most gentle, swift, and effective trauma-healing modalities available.

Re-regulating Trauma Physiology with the Heart-Brain-Body Connection

Here's what we need to understand about trauma and the heart-brain-body connection: trauma is a physiological process resulting in brain-based dysfunctions including a biochemical freeze response when we are confronted with overwhelming fear. In effect, we become frozen in our lower reptilian brain and central nervous system survival mode when our unresolved trauma is triggered.

Now consider that our physical heart has a collection of neuronal cells—cells in the heart that monitor and influence all the functions of our body, brain, and mind—that communicate with the neuronal cells in our brain. In effect, the heart has its own brain. Neuronal cells govern the interactions between the heart and the emotional and cognitive structures of the brain. Healing our traumas regulates our physiology so our heart can communicate more effectively with our brain's prefrontal cortex. This relationship activates additional peace-building gifts such as intuition, creativity, connectedness/oneness, and transcendence.

Leading-Edge Therapies for Healing

In my work, I have found that these two healing modalities most effectively repair our heart-brain-body connection:

Evidence-Based Emotional Freedom Techniques (EFT)

Also known as "Tapping" and "psychological acupuncture," this technique combines psychotherapy and acupressure, bringing together elements of exposure, cognitive therapy, and somatic stimulation. EFT is applied by someone simply focusing on an issue they would like to address with a related acceptance statement along with a simple two-finger Tapping technique on various pressure points on the face and body. In a therapeutic session, the therapist leads the client through the Tapping points and the client repeats the action. The technique can also be self-administered by the client outside of the session.

Evidence-based EFT has three features that distinguish it as an emerging fourth-wave therapy. Historically, psychotherapy is viewed as having three main waves to date: the psychodynamic approaches (Sigmund Freud, Carl Jung); the behaviorists (B. F. Skinner, Ivan Pavlov); and the cognitive behaviorists (Aaron Beck). Now, somatic body-based therapies like EMDR (Eye Movement Desensitization and Reprocessing) and EFT are gaining recognition as providing more effective, rapid relief.

It is a true heart-brain-body approach that quickly and permanently shifts dysfunctional emotional learnings. Research from Harvard Medical School has documented that the most effective therapies for trauma are brain-based somatic release techniques such as EFT/Tapping.[1] The stimulation of certain acupressure points on the body have been shown (through fMRI and PET scans) to calm the amygdala (the stress center in the brain) and stop the fight-flight-freeze response. With EFT, memories are retained, but they no longer trigger a physiological response in the body, thus allowing a full healing of the original trauma. Studies indicate that EFT positively alters the expression of a variety of genes implicated in stress hormones, cell repair, the immune response, tumor suppression, neural plasticity, and neurological signaling.[2]

The Grace Process

The Grace Process is a psychospiritual alchemical practice I received after my first near-death experience. The practice allows us to transcend our negative egos, and live in and from our highest heart-brain-body state rather than staying stuck in the lower reptilian brain. It is a formula for releasing judgments, opening to forgiveness, and accessing our highest human gifts through gratitude, love, joy, and wonder. When combined with EFT/Tapping, the alchemy of inner peace and transformation, unfolds more effortlessly. When combined, both modalities offer potent outcomes for trauma healing as well as strong implications for transgenerational trauma healing.

Building an Army of Peace-Builders

These practices became the foundation of my trauma healing work in Rwanda in 2007 with orphaned genocide survivors. In 2011, I developed a new form of humanitarian aid called Project LIGHT. LIGHT is an acronym for heart-centered Leadership Inspires Global Healing and Transformation. Project LIGHT: Rwanda became the world's first international youth healing program for traumatized young people based on trauma healing, economic sustainability, and heart-centered leadership training. The healing results were beyond our expectations. (Their transformation is chronicled in our award-winning documentary *When I Was Young, I Said I Would Be Happy.*)

Over the last twelve years, the miracles of this work continue to lead me into the heart of service with people who have experienced the worst of human tragedies in the form of war, school shootings, violence against indigenous people, and the conditions refugees are forced to endure during political and religious persecution. In each community, from Rwanda to Australia, from Sandy Hook, Connecticut to Parkland, Florida, we have worked with hundreds of young people and their caregivers to alleviate their suffering, heal their traumas, restore their resiliency, and open their hearts to inner peace and peace in our world. If these trauma survivors can find peace in their hearts and work toward peace in their communities and countries, who are we not to do the same?

My vision is to cultivate an army of peace-builders—parents, educators, mental health professionals, and young people themselves—dedicated to peace from the inside out. These peace-builders will establish Project LIGHT Centers around the world, offering young people the opportunity to heal their traumas, find successful work, and become heart-centered leaders. As incubators of peace, these centers can foster global citizens in connection with each other to cocreate innovative solutions for the worldwide challenges we face.

Our Hearts Really Do Have the Answers

We are truly in "the heart of service" when we realize that while there appears to be a giver and a receiver, meeting in the sweet spot in the middle of the infinity circuit connects our hearts to the Divine One Heart: there is only love, and we are all transformed. This "heart presencing," as I call it, which is only possible when our traumas are healed, is why I am able to experience the miracles that can and do come from tragedy.

Healing trauma in order to consciously evolve the power of our hearts to cultivate global peace *is* possible and *is* already underway. We have the heart-brain-body technologies to scale healing throughout our world with practices such as the Grace Process and evidence-based EFT/Tapping. As we heal our traumas, we change our genetics, our brain chemistry, and the ability of our hearts to connect, conspire, and cocreate new possibilities for healing ourselves, our children, and our world.

Imagine there is a computer system for activating that part of our DNA that "heart-wires" us for Divinity. The hardware is our heart, and the software is gratitude, love, joy, and wonder. Once activated, this system gives us maximum speed for connecting with the universal internet where the Divine One Heart exists.

Now imagine 7.5 billion hearts beating within the Divine One Heart in compassion and shared visions of safety, abundance, and peace for all. What's possible from this place?

A Path to Becoming a Peace-Builder from the Inside Out

By building an army of peace-builders committed to healing from the inside out, we can nurture our next generation of young people to heal, work, and lead us into a peaceful future. I believe we *are* "heart-wired" for Divinity. In moments of gratitude, love, joy, and wonder, our heart secretes a master hormone (ANF) that creates a connection between our heart and our prefrontal cortex—the part of the brain that activates our highest human gifts: creativity, intuition, transcendency, and connectedness.

To extend the phrase *peace is an inside job*, finding peace from the inside out is more of an ongoing practice. I experience inner peace when my heart-mind-body-spirit are in balance. Inner peace and grace mean experiencing a sense of connectedness and oneness in moments when the ordinary feels extraordinary and the extraordinary feels ordinary. In the experience of Oneness, the ego drops away, and in that connectedness, our hearts connect with the Divine.

Will you join us?

Chapter 17 Spotlight

Bringing the transformative process of healing ourselves and the planet back to the heart level, Lori Leyden leads people into heart coherence—a state when the heart, brain, and body are in physiological alignment. From this state, we have access to our highest human peace-building gifts: forgiveness, inner wisdom, creative problem-solving, spiritual connection, and cooperation. Her vision is to use innovative healing modalities, such as EFT and the Grace Process, to connect the heart, brain, and body for healing trauma and cultivate an army of parents, educators, mental health professionals, and youth dedicated to becoming peace-builders from the inside out.

Call to Action

Choose an incident from your past that you can drop judgments about and be open to forgiveness. Become a peace-builder from the inside out. Make gratitude, love, joy, and wonder a way of life.

18

The Noble Future: Becoming Fully Human

Gordon Dveirin, EdD, and Joan Borysenko, PhD

Transcending the Essential Contradiction

We are living in an era of interlocking environmental, technological, educational, and moral complexities as tangled as the fabled Gordian knot. According to prophecy, whoever could unravel its twists and turns was destined to become the supreme ruler of all Asia. In 333 BCE, Alexander the Great finally solved the "naughty-knotty" puzzle with a single swipe of his sword, rendering the ancient puzzle moot. Unfortunately, the problems facing our world today require a more Hegelian solution—a synthesis that includes yet transcends a variety of apparently contradictory polarities.

For instance, must we choose educating our children in STEM—science, technology, engineering, and mathematics—requiring them to stare at screens for hours each day, *instead* of enriching their inner capacity to use their new tools wisely and compassionately in a learning environment that fosters deep humanity?

A central contradiction of this perilous yet promising time is that we are at once super-empowered by technology and disempowered by our dissociation from resulting existential consequences. Consider this developmental ratio formulated by computer scientist, Bill Joy: human culture evolves at one thousand times the rate of biological evolution, while technology is evolving at one thousand times the rate of human culture.

Stop for a moment and think about that.

Marshall McLuhan, the late Canadian philosopher of culture and technology, called this dissociative condition "technological narcissism."[1] He viewed all technologies as extensions of the user. The hammer extends the arm; the tower extends the eye. But when the extension goes too far, so does the stress of maintaining its connection to our own deep selves and of expressing through it our most noble human values, motives, and sensitivities. The technology takes on a life of its own, like the rogue computer HAL in the movie 2001: A Space Odyssey.

Films are public dreams, making conscious the hidden content of our collective unconscious. Dystopian images abound in these dreams throughout the history of cinema, reflecting our shared sense of dissociation, of disconnection from feeling we can choose our own future rather than having it "happen to us" like fate.

How can we heal this disconnection and reconnect at a human level?

Shifting Perspective—Again

Wait. The earth revolves around the sun? We are not the center of the known universe? There is more to the world than meets the eye? The Copernican Revolution, as this seventeenth-century shift to a heliocentric perspective is called, marked the dawning of a new age of detached scientific observation.

The shadow side of such science is the co-occurring phenomenon of objectification. The late environmentalist and priest Thomas Berry lamented the resulting view of life as a "collection of objects rather than a communion of beings."[2] This dissociative viewpoint, sadly, gives license to manipulate, exploit, and control people as well as trash the environment, which is perceived as outside ourselves.

Science can help us pry loose nature's secrets to create a noble future, but as Francis Bacon, the seventeenth-century father of the scientific method understood, "knowledge without charity"—and, we add, intellect without heart, and power without love—produces "monstrous" results. The legend of Faust that emerged in Bacon's time foreshadowed that dark possibility.[3] J. Robert Oppenheimer, dubbed American Prometheus by his biographers in a book of that title,[4] fulfilled the Faust legend with horrific abandon three centuries later.

In *Hacking Darwin: Genetic Engineering and the Future of Humanity*, a former White House National Security Council member, Jamie Metzl, describes human biology as a form of hackable information technology. He writes, "After nearly four billion years of evolution by one set of rules, our species is about to begin evolving by another." However: "*Who* [italics added] has the right," he asks, "to make individual and collective decisions that could ultimately impact the entire human gene pool?"[5]

Who Are We, Anyway?

Who, indeed, do we imagine ourselves to be, and what values, reflecting either humility or hubris, will guide how we shape the world? The most important questions to ask are these: what do we imagine it means to be human, and who do we imagine ourselves becoming in the twenty-first century and beyond?

In an *Atlantic* book excerpt, "Why Technology Favors Tyranny,"[6] historian Yuval Harari shares his concern about the dangers posed by artificial intelligence. Alarmed about the growing concentration of information and power outside common control, he throws up his hands and asks: "So now, what should we do?"

His answer: "For every dollar and minute we spend on developing AI, we need to spend a dollar and a minute developing human consciousness," especially the cultivation of "our own wisdom and compassion."

Otherwise, increasingly tempted to surrender inner authority for algorithms available with a keystroke on platforms like Google, we seem poised for an automatic, driverless journey into a post-human future.

Do We Connect or Protect?

The capacity to connect is one of the quintessential human qualities. The neurobiology of connection begins in utero. What is the mother eating, drinking, thinking, feeling? Is she safe or in danger? Loved or neglected? After birth, does a child's primary caretaker respond to their needs? Are they bonded, well-attached?

As a lifelong need, during a pandemic, when we are asked to be socially distant, we see even more clearly how critical connection is at any age. Strong attachment leads to normal brain development. Abuse, neglect, violence, addiction, or other trauma, however, can stunt development of the brain's executive area: The prefrontal cortex (PFC)—the most evolutionarily recent part of the brain—enables us to think, reflect, set goals, plan strategy, and regulate emotions. It mediates the conversation between our interior world and the external environment.

Intelligence, the capacity of living systems to co-evolve and flourish through challenging conditions, is responsively relational. As the science of interpersonal neurobiology has shown, our hope to create a world of harmony and balance requires optimizing our human development—our ability to empathically connect with, rather than fearfully protect ourselves from one another.

In contrast, the limbic system—the most evolutionarily primitive part of the brain—overdevelops as a result of trauma. Thus, the biologic imperative of trauma is the perception of the world and other people as threats. Alarm, anger, and self-protection can take precedence over empathy and wise, compassionate action.

A robust movement in the fields of psychology and neuroscience has recognized the need to understand and mitigate trauma. The goal, of course, is to work toward minimizing the frequency of trauma and to educate and nurture our children in a way that leads to healthy, happy brain development and generosity of spirit.

Reviving the New Copernican Revolution

Developing human consciousness, including wisdom and compassion at scale, is now not only a possibility but a transformational movement in progress. In 1969, while directing the Stanford Research Institute's Education Policy Research Center, the late futurist Willis Harman wrote a classic paper[7] describing the "New Copernican Revolution" as a historic return to the inner life of consciousness that connects us to a larger whole. He wrote, "Today, the science of man's subjective experience is in its infancy. But if it gains momentum, its consequences may be even more far-reaching than those which emerged from the Copernican, Darwinian, and Freudian revolutions."

Harman was deeply immersed in the counterculture revolution of human potential that arose in the 1960s, intrigued by "the vast, imperfectly known universe of our own being" that encompassed transcendent experiences of the "higher self" and of human capacities for creativity, compassion, and unitive consciousness.

As an educator, Harman knew that we need a guiding vision that helps us imagine our way into a nobler future. That vision, he believed, "is to be found in a nobler image of man and of a society in which his growth may be better nurtured."

Nurturing the Noble Human

In 2019, we took a giant step toward realizing Harman's vision when the Aspen Institute issued the recommendations of its National Commission on Social, Emotional, and Academic Development: *From a Nation at Risk to a Nation at Hope*.[8] This document is a Magna Carta for humanizing education in the original sense of the word: "to unfold from within."

This is in contrast (and a response) to a 1983 report entitled *A Nation at Risk*, which was a national security appeal to regain academic advantage over our Cold War enemy, the Soviets, by "developing" better math and science skills in our students. Skill development was the overarching, though reductionist, aim of education.

A Nation at Hope recognizes our present need for a more fully integrated mode of human functioning if we are to creatively *respond* rather than simply *react* to the daunting challenges of our complex and rapidly changing environment. It sees its work as part of a wider cultural movement "to transform schools into places that foster empathy, respect, self-mastery, creativity, collaboration, civic engagement, and—on the strength of these values—academic excellence."

A Nation at Hope bases its approach on the overwhelming scientific consensus: "Human development happens in relationship. . . . Children learn best," it asserts, "when we treat them as human beings," which suggests relating in a personal "soul-to-soul" manner as opposed to an impersonal "role-to-role" manner, a shift that educator Parker Palmer has long advocated.

A warm, relational learning environment is optimally inclusive, helping children feel safe and be *seen* as unique and whole persons, respected in their cultural identities. Half of US children have a history of trauma.[9] A nurturing classroom has the potential to be an emotionally corrective experience for some of them. For example, if a child comes to school angry and acts out, the empathic teacher asks how they are and about what happened to make them angry. This mindful approach is in stark contrast to punishment. Such a trauma-informed approach to behavior at school is a key recommendation of the Aspen Institute's report. By definition, trauma anchors us to the past, diminishing our ability to be present and learn our way into the future.

That ability, to be fully present, deeply interconnected, and able to imaginatively learn our way forward together, is our passport to the noble future that reflects who, in our heart of hearts, we know ourselves truly to be.

Chapter 18 Spotlight

Taking an inner-oriented approach to bring about harmony and heal the whole system, because we are more than we think we are, Gordon Dveirin and Joan Borysenko envision a noble future in which everyone becomes fully human by returning to the *inner life* of consciousness that connects us to a larger whole. Developing and helping our own consciousness to evolve means tapping in to and aligning with our inner wisdom and compassion; this is the transformational movement of our time. This process of conscious evolution needs nurturing by transforming schools into places that foster empathy, respect, self-mastery, creativity, collaboration, civic engagement, and excellence. It is our passport to a noble future.

Call to Action

Commit to living into your own noble future. Choose to be part of the process of conscious evolution by becoming more empathic, respectful, and creative in all your relationships.

19

Elevating Our Spiritual Nature: The Pathway to Healing Humanity

Reverend Sylvia Sumter

With the needs of our world today, here's the question on so many minds: how can we heal our planet and humanity as a whole? Collectively healing the world is paramount; however, it must start with the individual. Salvation and evolution lie within our hands and hearts—this is our moment of choice! And thank goodness that is so.

Albert Einstein said, "No problem can be solved from the same level of consciousness that created it."[1] So, keep in mind that if we are to heal and create a new paradigm and a new earth, we must transcend human consciousness and human nature: we must see ourselves in a new light.

Under the old paradigm, we identified our threefold nature: mind, body, and spirit, with greater emphasis on the mind and body. The truth is, our primary nature is spiritual, and the order of dynamic expression is spirit, mind, and body, with the greater emphasis on spirit. Pierre Teilhard de Chardin aptly reminded us, "We are not human beings having a spiritual experience. We are spiritual beings having a human experience."[2]

We must awaken to the notion that we are spiritual beings, living in a spiritual universe, governed by spiritual laws. For this next quantum leap in our evolution, we have to get comfortable seeing and identifying ourselves as spiritual, not merely human. We are becoming a new order of beings that can and will manifest the creative essence of Spirit. We must put on the mantle and image of our Divine nature as spiritual beings! This is where our greatest power lies, for we have the ability to transform ourselves and the world through the unifying healing power of Spirit, within us and as us.

The time has come for a massive spiritual awakening! This is our moment of choice.

We must choose spirit, over mind and body, for the creative force of life lies within the spirit. The spirit brings inspiration to the mind and life and wholeness to the body. The scriptures remind us in Genesis 2:7, when we received the breath of life into our nostrils, that was the very moment we became living beings, or as some would say, living souls— the Spirit of God animating life itself. It is the creative energy and infilling of the Divine into all living things.

Our spiritual being is the highest facet of our existence and makeup, and we have the ability to bring forth the qualities and essence of spirit into our mind and body and hence into our world. The Divine qualities of Love, which unifies, harmonizes, and heals; Substance, which fulfills every need; Wisdom and Intelligence, which give us awareness and elevate our consciousness, are all aspects of Spirit. And as we raise and amplify our individual spiritual nature and consciousness, by drawing upon these qualities within us, we can and will collectively lift up humanity. We will make choices that speak to and serve the highest good for all concerned.

Spirit Dwells within Every Person

Here is the good news: Spirit is universal. It transcends nationality, race, gender, religion, culture, and any other variant we use to separate ourselves from one another. Any person who consciously chooses to express from a spiritual consciousness will lean toward expressions of peace, harmony, unconditional love, compassion, generosity, inclusivity, acceptance, connection, openness, and oneness.

Spiritual consciousness must lead the way if humanity is to heal. For when we rely solely upon our human nature and mind, we demonstrate a tendency, evident throughout our development as a species, to focus upon separation, superiority, greed, dominance, and other base qualities of human consciousness, as opposed to the higher and more refined qualities of spiritual consciousness.

But here is another encouraging truth: the more people awaken, the more people will awaken! Growth is exponential, and we impact one another through the matrix and interconnectedness of life. It is our responsibility to keep putting forth high thoughts, vibrations, and possibilities into the collective consciousness, so others may hear and feel the call to awaken.

Heart-Opening Techniques

Fortunately, the expression of spiritual consciousness and spiritual awakening do not require your typical spiritual practices such as meditation, yoga, mindfulness, and the like (although those are indeed excellent portals and highly recommended, especially for those interested in the spiritual path). Spiritual consciousness and awakening can be developed quite simply by opening the heart—something universal that appeals to anyone steeped in the human condition and consciousness. In fact, the heart can be thought of as the abiding place for spiritual consciousness, and a pathway for spiritualizing the mind.

It's popular to talk about keeping an open mind, but it is here we often find ourselves close-minded and trapped in our own views, beliefs, and ideologies. Something else is needed that carries the energy of the Spirit. With an opened and flowering heart, one becomes more accepting, forgiving, tolerant, understanding, and compassionate, ever widening the circle to draw everyone in. An opened heart is the repository of the Divine and powerfully radiates energy from its center, drawing everything unto itself. This is the magnetic power of Divine Love moving beyond human consciousness: When we touch it from within, we become a radiating center of loving and transformative spiritual energy that touches everyone in our path and beyond.

Practice Heart Breathing

One easy and natural way to open the heart is to consciously practice breathing in and through the heart. Focusing your mind-body connection on the heart will stimulate your spiritual consciousness. A calm mind and relaxed body make it easier for Spirit's higher guidance and wisdom to enter into your awareness. Engage in conscious heart breathing as often as possible and your thoughts will change and carry a higher vibration. When the heart is opened, the mind will follow!

Ask a Clear Question

Asking this clear question can also help: "Will this action, deed, or thought keep my heart open and connected to others, or will it bring about a sense of separation, alienation, and disconnection?" Then, consciously and consistently choose the former. Get into the habit of asking yourself questions that point to a higher consciousness. Ask with your attention upon the heart and not from your head! The heart has a wisdom that is far greater than the mere intellect.

Practice Visualization

Envision your heart surrounded by and infused with light. Light is a primary element of creation. There can be no life, no growth, no illumination or revelation without it. Light radiates in the same fashion, and all manner of life-affirming conditions come into being when your heart (as well as your mind and body) is imbued with Light and Love. Inspiration is received, healing takes place, and evolution unfolds; we create a world that works for all. We are equipped, empowered, and called to bring light into the world!

Consider this: the greater the plunge into darkness, the greater the urge to move toward light. As we witness the state of our world, the clarion is sounded. People are awakening and coming together in vast and beautiful collaborations, connecting to honor the planet, its people, and creatures. We are discovering the power of the collective consciousness to hold sacred intentions for the greater good of all. Holy alliances are being formed in all corners of the Earth as people recognize our shared humanity. People are being moved to Stand Up For Humanity—in general and also as part of this global movement, inspired by Unity of Washington, DC. Their mission is to encourage people to make a commitment to lift up humanity according to their own talents, abilities, positive expressions, and shared humanity, to raise the collective consciousness by honoring and taking a stand for all people. What good can and will you do for the good of all?

Stand Up For Humanity is about embracing those qualities that serve the highest and best of our humanity and spirituality as we connect and act from our universal and common good. Even one small act of goodness taken by an individual can make a world of difference and contribute to healing, transforming, and lifting humanity.

Beloved Ones, this is our moment of choice. Let's do this!

Chapter 19 Spotlight

Reverend Sylvia Sumter beautifully shows the path to healing humanity leads us toward elevating our spiritual nature. This is the underappreciated component of the mind-body-spirit wholeness of who we are and what we are intended for. As we awaken to—and live by—the notion that we are spiritual beings, living in a spiritual universe, governed by spiritual laws, we will accomplish the next quantum leap in our evolution and in the process keep our heart open to the Divine qualities, such as Love, which unify, harmonize, and heal all things. This is also the path that enables us to stand up for humanity by embracing the qualities that serve the common good.

Call to Action

Stand up for humanity with an open heart. Find the people in your community who are the least loved—the elderly, the poor, the sick—and then take action to bring your radiating energy of love to those who need it most.

20

Conscious Evolution: A Theory We Can Thrive With

Bruce H. Lipton, PhD

Human civilization is at an evolutionary crossroads where unsustainable human behavior is precipitating the planet's sixth mass extinction event.[1] Five times in Earth's history, life was thriving when some event precipitated a wave of extinction, eliminating 70 to 90 percent of all plant and animal species. The last mass extinction event, 66 million years ago, noted for wiping out the dinosaurs, was apparently due to a massive asteroid impact in Mexico that upended the global web of life.

Today's severe environmental imbalance is, in large part, attributable to the cultural consequences of Darwinian evolution theory. Since the 1900s, neo-Darwinian theory, with its emphasis on the "survival of the fittest in the struggle for life" and on genetic mechanisms as the metric determining species survival, has shaped the behavioral character of civilization by giving scientific legitimacy to the use of power, greed, and violence to "advance" civilization. However, new insights from epigenetic science and the results of the Human Genome Project have completely undermined basic tenets of Darwinian theory.

Cooperation as the Impulse Guiding Evolution

Conventional science formerly thought the gene-containing nucleus was the cell's "brain," but new research points to the membrane as the information processor that controls a cell's fate.[2] Molecular switches built into the membrane translate environmental information into cell behavior and represent the basic physical units of perception, the building blocks of consciousness. Epigenetics recognizes that the environment, and more importantly, our *perception* of the environment, controls genetic activity and behavior and thus shifts the focus of evolutionary theory to the role of the nervous system and consciousness.

Modeling membrane evolution using fractal geometry offers profound insights into the origin and influence of consciousness and the role of cooperation within and among species. Because conscious evolution theory elucidates the fact that cooperation, rather than competition and struggle, is the driving force of evolution, it can support the survival of human civilization. "Survival of the fittest" is giving way to a more scientifically accurate and more positive theory of evolution, one that emphasizes the role of cooperation, interaction, and mutual dependence among all life-forms. In the words of Lynn Margulis, "Life did not take over the globe by combat, but by networking."[3]

Today's world crises are precipitating a major evolutionary upheaval that will profoundly alter the fate of human civilization. The chaos produced by global crises, symptoms of our unsustainability, is destabilizing the structure of civilization and its institutions. While the current system is collapsing, new insights, understanding, and visions offered by cultural creatives (individuals seeking alternative solutions to today's problems) from every field of human endeavor are pointing the ways to reorganize human civilization so we may thrive into the future. The theory of conscious evolution was first offered by John Baptiste de

Lamarck, in 1809, and provides the blueprint for a more enlightened future, as does our new understanding of cell evolution.[4]

Analysis of the development of the cell membrane as the primal nervous system has revealed, as just outlined, a previously unobserved repetitive pattern of evolution with two phases: Phase 1 starts with the origin of a new organism and proceeds to create the most conscious version of that organism. This phase ends when physical limitations prevent further enhancement of the organism's nervous system. Phase 2 advances evolution by increasing consciousness through the assembly of individual organisms into cooperative information-sharing communities. This phase ends when the most conscious communal organization transforms into a new organism. The presence of a new organism initiates the repeat of phase 1, this time expressing a higher level of evolution.[5]

Interestingly, this progression represents the same evolution pattern observed in creating a computer:

Phase 1: Make the smartest chip.

Phase 2: Assemble the single chips into a cooperative information-sharing community (in other words, a computer).

More interesting, a cell is a "programmable chip," and their assembly into a cooperative information-sharing community creates the most powerful "computer" in the solar system: the human brain.[6]

Humanity as a Butterfly

We can get to that higher level of evolution but only if we change our rapacious ways. The potential positive future our species can be likened to is the metamorphosis of a butterfly. A caterpillar's body comprises several billion cells. In the body of the growing caterpillar, the economy is booming and the cellular community is actively employed. This organism's voracious appetite leads to it devouring the leaves of the plant on which it is living. Caterpillar growth slows and eventually comes to an end as the available resources are consumed. Within the pupa, the cells are out of work and their highly structured community begins to fall apart. Specialized imaginal cells within the ensuing chaos provide organizing information and direction to create a different, more sustainable future. Metamorphosis is complete when the unsustainable caterpillar civilization transforms into the ecologically sensitive butterfly civilization.

The parallels are clear. By behaving as a caterpillar, human civilization's voracious appetite to grow and consume has undermined the environment. The global crises we face today are Nature's wake-up call for humans to realize that civilization itself needs to undergo a metamorphosis, so our current incarnation as the environmentally destructive "caterpillar" must transform into a new, sustainable organism: humanity. The looming fall of civilization as we know it is a necessity; we simply cannot build a future for humans to thrive on the unsustainable foundation supporting today's world.

Will human civilization survive its metamorphosis? We're balanced on the knife-edge of extinction or conscious evolution. Our uncertain future is dependent on the actions we engage in today.

Chapter 20 Spotlight

Working from a whole-system approach, Bruce Lipton looks at our collective evolution as a process of increasing consciousness from individual organisms to cooperative information-sharing communities, which eventually take in all of humanity. He sees a metamorphosis as needed to get us to that higher level of evolution, fulfilling our innate potential. Depending on the actions we engage in today, the current environmentally destructive, separate, "caterpillar" version of civilization may transform into a new, interdependent, sustainable organism—humanity as a whole.

Call to Action

Find ways to choose cooperation, collaboration, and interdependence with those you interact with every day. Less "I," more "we." In this way, you can play an active part in humanity's current transformation.

21

Is Wholeness Really a Choice?

Deepak Chopra™, MD

Thanks to its positive connotations, *wholeness* has become a buzz-word in areas of life as diverse as holistic medicine, whole-foods nutrition, and the human potential movement (which aims to create a whole person rather than a separate, fragmented one). What these various applications have in common is that wholeness is seen as a choice—and there the problem lies.

If you are talking about whole foods versus processed foods, whole-ness is certainly a choice, and the same can be said for holistic as opposed to mainstream medicine with its reliance on drugs and surgery. But speaking about a whole person is somehow different. Becoming a whole person is involved in the most fundamental questions about what it means to be human. The nature of human consciousness is such that we can take any viewpoint we want toward our own existence.

Each of us decides how to relate to reality. In the modern era, society teaches us to relate to reality through scientific, rational, logical means. Nature, including human nature, is thus quantified, measured, mined for data, and arranged through rational explanations. This means the human mind must be the product of the brain, following the basic logic that brain activity can be measured and quantified. Thus, neuroscience claims to be the prime, perhaps the only, way to explain how the human mind works.

Yet this claim runs afoul of the entire subjective world, which obviously exists—everyone is aware of sensations, visual images, sounds, thoughts, flashes of memory, etc., that occur "in here." This entire realm of human existence cannot be turned into data or quantified. You cannot assign a number to an insight, intuition, creative idea, or spiritual experience. The result is a clash of worldviews that runs deeper than the exhausted topic of science versus religion. To choose either the outer, objective world or the inner, subjective realm as dominant squanders any hope of achieving wholeness.

Since we all rely on our minds in order to navigate through life, what is most needed is to stop assuming that the objective world is real. There is a reason ancient spiritual traditions see the outer world as a distraction, illusion, or snare. This isn't due to moral distaste for worldly things, although there is plenty of that in religious beliefs, past and present. Something more fundamental is at stake. Anything you can count, weigh, calculate, or measure is part of an all-embracing illusion—to grasp this fact will put you on the threshold to the "real" reality, which is wholeness.

In the Grip of Illusion

Let me make clear that I am using *illusion* in the most common sense of the word, the way a dream is an illusion. Imagine that you are dreaming one night, and inside your dream you can use numbers, measure things, and even pursue science. Obviously, the ability to do these things would reassure you of the reality of your dream. But once you wake up, all the counting, measuring, and science you did in your dream would become instantly irrelevant, revealed as an illusion while you were sleeping.

Do you think this example doesn't apply to the waking state when you aren't asleep? It does. To burst the bubble of numbers and the illusion they create, here are a few facts about a basic property of nature, namely, light.

○ Photons, the elementary particles of light, are invisible and have no brightness.

○ Light has two incompatible states: a particle and a wave. Both can be measured, but how one state turns into another is a total mystery. We can only observe that it happens.

○ Color as a perception cannot be explained. Why red is red has nothing to do with its frequency or wavelength, any more than the sweet taste of sugar is explained by counting the carbon atoms in a sugar molecule.

○ The visual images in your mind's eye cannot be explained by examining the brain. The brain's visual cortex has no pictures in it; it is totally dark and devoid of light.

If not shocked, I hope you are at least surprised to learn these facts. What ties them together is one thing: consciousness. Your consciousness gives light its brightness and color, creates images in your mind's eye, and experiences the world as a theater of events in time and space. Let's concede that data, fact-gathering, and mathematical formulas can't explain consciousness. So what? Everyone depends on the world of science and technology, and the course of civilization has depended on mathematics ever since the first architectural measurements were made thousands of years ago using knots evenly spaced on a rope. Theorizing that the whole structure is based on an illusion wouldn't seem to change anyone's daily life.

To get past "So what?" isn't easy, but existing inside an illusion has huge practical implications. If you delve deeply into the fabric of nature, the most basic level, the quantum field, is where "something comes out of nothing," as physicists call the process of creation. Ripples in the quantum field, arising from the vacuum state, are the basis of the universe. And that's an enormous clue to escaping the illusion.

There is a convincing argument that these ripples are products of consciousness; in other words, the universe thinks itself into existence. Decades ago, the eminent British physicist Sir James Jeans declared that the universe was beginning to look much more like a great thought than a great machine. Mind-like behavior has been spotted in the action of elementary particles, as noted by the prominent physicist Freeman Dyson. Moreover, if the universe isn't a product of cosmic consciousness—indeed, if existence isn't the same as consciousness—science is totally unable to explain how consciousness came about. Physical explanations for mind are the ultimate apples-and-oranges mistake.

Healing the Separation

When consciousness created something out of nothing, two tracks emerged and separated as the objective and subjective domain. Human beings are extremely good at balancing the two. A physicist can measure Higgs boson particles and also fall in love. But this balancing act is what keeps wholeness from being realized. Both worlds, as long as they are separate, falsify reality. Our inner experiences are solipsistic without an external world.

The "real" reality dawns when the illusion of separation is replaced with wholeness. Reality is wholeness, but we won't experience it until we are whole. You might suppose that relating to reality through separation is the only way to relate. If so, then aiming to be a whole person would be futile. Wholeness lies beyond any kind of split or fragmentation.

How do we actually get there? It can't be done, if the recent history of science has anything to say about it. In physics, more than a century has been spent attempting to fuse two irreconcilable domains, the quantum world of microscopic phenomena and the so-called classical world of macroscopic phenomena. This split pertains to everyday life because there should be a seamless connection between quanta, the basic building blocks of nature, and all the things we see around us—rocks, trees, mountains, and clouds.

Einstein devoted the last three decades of his life to merging the biggest and smallest things in the universe, without success. Sixty years after his death, the split remains, and physics exists with a rift down the middle that no one has been able to bridge. The same is true in the human mind. The world "out there" operates through things like cause-and-effect that should seamlessly connect to our subjective responses. Sometimes there is no serious rift. If you poke someone with a pin, they will go "ouch" almost without exception. Yet any predictable response runs up against the unique ways in which 7 billion people are building a life story based on their own beliefs, memories, desires, fears, and predilections.

You cannot robotize a human being, no matter how hard authoritarian regimes have tried. There is always the unknown, unpredictable possibility of a new and unexpected thought. That's the source of our greatest human gift, creativity. But it is also the source of our suffering. The unpredictable mind is intimately tied to the uncontrollable mind, which afflicts us with guilt, shame, doubt, hostility, anxiety, and depression. Those afflictions give evidence enough that we cannot confront the subject-object split with a shrug of "So what?"

Finding a Way Out

For centuries it has been declared, usually in a religious or spiritual context, that the cause of suffering is the separate self. Isolated and alone, building our individual stories, we have no connection to wholeness. We are like coral reefs amassed from tiny grains of experience, and that's that, unless we can exchange the subject-object split—the very thing that placed us in separation—for a new relationship with reality.

Let's say that you accept the terms of this argument so far, or if you don't, let's say you have other reasons for believing that wholeness is worth attaining. How would you get there? What would it feel like? Might you not be better off with your present life, warts and all, than pursuing chimera? The answer to all these questions is the same: they are the wrong questions. They presuppose that wholeness is a choice when in reality it isn't.

Wholeness is everything. It is the One, the All, or Brahman, as it was known in Vedic India. Being whole, it cannot be accepted or rejected. Neither can it be lost. To choose wholeness is like saying, "I chose not to exist yesterday, but I have decided to exist today." Another nonintuitive implication that surprises almost everyone is that you cannot relate to wholeness. Between two separate things there can only be a relationship; wholeness has no separations, no divisions, no "this and that," no "yes or no."

As a result, wholeness offers only the possibility of choiceless awareness. In choiceless awareness, you experience yourself as whole: as pure existence and pure consciousness. You still accomplish the things you ordinarily do in the world—you go to work, meet deadlines, take the family on vacation. But at bottom, your experience is seamless and unified. I realize that choiceless awareness sounds arcane if not impossible. We are so used to relating to reality through the subject-object split that everything is a matter of A or B. Countless choices fill our lives.

In the bigger picture, however, these choices have not made human beings happier, wiser, or more certain about who we are and what our place is in the universe. Indeed, no ultimate questions have been solved, which is the legacy of separation. We peer into reality like children with their noses pressed to the window of a candy store. This isn't the place to detail what the journey to wholeness actually is (for that, please see my book, *Metahuman*, which is devoted to escaping the illusions we live by), but the road to wholeness begins by knowing what's at stake: a complete shift in how we relate to reality.

J. Krishnamurti referred to this as the first and last freedom. The vision of wholeness gets you on the path; the same vision supports you along the way, and it stays with you after you realize that you are whole. There could be no first and last freedom if the journey was a straight line or if it had any divisions, including a beginning or end. Wholeness, which is what you are, cannot depart from itself, lose itself, or come back to itself.

There is only the process of waking up to reality. From there, the possibility of higher existence opens up. From any other starting point, I think the illusion created by the subject-object split will endure.

Chapter 21 Spotlight

Deepak Chopra™ challenges us to consider whether the question of wholeness is even a choice at all. If we can see the outer world as a distraction, an illusion, as ancient spiritual traditions did, we can focus on the one reality, which is a complete wholeness already, with everything existing within it. Consciousness ties everything in the entire universe together; it gives light its brightness and color, creates images in our mind's eye, and adds meaning to everything. Our overarching challenge in healing this false separation, which is the cause of all suffering, is making a complete shift in how we relate to reality. If we practiced seeing all things with the eye of wholeness, we would eventually live into the understanding that wholeness is everything, the One, the All, where there is no separation, no division. Here, there is only choiceless awareness, while we continue to do all the things in the world we would ordinarily do, where everything we see and do is a seamless, unified whole.

Call to Action

What does it mean to choose wholeness? Meditate for ten minutes on how the world might appear if you look through the eye of acceptance and nonjudgment.

Circle Five
Integrating Science and Spirituality

We utilize research and education to awaken, elevate, and evolve consciousness.

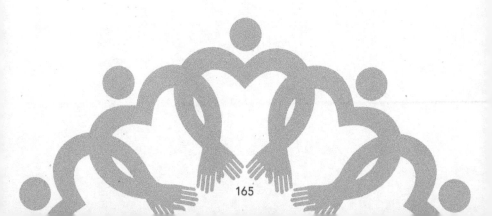

22

The Power of Eight

Lynne McTaggart

By 2004, I had grown especially curious about the idea that thoughts are an actual something, with the capacity to change physical matter. A number of bestselling books had been published about the law of attraction and the power of intention—the idea that you could manifest what you most desired just by thinking about it in a focused way—but as an investigative reporter by background, to all of this I maintained a certain incredulity, overwhelmed by a number of awkward questions.

Is this a true power? Exactly how "all-purpose" is it? I wondered. What can you do with it? Are we talking about curing cancer or shifting a quantum particle? And to my mind the most important question of all: What happens when lots of people think the same thought at the same time? Would this magnify the effect?

I wanted to examine whether this capacity was powerful enough to heal individuals, even the world. Like a twenty-first-century doubting Thomas, I was essentially looking for a way to dissect magic.

In my book *The Intention Experiment*, I compiled all the credible scientific research I could find into the power of mind over matter. But its purpose was also an invitation: very little research had been carried out about group intention, and my plan was to fill that gap by enlisting my readers as the body of group intenders involved in an ongoing scientific experiment.

I gathered a consortium of physicists, biologists, psychologists, statisticians, and neuroscientists highly experienced in consciousness research. Periodically I invited my internet audience, or a physical audience when I was delivering a talk or workshop somewhere, to send one designated, specific thought to affect some target in a laboratory set up by one of the scientists I was working with, who would then calculate the results to see if our thoughts had changed anything.

Eventually this project effectively evolved into the world's largest global laboratory, involving several hundred thousand of my international readers from more than a hundred countries, in some of the first controlled experiments on the power of mass intention to affect the physical world.

As it turned out, the experiments did work. In fact, they *really* worked. Of the thirty-three experiments I've run to date, twenty-nine have evidenced measurable, mostly significant change, and three of the four without a positive result simply had technical issues. To put these results in perspective, almost no drug produced by the pharmaceutical industry can lay claim to that level of positive effect.

But as amazing as that is, it isn't the most interesting part of the story.

In 2008, in one of my early workshops, I placed participants in small groups of about eight, to see what would happen if group members tried to heal one of their group through a collective healing intention.

I thought the group effect would be a feel-good exercise—something akin to a massage or a facial—but the following day I was shocked to observe more than an hour of instant, near-miraculous healings.

For the next year, in every workshop we ran, whenever we set up our clusters of eight or so and gave them a little instruction to send intention to a group member, we were stunned witnesses to story after story of physical and psychic transformation:

○ Marekje's multiple sclerosis had made it difficult for her to walk without aids. The morning after being the target of a

Power of Eight group, she arrived at the workshop without her crutches.

○ Marcia suffered from a cataract-like opacity blocking the vision of one eye. The day after her group's healing intention, she claimed that her sight in that eye had been almost fully restored.

○ Diane in Miami had such pain in her hip from scoliosis that she'd had to stop working out. During the intention she'd felt intense heat and a rapid-fire, twitching response in her back. The next day, she declared, "It's like I have a new hip."

There were hundreds, even thousands, more like this, and each time I was standing there, watching these changes unfold right in front of me.

Sande's Story

At a talk I gave in Denver, I met Sande, a sixty-three-year-old lifetime athlete—but now, one of her knees was shot. "When I walk, I can feel when my knee is going to pop out, which it does, and then I fall. I'm in a lot of pain." Fearful she would break a bone if she didn't take care of it, she had scheduled knee replacement surgery in a month's time.

During the talk, when I put members of the Denver audience in Power of Eight groups, tears rolled down her cheeks as she felt what she described as pressure around her knee on both sides, "as if somebody with big mitts was holding my leg. It was warm, not hot. I never felt that before. It went down my whole leg, going down to my ankle—and I hadn't told them about my ankles. When we opened our eyes, we looked at our hands, and everyone's hands were vibrating, with lots of tears."

When I asked the audience if anyone had had an experience, Sande was the first to put up her hand. "Look," she said, "I can bend my knees." She leaned over and squatted down. "I could not do that before." Three days later, the healing effects persisted. "When I walk, I don't get that feeling that the knee will pop out," Sande said. "I can go upstairs without pain." Since the Power of Eight group, she no longer needed her brace and was able to cancel her surgery.

Beverly's Story

Beverly, a massage therapist, hadn't planned to come to my Denver talk because she'd been recovering from a car accident. "My crunched ribs were uncomfortable; my shoulder was singing a high-pitched, exquisite pain and wouldn't stay in place without support," she said. Nevertheless, a church group member was particularly persuasive, and Beverly arrived, holding her shoulder in place.

She described that during the Power of Eight circle, "I felt all the tension of the car wreck fall out of my left side. Supported by my groupmates, bubbling, Kundalini-type energy poured out onto the floor through my arm. My shoulder slid back to normal position, my rib cage released, and I took a full breath for the first time in the six weeks since the accident." Nearly two months later, Beverly wrote a progress report: Her shoulder had remained in place, "almost exclusively pain-free."

And there were many others, even among the senders: a woman who'd had a stroke and could no longer focus her eyes went back to seeing normally; a fellow with bursitis could raise his arm all the way up again. Another woman, who had arrived with a migraine, said her pain had completely cleared. One of the senders arrived with a cane and walked away from the event no longer needing it. Someone else felt the ache in her back immediately begin to dissipate. "I'm a real skeptic, and yet it worked."

For many years I believed I was witnessing a placebo effect—until I began to realize that the senders were getting healed too.

Wes's Story

Wes Chapman, for instance, was in college working on a science degree when he was drafted and sent to Vietnam for the final year of the war.

The experience so traumatized him that he did not finish his university degree and was left in a state of depression. His bad luck seemed to carry on; even the high point in his life—his second marriage—was quickly extinguished when his wife died from cancer.

At sixty-five, he'd gotten to the "What's the use?" stage, where it was difficult for him to even make breakfast. One August, he volunteered to be part of a Power of Eight group, as a sender of healing intentions to two group members.

Afterward, he said, he experienced his own amazing shift—a feeling of intense joy. All the activities that had derailed him for years he now was able to handle with ease.

The second night after the group intention, he had a vivid dream. He was back on his college campus, where met his nineteen-year-old self, who told him, "There's still time." Suddenly Wes felt compelled to reengage in writing and even intense exercise, including weight-lifting and ninety-minute power walks. "It feels like I'm twenty-five, not sixty-five," he says.

Andy's Story

What would happen if people met regularly in groups of eight? I wondered. Would everything in their lives begin to heal? I decided to run an intention masterclass, with members meeting in groups while I monitored their progress for an entire year.

Andy Spyros had tried everything to remove old patterns that had interfered with her ability to make a good living. When she joined a Power of Eight group, she shared her intention to find a dream job with ample income.

None of the intentions the group tried were working for her. So, at my insistence that she "get off of herself," she started shifting her intention to a young boy who'd tried to commit suicide. "Two days after that," she reported, "I got an unexpected offer to do product development and strategy for an online organization involved in human development—a job that would joyfully bring me money doing work I love!"

The Science Behind It

Working in large or small groups and doing something altruistic activates the vagus nerve, which connects with all the communication systems involved with caretaking. It slows down heart rate, calms the effects of any fight-or-flight autonomic nervous system activity, and initiates the release of oxytocin, a neuropeptide that plays a role in love, trust, intimacy, kindness, and compassion.

Increased oxytocin levels also have a marked healing effect on the body: they lower inflammation, boost the immune system, aid digestion, lower blood pressure, heal wounds faster, and even repair damage to the heart after a heart attack. If oxytocin is considered the "love hormone," the vagus nerve is the "love nerve."[1]

Other evidence from neuroscience studies that scientists have carried out on Power of Eight groups shows that members of the group undergo major brain-wave changes akin to those of a Buddhist monk during a state of ecstatic prayer: a feeling of blissful oneness. Intending in a group is a fast track to the miraculous.

The powerfully transformational mechanisms at work in my healing intention groups appear to be the unique power of group prayer coupled with an amazing mirror effect and the power of altruism.

Focusing on healing someone else often heals the healer.[*]

---

[*] Adapted from Lynne McTaggart, *The Power of Eight: Harnessing the Miraculous Energies of a Small Group to Heal Others, Your Life, and the World* (New York: Atria Books, 2018), which includes full instructions about how to do group intention and construct your own Power of Eight group.

Chapter 22 Spotlight

Using research, education, and ample personal experience from her workshops to integrate science and spirituality and elevate consciousness, Lynne McTaggart has extensively researched the power of intention—manifesting what you most desire by thinking about it in a focused way—by gathering a consortium of scientists and creating the world's largest real-life laboratory. With highly controlled scientific experiments involving hundreds of thousands of people, they have carried out thirty-three Intention Experiments to date—from simple seed-and-water experiments to those attempting to heal ill people or lower violence in war-torn or highly violent areas—with twenty-nine showing measurable, positive, mostly significant effects, and many evidencing healings among the participants themselves. She's also worked with thousands of Power of Eight groups, showing consistent miraculous results and healings through collective intentions. These phenomenal results are supported by neuroscience studies and reflect the collective effects that altruism has on all involved.

Call to Action

Gather a group of around eight friends together. Meet in person or virtually. Have each person choose an intention most closely aligned with each person's deepest desires. Be highly specific. Make sure each person quantifies the kind of change they'd like to see and when they'd like to see it happen. Write an intention statement for each group member and hold those intentions collectively, one by one. Keep a record of how many of your intentions come to pass, particularly when you intend for someone else.

23

The Current Science of Awakening

Loch Kelly, MDiv, LCSW

I am still alive and have found nirvana.

And if I have found nirvana and I am still alive

then everyone who is still alive can find nirvana.

—Jill Bolte Taylor, PhD, *A Stroke of Insight*

When I was fourteen years old, I died. Or so it seemed, because I am here to report it was a return from death, or a near-death experience (NDE). While in school one day, I had a terrible stomachache; I waited until near the end of the day to go to the school nurse. When I did, I was rushed to the hospital with acute appendicitis.

While I was being put under anesthesia for emergency surgery, my heart stopped. But I remember looking down from above the operating table and clearly seeing everyone moving around, trying to revive me. I saw one nurse leave the room and come back with a doctor I had never seen before but was able to describe later.

Then in a split second I traveled from above my own operating table to a nursing station down the hall where a woman was crying while talking to her sister on the phone, saying that her husband did not look good and the doctors told her he might die. Even though I don't know how I'd gotten there, I felt that I was drawn to be with her by a sense of compassion and connection. Just as swiftly, I was back above my operating table.

Then, with a whoosh, I went up through a tunnel made of light. This was not just ordinary light—it had a palpable feeling like pure Love. Out of the loving light appeared a being dressed in white who showed me a book. The being, the book, the words: everything seemed to be made of this loving light. Things were shown to me on all levels, and then in an instant, I was given a choice to stay or return. I knew I would come back to this reality. I did not hesitate to choose to return to the human realm. I was told that I would not remember all of this but would retain some sense of it.

The next thing I remember is waking up in my hospital room. A nurse and my mother were standing next to me. My mother asked me how I was feeling, and I responded, "What does C stand for?"

"What do you mean, C?" she said.

"$E=MC^2$," I answered. "What does C mean?"

It was very strange to hear myself ask this question, as I was not really interested in science as a kid and had never read anything about physics. Later that afternoon, my mother returned with an encyclopedia, from which I learned that C stood for the speed of light. C was also a significant part of Einstein's theory of relativity. It had to do with everything being relative and not as fixed and solid as it seemed.

Most people I told had no idea what to make of my experience. Some said it might be related to the anesthesia or that it was a dream. I asked a nurse to check about the second doctor, whom I had seen come into the room when I was above the operating table, and the woman at the nursing station who was crying. She later confirmed that both things had happened just as I had seen them. She seemed to be kind and comforting but not very interested. My doctor looked at me with a smirk and dismissed me outright.

This was a glimpse into another dimension. It was nothing like a dream or a drug trip. It was as real as anything in this world. It was like I emerged from a fog to really be here, alive and free and connected. It lifted feelings of separation, fear, and alienation I didn't even know I had. This shift of perspective helped me realize that there is something bigger going on than just relative reality.

I have continued to be inspired by Einstein's insights into deeper levels of reality. To this day I try to keep my spirituality grounded in the scientific method by asking: Is this repeatable? Is it verifiable by others? And does it produce results?

The Art and Science of Effortless Mindfulness

For many years, the contemplative practices within religions, within spirituality, and within certain cultures were based on assumptions and beliefs that became codified and sometimes rigid or fundamentalist. But there were always people who took what they learned and made it more contemporary, brought it into a new form, a new culture, and adapted it.

As these contemplative traditions come West, they met with Western science and Western psychology, which is a wonderful thing because science helps us discover what's true, what's real, and what works.

Looking at these traditions of meditation and contemplative practice, we can apply different ways of measuring what we see. Some of the new research relates to the practice of *effortless mindfulness*. The foundation of effortless mindfulness is an awareness-based knowing, called *awake awareness* or *nature of mind*. It is similar to a flow state, described by psychologist Mihaly Csikszentmihalyi as a way of optimally functioning: in a flow state, we are effortlessly mindful, using implicit memory—what we already know—so we are not continuously self-referencing. From this state of effortless mindfulness, you can even move your hand or use thought as a tool and then return to awareness-based peace of mind.

Functional magnetic resonance image (fMRI), gives us the remarkable ability to look at the brain functioning in the midst of meditation. I've participated in some of these studies as a research subject, and it's like being put inside a big magnetic machine. As an advanced practitioner of various types of meditations, I found it fascinating to learn the differences show up in measurable ways. And it was exciting to get third-person scientific validation of the positive first-person experiences that I had experienced.

The Effortless Mindfulness Solution

Traditionally, deliberate mindfulness refers to two primary forms of practice: *shamatha*, translated as "calm abiding," and *vipassana*, translated as "insight meditation." Researchers have extensively studied both types of deliberate mindfulness in recent years, and they refer to shamatha as "focused attention" and vipassana as open monitoring.

Recently, a third type of mindfulness, called *nondual awareness*, referring to the wholeness of all things, has been added to the research studies as a form of effortless mindfulness. In a recent research study, only the nondual type balanced external and internal networks with the experience of being undistracted without effort, aware of what's going on inside and outside as a continuous, seamless flow state.

When one of my teachers, Tsoknyi Rinpoche, first came to the United States from Nepal, he noticed that many meditators here seemed to be practicing what he called "stupid meditation," referring to "doing only shamatha practice of watching your breath." This kind of meditation suppresses chattering thoughts, but it reduces your alertness and ability to fully function. Although forms of mindfulness like (focused attention) that are heavy on concentration are relaxing, it's not the type of relaxation accessed in the alert intelligence of awake awareness.

The researcher Zoran Josipovic concluded, "Our results lend further evidence to the claims that nondual awareness meditations are different from both focused attention and open monitoring meditations. While focused attention and open monitoring meditations are traditionally regarded 'as constructed' states created through deployment of specific attentional strategies, nondual awareness meditations are thought not to involve intentional effort, but to be based on identifying a reflexive awareness that is regarded as 'unconstructed' (Mipam and Hopkins, 2006) . . . Nondual meditation is different from both focused-attention and open-monitoring meditations in that it enables an atypical state of mind in which extrinsic and intrinsic experiences are increasingly synergistic rather than competing."[1]

Effortless mindfulness, therefore, balances our brain's activity so that we are equally aware of what happens inside and outside. We are in full command of our abilities and awareness, while perception becomes uncommonly acute. Time may seem to slow down, and there is no sense of rush. This so important because the next stage of mindfulness meditation also marks the next stage of human development.

We are calming our everyday mind while upgrading to a new level of mind, which we may not have realized even existed or was possible for us to access. Surrendering, letting go of ego-identification, can open us to greater resources and a new foundation of identity. Letting go can help people achieve difficult goals more easily. During meditation or prayer practices, feeling less ego-centered while experiencing a boundless unity is often reported, along with an increase in the positive qualities of unity, alertness, clarity, boundlessness, freedom, joy, love, and connection.

When we use spiritual practices like these, our sense of identity is untied from the physical-boundary program and begins to experience our true nature's boundless condition. Learning meditation and awareness practices, that reduce the activity in this brain area, can help facilitate decoupling the normal physical sense of our body's boundaries. By opening and looking from spacious awareness, we feel even safer and more relaxed, sensitive, open, and responsive—like a tai chi master. In this way, we shift from feeling that our identity is located in our heads behind our eyes to a more spacious, yet embodied and interconnected, experience. This openhearted awareness also allows us to feel the timelessness of being fully involved in the "now."

It's important to keep in mind that the practice of meditation—or awakening training, which transforms the brain and biology—is not just for full-time yogis or hermits but is also possible in the midst of daily life, as practicing mindfulness in whatever way available to us becomes effortless and leads to the possibility of awakened living, resulting in restfulness, creativeness, interconnectedness, and natural compassion.

Chapter 23 Spotlight

Drawing from what he learned from his own example of authentic experiential education, Loch Kelly tells how his near-death experience led him to the life-changing awakening that relative reality is not all there is. This experience gave him a glimpse into another dimension, as real as anything in this world, from which he emerged more alive, free, connected, and committed to grounding his spirituality in the scientific method of replicability and verifiability. His subsequent life has been devoted to effortless mindfulness practice, which he says marks the next stage of human development and is therefore accessible to all. It has been confirmed to calm our everyday mind, put us in a state of flow, give us a sense of boundless unity, help us achieve difficult goals more easily, and result in restfulness, creativeness, and interconnectedness.

Call to Action

Imagine yourself awakening from within. What is your greatest talent? What are you most passionate about? Spread that passion and joy with others and encourage them to discover and manifest their own awakening.

24

Awakening to Our Limitless Mind

J. J. Hurtak, PhD, and
Desiree Hurtak, PhD, MSSc

Accessing the Consciousness Field

To end suffering, we need to discover our limitless mind. Our minds are part of a vast macrocosm, and to experience this greater reality, we need only to reach out: into our local environment, into the surrounding subtle currents and fields of energy. We are capable of reaching out into the vastness of creation itself. Through a greater consciousness network—what Lynne McTaggart calls the "consciousness field"[1]—we can gain access to information around the world, even into different realms of reality.

With higher levels of information, humankind enters new horizons beyond the status of a highly evolved animal into open, and apparently endless, multidimensional frontiers. According to our research with Dr. Elizabeth Rauscher, our mind is far more than a computer-like system for information-gathering, storage, and retrieval.[2] Many realize this when they experience an epiphany, which culminates in the unfoldment of knowledge beyond our normal senses. Others have developed it in studies involving "remote viewing," gathering information from sources our five senses normally cannot consciously access, using a technique of "mind projection."

Attuning to a Higher Consciousness

Where does information come from that is beyond the scope of our immediate knowledge? We believe this comes through attunement to a higher consciousness, to multidimensional levels of information beyond the familiar three-dimensional realm. Rauscher, for example, describes an eighth dimension (Eight Space) beyond both space and time as we know it, where the past, present, and future exist simultaneously. Our brains can access this space to acquire information from other dimensions and "infinite time," far beyond our three-dimensional world of the local space-time that we physically inhabit.

Humans as Biotransducers

Several centuries of development in physics and mathematics have taught us, as the ancient wisdom traditions and scriptures also did, that we are part of an infinite reality; we simply do not know it. Our research brought us to the important realization that we—even while in the physical world—have access to higher-dimensional sources of information. We are "biotransducers," able to receive, process, and give out information. Of course, we also have the free will to choose whatever information we want to access.

Practicing Image Construction

Through the process of greater self-discovery, we begin to understand that our minds are interconnected, which releases us from the boundaries of our limited awareness and makes us part of the greater totality. Reaching out into the consciousness field, we practice "image construction" by gathering resonating thoughts and constructing our "chosen" positive or negative life events, which become our reality. It is also possible to construct an image of superconsciousness—that which exists in realms beyond our space-time, also to be perceived and made known.

Finding Our Frequency

We are now learning that our bodies are constantly affected by things we cannot see, such as infrared, microwave, radio, and other invisible frequencies from cell phones, Wi-Fi, computer systems, and even cosmic waves at extremely low frequencies. In electromedicine, choosing the right frequency or frequencies, as seen in the FDA-approved "tumor-treating fields" device from Novocure,[3] can heal our bodies. Just as each molecule is engaged in a constant vibratory energy exchange, so too our thoughts and our experience of reality correlates with greater multidimensional and omnidirectional realities.

Exploring Our Entangled Universe

Our work supports the idea that consciousness exists throughout all realms of life in an entangled universe. Quantum physics research is already starting to explain this. Specifically, the information transmission from our brains is not limited to the speed of light, nor is it working with "faster than light" particles, but it has interconnectedness (nonlocality), meaning it can be simultaneously everywhere. In various experiments involving the production and separation of pairs of photons, each photon, regardless of spatial separation, could instantly sense its twin's behavior. Each reacted to the other without any apparent direct communication, faster than the speed of light. This is understood as entanglement, and the results do not violate the laws of Einstein's general relativity; rather, it is as though the universe is like a spiderweb or matrix, and each part can feel every other part, no matter how distant.

Perceiving the Greater Consciousness Network

Our mind can perceive information beyond the normal scope of our reality when it knowingly works with the greater consciousness network. Remote viewers are showing how our human brains are capable of perceiving these sophisticated levels of networking. When we are able to understand the collective field of consciousness (including the human mind-body-spirit) as a dynamic, fractal-like process, like a growing tree, we arrive at a state of mindfulness, where the choices we make in accessing information from the consciousness field create either positive or negative events in our lives. It is up to us to comprehend the map, the energy pathways, as we build libraries within our brain while learning how to make greater positive and productive choices out of the infinite possibilities.

If consciousness connects us with all surrounding energy fields, then we also have infinite thought possibilities throughout the universe. If consciousness is the hidden variable and multiple dimensions exist, we can also see ourselves as multidimensional beings capable of building bridges, not just to any *object* in the universe but to any *thought* throughout the myriad dimensions. A practical application of this would mean that we are all multidimensional transmitters of information through a higher state of consciousness, generated originally from a Divine Universal Mind.

The Buddhists call this self-realization, which ends the separation between the personal "I" and the collective "we." Others, like Teilhard de Chardin, call it the *noosphere*—that is, the arena (sphere) in which human consciousness and thoughts influence the way biological life evolves.[4]

Love as Divine Consciousness

Amid all the theories and terms, we assert that life is a function of flow, which at the highest level is called Love. Today, we are learning how we are a part of a greater collective consciousness that welcomes our input into the field through Love. Love can be seen as a higher resonance that allows for us to best integrate our life energies and frequencies into the consciousness field.

The experience of Love or recognizing the need for Love in any moment can be understood in building up the network in a direction that can improve the lives of everyone. We can thus state the following supposition for living creation-recreation: the positive, sustaining power of "active love" is behind the harmonious interactions and energy balances that are the basis of the true sustaining physics of the universe.

When the transcendent Consciousness comes into human experience, the Living Mind manifests, expressing higher thought-forms of light, made up of "love-powered emanations."[5] When we share in Love, we are aware of our true inner strength, revealed through our inner Spirit. We are now learning to share the power of Unconditional Love with the world as an ever-evolving, ever-reflecting, and ever-sustaining power of Divine Consciousness.

In this realm of material existence, our life experience is short. Humankind is going through experiences of energy incarnation, extension, and radiation. Change and love-powered emanations, or higher-resonant radiations, are what sustain the evolution of humankind. As a result, we continue to gain the inherent powers of Consciousness memory and a "knowing" of the experience of Universal Awareness.

To experience the fullness of who we are and realize our true potential in life, we seek to dynamically unite with the consciousness awareness of Love and our greater potential. Understanding our interconnectedness releases us from our limitations and makes us part of the greater collective totality.

Each part of the world will need new social and spiritual wisdom to prepare us for working together with realistic strategies for new energy needs and food alternatives, while creating and sustaining a higher spiritual vision. This will come about through realizing and experiencing that we live not simply in one physical universe but within the layers of many consciousness universes, containing all variations and possibilities.

In effect, we have already reached the threshold of the noosphere revealing itself and showing us a Higher Pathway we can choose to follow. Let us begin to use our inherent powers, intuitive perception, self-regeneration and healing, creativity, and direct awareness of the Divine Consciousness, known to the ancients as the Divine Presence, to partake in the Universal Love.

Chapter 24 Spotlight

Building upon the perspective of integration and wholeness to evolve consciousness, J. J. Hurtak and Desiree Hurtak illustrate how we can awaken our limitless mind, as it is in reality part of a vast macrocosm. By extending ourselves out into our local environment, and into the surrounding subtle currents and fields of energy that vibrate all around us, our minds are capable not only of reaching out into the vastness of creation but also accessing and acquiring information beyond both space and time. This means we are part of an infinite reality and can evolve into more sophisticated levels of networking and interconnectedness, which releases us from our limitations, makes us part of the greater collective totality, and through our own higher state of Consciousness, connects us at the highest level to what is called Divine Love, that which also sustains the evolution of humanity.

Call to Action

Prepare for a positive future. Let your limitless mind be a sacred space of love and compassion in service to every expression of the Divine.

25

Authentic Education to Awaken, Elevate, and Evolve Consciousness

Nina Meyerhof, EdD

The twenty-first century holds the greatest possibilities in history for an integrated, peaceful, and prosperous global community. Connected by telecommunications and a growing spirituality, with more access to education and healthcare than ever before, humankind has a chance to actualize an evolutionary state of being. At the same time, never before has the future been more challenged by worldwide geopolitical unrest, terrorism, poverty, climate change, and inadequate education and healthcare. The kind of world that the next generations will experience depends upon our collective vision and intention now. As long as the global culture is grounded in fear, greed, and scarcity, we will continue to waste our human and financial resources on war and destruction. But we're called to shift toward love, to integrate deep compassion into the education system, and to deploy resources for the common good, and with that approach, we will be able to lift up all people to a life of hope and security.

Today, science and spirituality are coming to the same conclusion—that all people are intrinsically similar. The Human Genome Project has proven that we are genetically 99.9 percent alike with only one-tenth of 1 percent making us different. As we realize that "I am you, and you are me," right action and thought are supported by the universal laws of nature. When we concentrate on what makes us the same instead of what makes us different, we are able to deal with the challenges ahead. Our similarities in this case means we all hold peace and happiness as our deepest personal goals and desires. The existing layers of differences are only a result of what time, religion, and culture you were born into, as well as parental influences. Thus, underneath, we are one family of humankind with individual differences, exemplifying diversity in unity.

Raising Up Young Leaders and Innovators

To foster this consciousness and have it become a visible reality, to have our minds adjust to the collaborative model of humankind, we must consider future generations and their role in this change to systems thinking. It is imperative that we direct resources to young people and support this with educational experiences and leadership opportunities that promote authentic personal learning while building a climate for respectful communities, common ethics, sustainable practices, peace, and economic opportunities.

Our children and youth are poised to be the innovative leaders of building new systems, but we need educational systems to contribute to this focus. The time of information building is over. We no longer function in the industrial era. Educational systems now need to allow their own evolution to occur with these changing times. We need an open environment of ideas that support a deeper understanding of human evolution. Schools need to keep up with the pace of change. There is so much more they can do to nurture creativity and higher-order thinking. We can no longer live in that past.

Wholeness: Education's New Conceptual Framework

Humanity is now preparing for a major leap into a collective understanding that we are One. We are moving into the age of conscious understanding by tapping into a consciousness that gives us a new way of thinking, confirming we are an interconnected and interdependent species. From this, we learn the attributes of caring, sharing, and feeling deep compassion for the other. Education needs to focus on the individual's inner character as the basis for this emerging culture of oneness and the systems that will be aligned to this in order to offer a holistic understanding of all of life. The clarion call of this coming age is to stay present in one's own authentic self while feeling connected to the greater whole. This understanding of wholeness should be the conceptual framework of education.

Education comes from the word *educare*, meaning "to draw forth or lead out." Authentic education is to draw out the true purpose of the "I-ness" and remember the actual meaning for life as it relates to all surrounding life. The authenticity comes from recognizing the true internal self's inner calling, which evokes a cognizance of the laws of nature and a desire to become an active participant in the magnificent web of life.

As we head into the next phase of cultural evolution, young people, inspired by a deeper exploration of their personal spiritual awareness of conscious mindfulness, become a driving force on all the issues that challenge us today. Each generation becomes more consciously aware of connecting to the whole and where we stand in history by recognizing themselves as part of the natural evolution of humankind.

The next generations—with greater inner consciousness connected to the higher consciousness that surrounds us all—are the future architects of the coming phases of social, cultural, and global development. Young people have the potential to move beyond imitating what has come before, imagining new models of structures for systems and governance that become the scaffolding leading us into a unified whole, a better possible future.

Our children and youth are primed to move forth into a new era. They are rising up in a groundswell, expressing the feeling of this urgency toward building a momentum for a new humanity, one of caring for the other, interconnected and interdependent with all of the planet.

As we learn to practice authentic education, we support individual exploration of personal consciousness, growing the number of fully expressive individuals who apply their inner knowing to the world and further actions for the greater good.

Three Phases of Authentic Education

Three phases of authentic education help learning fulfill its role in this emerging era: awaken, elevate, and evolve consciousness. They are interwoven and in no particular order. These components encourage the learners to mindfully seek answers from the Self, then to apply their internal realizations to daily life challenges and come up with a plan for the future. This leads us to an evolution of consciousness within the self and in interfacing with all of humanity. Each action step creates a momentum for becoming conscious of our Self in relationship to the whole. It's an interplay of inner and outer; as above, so below.

Awaken the young to their inner knowing!
They are the ones who will help birth a new understanding of how we must share our space on this planet. Some must be awakened to remember, as it is in remembering that change will come. Some will already know.

Moment to moment, a new now is created. We are all who we are, yet we are constantly evolving. It is no longer necessary to be unconscious; we can choose to consciously live our lives. Our destiny will reveal itself. Children are much more conscious than the past generation and are ready for a major whole Earth paradigm shift. The deeper truth that connects us is becoming evident, and its actual facts are becoming clear: We are here to live in the great story of finding a sense of unity for individual and collective balance. Awaken to the call of the authentic self to foster a love of living in mutuality and oneness.

Elevate our young into the position of knowing they must design their own future.

Already fewer young people are developing as professionals who wish to climb the ladder of material success. More and more they are planning their own futures as independent social innovators and entrepreneurs. They need help understanding that this is not a final phase but rather a stepping-stone to standing as an individual connected to all others in a complex structure of a hologram. It is in right relationship to each other and to all of life that Mother Earth can best flourish.

Evolve consciousness to further inner exploration of how to live a life of meaning.

Today, schools often offer mindfulness as a first step toward understanding how each individual is able to direct the outer self to construct a better reality. In the future, we will tap into our global consciousness to recognize that beneath the surface self lives the authentic self, requesting to participate in life in a meaningful manner. When we are coherent in consciousness, we create what Teilhard de Chardin calls noosphere (a planetary "sphere of reason") that helps us accept oneness as the modern wisdom.

Authentic education fully understands that to educate means to draw forth the inner purpose of each individual. The teacher, as educator, is a guide rather than an enforcer. Information and skills are still learned but for navigating the terrain of life in a constructive integrative manner versus conquering life as the individual. Cultural values, religion, personality variations, and other elements are the tools used to construct a future society. Our consciousness holds us together as humanity. We educate to experience the self as related to the whole.

We must lead with our hearts and use our minds to further our understandings of how our universe works, and then learn how to behave as this one family of humankind. Authentic education is necessary for us to experience unitive synergy.

Chapter 25 Spotlight

Education, a key to arriving at this understanding of interconnectedness and wholeness, is said by Nina Meyerhof to be *authentic* when it awakens, elevates, and evolves consciousness. Science and spirituality are coming to the same conclusion—that all human beings are intrinsically similar—but as we also accordingly shift and expand our field of love toward our extended human family and integrate this deep compassion into the education system by deploying resources for the common good, we will lift up all people to a better future.

Call to Action

What can you draw from within that will awaken, elevate, and evolve consciousness in others, especially children and youth? You can become a mentor, volunteer as a big sister or brother, or remember those who were kind to you when you were a child and then become that person for a child in your life.

26

A WholeWorld-View to Guide the Evolution of Consciousness

Jude Currivan, PhD

Healing Our Worldview

A worldview is a mindset, a set of beliefs or values, an outlook about life and reality that grounds and influences perception, thinking, feeling, and action, especially when informed by cultural, faith, social, and experiential factors. It's a framework for experiencing, making decisions, and behaving in the world. Our behaviors are ultimately driven by our worldview; what we believe about ourselves, each other, and the wider world—whether true or false.

Our collective worldview, in recent times, has focused too much on a fragmented, dualistic, and material Universe, and people are responding to traumas with separation-based behaviors. These are symptoms of an essentially "dis-eased" worldview—one which has brought us to our current healing crisis, existential threats to the continuation of our species, and catastrophic damage to our planetary home. Yet, as any doctor knows, trying to deal with symptoms without addressing the root cause of a disease will not, and cannot, heal it.

What though if those beliefs are fundamentally wrong? What if we can "re-member" the true and essentially unified nature of reality? And if we can, what could it mean to us and to how we treat ourselves, each other, and our planet?

A WholeWorld-View Unifying Framework

Mainstream science has long maintained that the seemingly separate and material appearance of the Universe is its true and sole reality. In that view, consciousness arises from the brain, as an accidental result of random occurrences and mutations that enabled the evolutionary emergence of biological life and subsequent "survival of the fittest."

These days, leading-edge science across all scales and domains of existence and across many research fields is instead revealing that our Universe exists and evolves as a unified entity. The appearance of separation is an illusion. Revolutionary experiments and discoveries of this emerging postmaterialistic science are showing that mind and consciousness aren't something we *have* but rather—as spiritual insights of all ages and traditions have told us—what we and the whole world *are*.[1]

This radical WholeWorld-View is of a fundamentally "in-formed" and holographically manifested Universe emerging from nonphysical realms of causation—literally a cosmic hologram—showing itself through self-similar and *meaningful* "in-formation-al" patterns, relationships, and processes.

Key experiments proving the inherent physicality of information and validating theoretical predictions support its premise that information literally informs the emergent energy-matter and space-time appearance of reality.[2] Whether cosmology, physics, chemistry, biology, or other complex systems, these patterns, known as fractals, occur at enormously differing scales of existence. Extending from individual atoms to vast, galactic clusters, they are all-pervasive throughout the informational appearance of our Universe.

The fractal signature of the "cosmic hologram" was even seen in early 2017 in the cosmic microwave background: relic radiation left over from our earliest epoch that fills all of space. Crucially, such relationships are being uncovered not only throughout the "natural" world but are also reflected in our collective human behaviors. For example, the "in-for-mation-al inter-play" of internet traffic, website links, and data routes all embody the same fractal patterns, as do biological ecosystems.

This emergent and integral model is also based on the framework and growing evidence for universal nonlocality. Within space-time, no signal can travel faster than the speed of light; this premise holds that the entire Universe is a nonlocally unified entity. In 2018, researchers at MIT proved this with cosmological scales by nonlocally connect-ing photons of light in their laboratory with starlight from six hundred light-years away and triggering the nonlocal entanglement with ancient starlight received from two incredibly powerful and distant quasars (respectively, 7.8 and 12.2 billion light-years away).

This WholeWorld-View offers a natural and inclusive framework for validating the intention around experiments and supernormal phe-nomena. It points to our shared psyche, operating at many levels of awareness, as the place where the reality of our communal behaviors manifests. It also reveals that the algorithms we call the laws of phys-ics and the exquisite fine-tuning of our Universe embodies an innate evolutionary impulse from simplicity to complexity. By remembering the unity of the whole world, instead of its illusion of separation, and instead of perpetuating separation-based behaviors, we can consciously cocreate thought patterns for love-based attraction, assisting the flow of conscious evolution.

The WholeWorld-View message supports the understanding, experi-encing, and embodying unity awareness, inviting a spiral of consciousness that moves our focus dynamically between "me," "we," and "all" levels of communication and engagement, and is an invitation to think cosmic, feel global, and act local.

"Re-Storying" and Restoring Our Worldview

These three keys are how we are beginning to "re-story" our worldview and what it means to be human; to heal and restore our relationships with ourselves, each other, Gaia and all her children, and the entire Cosmos.

Think Cosmic

We have never before had so much evidence that we are living in an interdependent and informed Universe that not only exists and evolves as a unified entity—but exists to evolve.

We are coming to realize that mind and matter are unified—and that our Universe is a great thought rather than a great thing. Leading-edge science is discovering that separation is an illusion. That mind and consciousness holographically informs the co-creation of our universal reality and states of existence. Every micro aspect of existence contains the informing codes of the macro Universe.

We are alive in a critical evolutionary moment: after 13.8 billion years of evolution, our Universe birthed a self-aware species. As we collectively remember the multidimensional and unified cosmos, we are on our way to becoming unity-aware beings and conscious cocreators with our Universe and its ongoing evolutionary impulse.

Feel Global

We are all indigenous to Earth. We are all Gaia's children. Like a healthy, resilient ecosystem within the wholeness of the All, our global experience manifests through the radical diversity of "me" and "we." But the illusionary story of separation is breaking down. We now either consciously evolve together globally or our species likely goes extinct. In this pivotal time of breakdown and breakthrough, we can remember and feel for our inherent connection to each other and Gaia and cocreate a thriving future for all.

Act Local

While the process of remembering unity is unique to each, all our paths are on the same journey of inner and outer evolution. In the coming years, the choices of each and all of us will determine the fate of our species and potentially all life on Earth. We can choose to become unity-aware beings, acting local and feeling global, to experience and embody wholeness. We are indeed in this together. We always have been.

Change agents and cocreative movements are designing, developing, and manifesting unity-based communications and structures in numerous areas, including finance and economics, science and technology, education, holistic wellness, politics, governance, justice, peace, media, arts and culture, architecture, and social entrepreneurship.

Locally, people and communities are embarking on quests and practices of "sacred normality"—reconnecting to each other, Gaia, and the universal pulse of evolution that flows through us. A recent example of this shows up in how we have come together: caring for the environment, initiating healing circles, and social connecting through numerous actions of kindness, focused intention, and even meditative care through the time of the COVID-19 virus that has swept around the globe.

We are remembering what it means to cocreate lives of meaning, purpose, and responsibility. Communities are rediscovering their ability to find local solutions to global challenges. Crisis is breeding opportunity and innovation. We are waking up, growing up, cleaning up, showing up—and progressively linking up and lifting up in waves of cocreative cooperation and empowered synergies.

The WholeWorld-View Adventure

A WholeWorld-View offers a salve to heal our fragmented perceptions and collective disease of separation while restorying and restoring a unified reality. This unified worldview converges with universal spirituality and the teachings from indigenous wisdom, guiding us in restoring our relationships with each other, Gaia, and the whole world. It empowers our stepping into the hope, to following action of the evolutionary impulses unfolding around us in these transformative times, and calls us to manifest the potential of our individual and collective conscious evolution.

Our WholeWorld-View movement invites an adventure that takes us from understanding the new story into experiencing it for ourselves (visit wholeworld-view.org). We are all invited to embark on our diverse quests into the world and help to transform it through our individual and collective experiences of unity in diversity.

Each of us can choose our narrative and consciously choose to live a story founded in unity consciousness; to connect with changemakers locally and across the world with positive intention to energize and embody our own vision and purpose. We can step forward to cocreate with others, Gaia, and the Universe, living and sharing our evolutionary purpose, discovering our unique cocreative toolkit that enables and empowers each of us to make a positive difference in the world.

Chapter 26 Spotlight

We can approach living into the wholeness all around us, and allowing our consciousness to evolve at the same time, by applying the power of a spiritually based science. Jude Currivan offers us a way to do this with a unifying framework developed by the WholeWorld-View movement, viewing ours as a holographic Universe in which similar and meaningful patterns and relationships exist at all levels throughout. This allows us to visualize a living wholeness of ecosystems all coming together as one inclusive system, giving us a needed perspective for remembering the unity of the whole, restoring how we see ourselves, and re-storying this new experience for ourselves.

Call to Action

Choose a situation that you don't like and try to see it anew with a WholeWorld-View. Can you shift your perspective? Do you see the situation in a new light?

Change Our Story; Change Our World

Gregg Braden

Since the birth of modern science some three hundred years ago, with Isaac Newton's formalization of the laws of physics, the story of our lives has led to a dangerous course of thinking—that we're little more than specks of dust in the universe and biological sidebars in the overall scheme of life. We've been led to believe that we're separate from the earth, separate from one another, and perhaps most significantly, separate from ourselves. As a consequence of our beliefs of insignificance and separation, we've felt that we're powerless when it comes to the healing of our bodies and our ability to influence cooperation and peace in our world.

Our story of separation includes Charles Darwin's belief that life is a struggle and we must fight for the good things that come to us in life. As children, many of us were conditioned to think this way through the mantra that we live in a dog-eat-dog world. The very phrase embodies the thinking that the world is like one big, limited pie, and therefore we must struggle and fight for our slice of the pie or miss out forever. This is the basis for the popular worldview of scarcity and lack and the violent competition that results from that perception. It may be no coincidence that during the same period we've held this view, the world has found itself facing the greatest crises of war, suffering, and disease in recorded history.

The Discoveries

New discoveries in the fields of biology, physics, archaeology, and genetics are revealing a new human story. They're also forcing scientists to change their thinking when it comes to who we are and how we fit into the world. In biology, for example, the publication of more than four hundred studies showing that nature is based upon a model of cooperation, rather than Darwin's ideas of competition and "survival of the fittest," has turned the thinking of evolutionary science upside down. In light of such discoveries, and others, some key assumptions of the past—now recognized as false assumptions of science—can no longer be taught as fact. Examples of these include the following:

False Assumption One: Nature is based upon survival of the strongest.[1]

Fact One: Nature relies upon cooperation, *not competition*, for survival.[2]

False Assumption Two: Random genetic mutations over time explain human complexity, capabilities, and origins.[3]

Fact Two: The timing, nature, and result of human genetic mutations, such as human chromosome 2, are beyond what can be attributed to random mutations and evolution alone.[4]

False Assumption Three: We live in a universe where the space between things, and us, is empty and we are separate from one another.[5]

Fact Three: The universe, our world, and our bodies emerge from a shared field of energy that reveals a previously unrecognized level of connection and unity.[6]

When we think about everyday life—the way we care for ourselves and our families, how we solve our problems, and the choices we make—it's plain to see that much of what we accept as common knowledge is rooted in false assumptions.

Rather than following the scientific imagery that portrays us as insignificant beings who originated through a miraculous sequence of lucky biology and then survived five thousand years of civilization as powerless victims separate from the world we've found ourselves in, the new science suggests something radically different. It reveals that we are part of, rather than separate from, our world and imbued with the power to choose the quality of our lives and relationships in the world.

The Truth of a Lie

While for some people the possibilities implied by the new discoveries are a welcome and refreshing way to view the world, for others they shake the foundation of long-standing tradition. It's sometimes easier to rest upon the false assumptions of outdated science than to embrace information that changes everything we thought we knew. When we cling to the false assumptions, however, we live in the illusion of a lie. We lie to ourselves about who we are. We lie about the possibilities that await us, and we lie to those who trust us to teach them the latest truths about our world.

Science-fiction author Tad Williams has expressed a reality check of the power of such a lie: "We tell lies when we are afraid . . . afraid of what we don't know, afraid of what others will think, afraid of what will be found out about us. But every time we tell a lie, the thing that we fear grows stronger."[7] The new discoveries tell us that the teachings of the past are no longer true. Now we must choose. Do we continue teaching the false principles, and suffering the consequences, of wrong assumptions? If we do, then we must answer an even deeper question: *What are we afraid of?* What is it about knowing the deepest truths of who we are, our origins, and our relationship to one another and the earth that's so threatening to our way of life?

From Fear to Fact: Our Moment of Choice

Emerging studies, such as those reported in *Scientific American*'s "Crossroads for Planet Earth," tell us, "The next 50 years will be decisive in determining whether the human race—now entering a unique period in its history—can ensure the best possible future for itself."[8] The good news the experts almost universally agree upon, however, is that "if decision makers can get the framework right, the future of humanity will be secured by thousands of mundane decisions."[9] It's in the details of everyday life that the "most profound advances are made."[10]

The key in this statement is that *we are the decision-makers*. Our moment of choice is our opportunity to replace the fear that's led to the hate and suffering of the past with the discoveries that spawn cooperation and healing as we make our everyday decisions. The fact that hate remains today, and that crimes of hate are accepted as a part of everyday life, tells us that we have yet to heal the thinking that makes hate possible.

Whether it's directed inwardly as the epidemic lack of hope expressed by young people regarding their future, and their acceptance of drugs to distract them from their sense of hopelessness, or directed outwardly with race-based, gender-based, and religion-based hate that frequents national headlines, the acceptance of hate is only possible because of a way of thinking. To douse the fear that breeds hate in our lives, we have to address the core belief itself—the thinking that tells us we live in a world of competition and scarcity, where the devaluing of human life is justified as the price for survival. To do anything less is the equivalent of merely placing a bandage on the wounds of hurt that are destroying our families and societies.

In the new human story, as we remember to revere the specialness of life and the role of cooperation in nature, it will no longer make sense to criticize, hurt, and kill one another with the ease and frequency that we see today. And by basing our children's education on these uniquely human values, we create the foundational shift—a complete sea change—that leads to our greatest destiny of realized potential as a species.

When We Change Our Story, We Change the World

American politician William Jennings Bryan remarked, "Destiny is not a matter of chance; it is a matter of choice. It is not a thing to be waited for, it is a thing to be achieved."[11] I believe there's a lot of truth to Bryan's observation, especially when it comes to our collective destiny and the world that awaits beyond the fearful thinking of the past. For the first time in three hundred years, the potential to shift from a world of competition and conflict to one of cooperation and sharing is now within our grasp.

To meet the challenges of our time, we must be willing to think differently, perhaps more so now than at any point in the past. We must be willing to change our story from one of powerless victims of circumstance to responsible masters of our experience. And to do so means that we must cross the traditional boundaries that have separated the discoveries in one area of scientific study from those in another. When we do, something wonderful begins to happen—we discover a mysterious history that reveals our extraordinary potential.

Fossilized human DNA shows that we appeared on earth 200,000 years ago with the same genome, and the same extraordinary capabilities of intuition, imagination, self-regulation of our biology, and healing that we have today. The new science of neuro-cardiology reveals that, from the time of our origin, we've embodied a nonverbal language based in our hearts that connects us with one another and communicates with all things. Discoveries such as these, and others, are revealing a new human story, and new choices for our future. The beauty of our moment of choice, is that there *is* a choice, and it's ours to make. We must choose to either learn from the discoveries of our past and embrace the potentials they reveal, or to deny these truths, and succumb to the consequences of our ignorance.

Without a doubt, each of us will be asked to make countless decisions regarding our future. I can't help thinking, however, that the most profound, and perhaps the simplest, will be to embrace what science is showing us about ourselves. If we can accept, rather than deny, the deep truths of our existence, then everything changes. With that change, we can begin anew.

Chapter 27 Spotlight

The integration of science and spirituality leads to an evolution of consciousness as advances in knowledge expand and deepen our understanding of reality as a whole. Our beliefs change in the process, as Gregg Braden clearly illustrates here. Old stories become outdated and even dangerous as new discoveries emerge, slowly take hold, and eventually supersede the old. This process of conscious evolution has played out many times in our history. Today, new discoveries are bringing with them new beliefs that are replacing false assumptions. A new story of breaking down old boundaries and living in connection and unity is changing our world.

Call to Action

Is some part of your story holding you back? Experiment with changing a belief about yourself or the way you see the world. Rewrite your story and then take an action that reflects the new you. If you've been a person who lacks resources, give something generous; if you've never felt loved, do something loving. You get the idea!

Circle Six
New Frontiers
Beyond Space
and Time

*From outer space to inner space, we view the cosmos
as a fully integrated whole.*

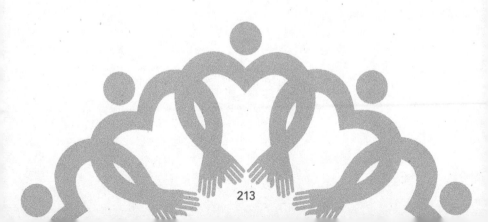

28

Liberating Human Potential

Eben Alexander III, MD, and Karen Newell

Over the last few decades, a major scientific revolution has been brewing over the nature of consciousness. The conventional scientific worldview of materialism, or physicalism, is a remnant of the determinism that originated with Isaac Newton, one of the most renowned scientific minds of all time. Many modern proponents, those who study the physical, or material, world, claiming to speak for the scientific community, would go so far as to claim that consciousness—our sense of self-awareness and existence—is merely chemical reactions and electron fluxes in the substance of the brain, and thus that free will itself is a complete illusion.

Dr. Wilder Penfield, a renowned neurosurgeon of the twentieth century, who spent much of his career studying results of electrical stimulation of the brain in awake patients, wrote *The Mystery of the Mind* in 1975 to address the possibilities of consciousness beyond what's explicable through brain mechanisms alone. Australian philosopher David Chalmers carried this further in his 1996 book, *The Conscious Mind*, in which he described the "hard problem" of consciousness as the impossibility of explaining consciousness based on our knowledge of physical brain's workings alone.

The assumption that only the physical world exists traps us into a false worldview. When we study human experience itself, and especially the rogue cases that populate the world of parapsychology, evidence that physicalism is false fully overloads the system of debunkers and deniers who remain willfully ignorant of the supportive data. In fact, scientific evidence supports the reality of such things as telepathy (notably in twins but also demonstrable in other settings), remote viewing, out-of-body experiences, psychokinesis (physical action accomplished through mental will alone), and near-death experiences (NDEs). Also of note are the closely related but more challenging cases of shared-death experiences, in which someone who is not "near death" takes the journey along with a departing soul, even to the point of witnessing a full-blown life review of their loved one, prior to returning to this world.

Although NDEs alone can never fully answer the question of what happens after we die, given that NDEers return, the evidence suggests that a spiritual, or nonphysical, realm exists, supported by thousands of reports from all continents, belief systems, and millennia.

Answering the Big Questions about the Afterlife

The only way to make sense of the afterlife question is to assemble all that we know, from every relevant line of inquiry, about the relationship between brain and mind that is the fundamental nature of our conscious experience itself. One of the strongest pieces of evidence to support a much grander vision of consciousness in the universe is the data on over 2,500 cases of past-life memories in children indicative of reincarnation, studied by doctors Ian Stevenson and Jim Tucker of the University of Virginia over the last six decades.

Consilience is the notion that lines of evidence from widely disparate fields of inquiry might strengthen a theoretical position as they converge on a similar answer. In the science of consciousness, such consilience involves the hard problem of consciousness as it applies to the neuroscience of consciousness and philosophy of mind, and multiple intriguing lines of evidence concerning nonlocal consciousness from the world of parapsychology.

It also involves the profoundly intriguing experimental results accumulating in the field of quantum physics, the most successful theory in the history of the scientific revolution. Progressively refined experiments over the last five decades have come to demonstrate in profoundly convincing form that the *primacy of consciousness* in the universe is inherent in comprehending the nature of reality.

In our book *Living in a Mindful Universe*, we propose metaphysical idealism as an emerging theoretical model that offers a more complete explanation. The grandest implication of this worldview is that none of the world exists independently of the observing mind. It appears that consciousness is a fundamental property of the universe, and the physical world is simply a projection out of consciousness itself. Fully understanding this primacy of consciousness concerns seeing the physical brain as a filter that only expresses certain states of consciousness, but that the origin of consciousness is at the basis of all emerging reality.

Arising from this discussion is the important idea that we are all sharing one mind, a concept brilliantly elucidated by Erwin Schrödinger in particular. The "overlap" of our mental space, as exemplified in empathic connections, telepathy, shared dreams and intuitions, and experimentally using the Ganzfeld technique to clear the receiver's mind to more easily receive the sender's signals, all suggest this unity. Of course, many who have undergone a near-death experience are quite familiar with this concept in their discussions of a life review, where the events of their lives are re-experienced not as themselves but as witnesses to the emotional impact of their actions and thoughts on those around them, experienced from the "others'" point of view. Through the life review, the Golden Rule—to treat others as you would like to be treated—seems to be written into the very fabric of the universe.

Swapping Our So-Called Reality for the View of the One Mind

As more of us awaken to this refreshing worldview, our so-called reality can be seen more as the dreaming of the one mind, with each of our individual perspectives more akin to a facet on the surface of the gem of the one mind. We all, at any age, seem to be sharing a communal journey of learning and teaching in this soul school of life. The vestigial, outdated views of separation and competition in the physicalist position, often with distressing and destructive conflict, are inconsistent with this emerging view of the one mind.

In the worldview of metaphysical idealism, the outer world is a reflection of our inner world, and science is rapidly moving toward confirming that reality. It is both a birthright and an imperative that we individually take steps to more fully understand and consciously manage our inner world. By developing the ability to go within using meditation, centering prayer, or some other method, we learn to identify with the inner observer—the part of us that is connected to the more expanded one mind. It is critical to evaluate limiting belief systems, manage distracting thoughts, and release reactive emotions. A concerted practice will bring clarity, providing an opportunity to instill a neutral state, unencumbered by worries and anxieties. This leads to alignment with the grander essence of who we truly are, rather than simply identifying only as the roles we play.

We all seem to be connected through the binding force of pure, unconditional love, as those with firsthand experience directly report through any sort of spiritually transformative experience. That same unconditional love, so comforting to the experiencer, provides the empirical evidence of the nature of that primordial consciousness—love is at the core of our existence. This is the profound lesson that humankind has been challenged to assimilate for thousands of years. Although the fundamental message of the prophets concerning love, mercy, and compassion has strayed through some conflicting religious dogma over the millennia, the current message of the neuroscience of consciousness concerning these extraordinary human experiences stands a much better chance of changing the world for the better. Religious beliefs can be augmented by scientific consensus and a secular spirituality, of sorts, that is common to us all. By bringing the knowledge-supporting power of scientifically supported models of the nature of reality and acknowledging transcendental personal experience, true awakening might finally occur.

We've had over five millennia of reports from prophets and mystics sharing their experiences and seeking the buy-in of humankind concerning realms beyond the material. As the scientific study of consciousness proceeds along a path that increasingly supports the primacy of consciousness in the universe, spearheaded by the voluminous explosion of near-death experiences over the last six decades (beginning with physicians' ability to resuscitate cardiac arrest patients by the millions since the late 1960s), we are finally awakening to a deeper truth of mutual purpose and connection through love, compassion, and mercy that will ultimately enable a more harmonious and peaceful world.

By actively cultivating feelings of love and compassion, we demonstrate the ultimate Golden Rule—where generating love from within serves to help others as the heart's electromagnetic field naturally radiates that energy to the world at large. By developing a richer relationship with our more-expanded consciousness through our inner world, we come to realize that all is well—that, in fact, it's a win-win situation that honors love, compassion, and kindness in our dealings with self and others. This maturation of understanding will serve to remedy much of the polarization and conflict in our current world.

Chapter 28 Spotlight

As Eben Alexander and Karen Newell explain, in both outer space and inner space, new scientific discoveries revealing the cosmos as a deeply connected and fully integrated system are liberating human potential.

Consciousness is a fundamental property of the universe. We have one mind that we all share, connected through the binding force of pure, unconditional love, which guides its evolution. We are finally awakening to a deeper truth of mutual purpose and connection through love, compassion, and mercy, which will ultimately enable a far more harmonious and peaceful world—as the cooperative energy of the Golden Rule radiates throughout the entire world.

Call to Action

Experiment with unconditional love! Love with no expectations and complete acceptance. Show your compassion; give your time freely. How does it make you feel?

Vibrational Intelligence: Tapping into the Language of the Universe

Eve Konstantine, MPH

Our planet's systems, both human-made and natural, are breaking down with greater intensity and increasing frequency. Yet the awakened mind also understands that we are on the precipice of a great breakthrough, with limitless power, intelligence, benevolence, and help available to us, both seen and unseen, in our grand multiverse.

Increasingly, lay, scientific, religious, and secular thinkers understand that we are living in an intelligent universe and that we are, in fact, an indivisible part of it. It is ours to learn how best to communicate and interact with the vastness of our magnificent home. Tapping in to and maximizing what could be infinite knowledge, wisdom, and compassion requires our understanding that this powerful help is always available to us. We can access this intelligence and cocreate accordingly in ease, joy, and beauty.

This is not a new idea. Well before the time of the ancient Greek philosopher-mathematician Pythagoras, the universe was understood to be a fully connected, indivisible whole, through an unending flow of vibration and frequency.

Our task is to learn to stand in the magnificence of what we are. To truly ponder the profound notion that we are indeed One with Source, One with this awe-inspiring universe, One with All-That-Is. How, then, do we want to live? How can we understand this, and what does it require of us?

Cultivating Forms of Intelligence

We have managed to understand and measure what we call our IQ, our intelligence quotient, and though it may be limited in its capacity to reflect diverse forms of genius, we have used it—for better or worse—as a barometer of an individual's raw capacity for learning.

As "success" came more and more to be measured in financial terms, researchers noticed that high native intelligence did not necessarily correlate to material gain. They discovered that a person's social aptitude was often a better predictor of professional advancement and dubbed this form of intelligence *emotional intelligence*, or EQ. Over the last two decades, a mini-industry of publications and trainings on EQ has grown.

I call our next level of intelligence our *vibrational intelligence*, or VQ©. Our VQ is the language of the universe. It is our key to unlocking our limitless cocreative capacities, now needed more acutely than ever before.

Our current challenge is to vastly broaden our perspective and step into and fully embody the fact that we are *one and the same as the Creative Force underlying this entire universe*. Short of this, we are living at a mere fraction of our total capacity and missing the point of who we are and why we came here. We are master painters at the easel without our brushes.

Could the immortal phrase inscribed at the Temple of Delphi, *Know thyself*, mean something even deeper than knowing the inner workings of one's psyche? Might it be a directive to ultimately realize the immensity of Who We Are? What if, as many Eastern and Western philosophies have long stated, we are more than our minds, more than our bodies? What if we could glimpse the magnitude of our truest and highest nature?

In the Bible we find the words, *That thou art*. The Vedas say, *Tat tvam asi*, "You are that," and *Soham asmi*, or "I am that." Islam declares: "Know that the key to knowing God is to know your own self." The Sufi poet Rumi, with laser-like precision and elegant simplicity, stated "You are not a drop in the ocean, you are the ocean in a drop."

Many other religions and indigenous traditions speak to this vast understanding of our essential nature. Is the admonition "Know thyself" leading us? Could it be directing us to finally see ourselves as being One with All-That-Is, One with the Divine?

Contemplating such an awe-inspiring idea is most humbling and takes us into the mystical, to a place of total wonder of the cosmos. Quantum mechanics states that everything is a vibration of light, constantly fluctuating between wave and particle. This continuous flow sets up a resonant field in which a measure of coherence between two or more entities may or may not exist and which are impacted by the mere act of observation.

So now we must ask, what tools do we have for exploration, play, and mastery of this dynamic? How might we create and expand upon the coherence potential when it is in the highest interest of life and the planet? Here our innate level of intelligence, largely unknown and untapped, comes in. Our $VQ^{©}$ measures our efficacy in reaching into and consciously cocreating with the field of pure potential, the field of all possibilities. One day, I predict, this will be as commonly understood as our IQ.

Re-creating Ourselves and Designing a New World Order

We are now, all of us, just untrained magicians. The beauty of this, as we face the possibility of a sixth mass extinction, is that once we understand its truth and stand in the magnificence of who we are, then the possibility of the human race to collectively respond to and influence the course of life on the planet soars to heights unknown.

With our collective backs against the cosmic wall, let us remember the words of physicist, astronomer, and mathematician Sir James Jeans, "The universe looks more like a great thought than like a great machine,"[1] and make the decision to intentionally cocreate ourselves not just out of this existential crisis but into a world yet unknown to all of us for its beauty, its love, its fairness, and justice. Indeed, its joy.

I hold the vision of a global people who understand and who have unhesitatingly stepped into the infinite power and magnificence accorded by comprehending the truth of who we are. I see the entire human race living our lives aligned with the unlimited, benevolent, creative forces that brought this whole multiverse into being. From this perspective, we as a human race, plus sentient beings of all domains, can address and resolve our many challenges. Accomplishing this may be the sole reason we've come to Earth in the first place.

Here are ways we can work toward achieving this potential:

○ Expand the limits of perception and entertain the possibility
   that we are one-and-the-same as the great intelligent
   vibrational forces that created our universe.

○ Align with and enter into resonance with the fundamental
   vibrational field in which we all dwell.

○ Develop a daily practice of tapping in to this field through
   whatever mechanism most efficiently raises your own
   vibration, for example, music, meditation, walking in nature,
   knitting, deep focus, getting "in the zone," running, cooking,
   painting, dancing . . . whatever draws you the most.

If all this seems too impossible or too magical, please at least temporarily suspend discouragement or cynicism that could block your learning. Give yourself the chance to experience and align with the infinite. Make a commitment to repeat the experiment daily for one month, maybe two. Surrender to what may be possible.

Globally, we may already have reached a positive tipping point in our social evolution if we combine all those already interested in the topics covered in this book: health, the environment, animal welfare, conscious business, medicine, education, politics, governance, and awakened spirituality. Casting a wide net, we may well have already reached or even surpassed the necessary very small percentile to flip the entire system.

Such a major evolutionary leap invites, even requires, new levels of thinking, perception, and action. Indeed, we *are* Nature, and as part of this beautiful, living, *benevolent* Universe, we have much to discover about our untapped capabilities.

Do you wish to help design a new world order of peace and prosperity for all? Develop your VQ© and join in! All it requires is for us to exercise spiritual courage and deeply explore the nature of Self. We must come to profoundly know ourselves, far more than what most of us have dared to believe.

Given the choice, I believe we would rather spread goodness and love than fear and separation. I believe that if we are willing, as so many already are, we are capable of doing anything.

I invite each of us to see ourselves as "the ocean in a drop." Make every decision a conscious decision. Then start noticing the effects of your conscious decision-making. You are already actively cocreating every moment of your divine existence. Now do so with greater intention and discernment. Breathe in the magnitude of Who You Are and see yourself for the truly magnificent being you are. You are that! And we are all in this together.

Chapter 29 Spotlight

We can tap in to the unifying language of the intelligent, compassionate universe, Eve Konstantine says, by learning to communicate and interact with the vastness of our home, which is connected through vibration and frequency and which makes it all one indivisible whole. We can unlock our limitless, built-in cocreative capacities, and we can unlock them by developing our vibrational intelligence. VQ© helps us reach into the field of pure potential and consciously cocreate a world in which we live in alignment with the benevolent forces that sustain us.

Call to Action

Consciously enter the natural world, connect deeply to the vastness of our earthly home, and listen for the language of the universe. Feel the living earth under your feet. See the galaxies above you. Feel yourself as the entire ocean in a drop.

30

Dawn of the New Day

Reverend Christian Sorensen, DD

*This is all wrong. . . . I should be back in school on the other side of
the ocean. Yet you all come to us young people for hope. How dare
you! You have stolen my dreams and my childhood with your empty
words. And yet I'm one of the lucky ones. People are suffering. People
are dying. Entire ecosystems are collapsing. We are in the beginning of a
mass extinction, and all you can talk about is the money and fairy tales
of eternal economic growth. How dare you!*

*For more than thirty years the science has been crystal clear. How
dare you continue to look away and come here saying that you're
doing enough, when the politics and solutions needed are still nowhere
in sight.*

> —Greta Thunberg (then sixteen years old) speaking at the
> 2019 UN Climate Action Summit

We are feeling the pain of a planet trying to rid itself of parasitical
consumption. Our outer world is crying for help, but fortunately, the
perceived trajectory is not the only possibility. Humanity is being called
to a finer way of being.

227

Times of distress lead to the development of a higher awareness and, ultimately, peace. In this era of fear and anxiety, to cultivate conscious evolution, we practice seeing a greater potential beyond and seek a supportive community. And, most vitally, we place confidence in the sustaining energy of life itself to help re-establish a new and positive story for humanity.

What's Happening in Our Outer World

People are in love with our things, with our gadgets and technology without consideration of what it takes to deliver it to our homes, to constantly update and dispose of. Our appetite for more has made us the most destructive species in this planet's history. The waste of our consumption is destroying the commons. We are burning and clear-cutting the Amazon forests, the lungs of our planet. Himalayan glaciers that feed major rivers in Asia are melting at an alarming rate. Antarctic ice sheets are breaking up. Africa's deserts are expanding.

All these things scorching the earth now are impacting our lives. These times we live in are not only calling us to open our eyes but are stirring our souls to take action! It's time to get back outside and remind ourselves that this planet is alive and that we share her with our brothers and sisters across the globe. We must be part of the solution by re-establishing the balance between carbon emissions and nature's capacity to sequester carbon.

Westerners have been insulated for many years, but the conversation is going to change. When it's personalized—when it's your tree being cut down, or your child going off to school in the morning wondering if she will get home safely, or your body that is toxically poisoned—it all becomes very real. It's no longer in a distant land, the pandemic of fear has come to our home to roost.

This is our moment of choice. Are we going to stay on the present path toward extinction, or can we participate in a conscious evolution, taking action to steer humanity toward a unified family who loves and walks in harmonious relationship with Mother Earth and all her creations?

We are being called to reevaluate the societal narratives from an inner higher observer who recognizes this precious moment.

Allow your inner space to reflect its vision of the new day into your outer world. What can you do to free yourself from the constraints of fear and anxiety? You were born to be who you are, not what society attempts to sculpt you into. We can no longer wait for the "the one" to save us. It will take all of us responding to this inner call. The hope of a new day lies within you.

Call from the Inner Higher Awareness

What if it's not all so dire as it sounds? What if what's taking place right now is a call for a higher awareness? What if a new evolutionary story is emerging, telling of the birth of a new world? Let's soulfully activate our hearts to participate in the conscious evolution that is unfolding.

Like earlier times that called for a leap in consciousness, this time is challenging each of us to wake up to a higher inner vision of what's possible, to live in harmony with this earth and each other. The new global story is of a collective new thought coming through each of us, that binds us together in support of one another.

The global heart and soul of humanity is awakening us from our apathy and ignorance. It is calling us to mindfulness so that we become more mindful of all that we see, think, and do. It's time to collectively recognize the potential in this transformative moment. It is a fertile time, and mindfulness helps us befriend the greater vision.

When spending time in mindful practices of meditation, contemplation, silence, prayer, or a stroll through nature, it is only a matter of time until our perception matches the higher frequency. We must spend time within this resonant field so we can be a more effective part of a great mobilization taking place right now. Sacred activism, passion in action, is underway. It is the energy of a mother defending her child: a proactive, unstoppable birthing; a realization of the interconnectedness of all living things.

Reaching for Integrated Wholeness

How do we get from here to a world that works for everyone before time runs out? Saving our planet is not a spectator sport. We need to pay attention to her calls and act quickly—to reverse Earth's environmental deterioration, eradicate poverty, and stabilize the population—or we will reach the tipping point of no return. Mother Nature has other options we haven't seen to bring balance back to the earth. We haven't responded to her previous calls, and if we don't take the initiative now, she will take back her planet. Could be with a pandemic, unusual severe weather, or maybe even an asteroid, but no matter what, it will be an event to get humanity to respond swiftly and to live together in harmony. We must do something different:

○ A world spending over a trillion dollars a year for military purposes while not protecting the fundamental systems that provide people's food, water, healthcare, and housing might be out of alignment with the priority of living in balance with the globe's life-supporting system. Wouldn't reallocating just a quarter of that spending seem to be a reasonable request to save humanity from self-destruction?

○ Commune with nature and journey within to the inner space, where you can see what the owl sees beyond this world. Listen to your soul. You might still hear the wind calling your name or tapping you on your shoulder.

○ Like a mystic always invited to see the mystery of the new frontier beyond time and space, take on your own mindful practice, so you too can be consciously aware of your oneness with all life. Let your spirit soar with the eagles, lifting you above the fray of struggle and allowing you to effortlessly know the elevated story.

○ Remind yourself of your place in the larger story of life. Not as a victim, but a participant in nature. Feel your inner connectedness to all of life, remember your inherent rhythm, return to your natural place.

○ Keep your eyes on the vision of possibility rather than the fall we fear. We are in the midst of a mystical renaissance. Our innovative expression, a unique characteristic of the human spirit, has always brought us through a time of crisis.

Humanity is connecting through the global heart of what Teilhard de Chardin calls the noosphere as it grows toward an even greater integration and unification. Sitting in stillness, mindfully exploring the inner frontiers, one can feel the stirring of the soul. When we are in service to something bigger than ourselves, it becomes a joy to share the vision for the potential of a greater possibility.

A new dawn is rising. We are beckoned to inspire action, write the new vision, and share the evolving narrative. See beyond appearances; be the mindful visionary who speaks it into being with passion and belief. We are all in this together, so help it become the new collective conversation. More people speaking in unison create an unstoppable tidal surge that displaces the old story with the new. Conscious evolution takes participation and you are being called to get involved now.

Manifesting Heaven on Earth

We all play an intricate part in moving away from imminent disaster and toward re-establishing the Garden of Eden on Earth. We do this by relying on inner sight, not form. To change old ways, we must live, move, and have our being in the dawn of the new day.

This means having faith in the good that lives in all people, speaking out on behalf of our children and our grandchildren and the generations who will follow and educating ourselves on present planetary issues as emotion-free witnesses to conscious evolution. This nonfearful way of seeing and being in the world is knowing that what is happening on our planet now is an alarm to get us collectively up and moving for the well-being of our planet.

It is our conscious choice to be part of the emerging pulse of the social uprising. Let our voice be heard: roar with passion in the streets, send letters to your representative, write opinions to newspaper articles, post on social media, share helpful information with friends and family. Integrate, implement, and instigate. Bless this revolution now gracing this planet. We are needed at this time more than ever before in our planet's history: to be difference-makers and transformers. It is time to answer the call and help usher in the change that will save our natural resources, our planet, and humanity!

Chapter 30 Spotlight

With a new day dawning, calling us to re-evaluate the prevailing social narratives from an inner higher-observer perspective, Christian Sorensen envisions us all participating in the conscious evolution of humanity by taking action to steer us all toward a unified family that walks in harmonious relationship with Mother Earth and all creation.

A new global story is emerging to get us moving for the well-being of our planet: the collective new thought coming through each of us, binding us in support of one another, calling us all to action and in service to something bigger than ourselves.

Call to Action

Help write the new story of humanity by walking in harmony with planet Earth and the whole human family. Commit yourself to expressing gratitude for each and every day. Do one kind thing for another person today.

31

Putting on Our Red Capes, Activating Our Superpowers

Diane Marie Williams

I t's our moment to upshift to the next level of human evolution. To operate at the most advanced level that human beings can possess. With our current climate emergency, global pandemics, and a worldwide human identity crisis, our very survival is at stake as well as the survival of all precious life on planet Earth. Our moment of choice is at hand. Do we choose mass extinction, destroying the planetary wholeness that gives us life, or mass evolution, where we usher in humanity's biggest collective consciousness shift in history? Those who are choosing the later know that something more is possible.

Ushering in a Great Leap of Consciousness

What is it going to take to usher in a great leap in consciousness on the planet toward a cocreated future, magnificent beyond our present imagining? The answer lies in putting on our red capes and activating our "superpowers" like our favorite action heroes. They always seemed to confidently know how to use their powers to save the world. If they were able to do it, why can't we?

Superman (a.k.a. Clark Kent) was originally from planet Krypton. When he was a child facing his planet's impending destruction, his parents put him on a spaceship and sent him to Earth, a more habitable planet. He in turn expressed his gratitude for his adopted planet by using his powers for good.

Everyone reading this book has a lot in common with Mr. Kent. Our superpowers are sourced by Source energy, not kryptonite, and we want to use them to become a force for all that is good, including saving our planet before it, like Krypton, becomes uninhabitable. But Superman relocated to our beautiful planet Earth. What's our backup plan?

Well . . . currently we do not have a feasible plan B. Earth is our home, and at the present there is no human technology that we are aware of that can take all of us to another habitable planet safely and for the long-term. So, until we find our Plan B, or get rescued by compassionate, interstellar Superbeings, we need to come to terms with acting—here and now. When Clark Kent took off his thick glasses and put on his suit and cape to become Superman, it enabled him to shift his perception of reality and become invincible. We also need to shift our perception of what we can accomplish because it's going to take the full recognition and activation of our inherent off-the-charts potential to reverse our current course. With over 50 percent of all individual animals lost since 1970 due to habitat destruction, hunting, pollution, human overpopulation, overconsumption, and climate change, unless we act now, researchers are saying that fish may disappear from the ocean by by 2048.[1] The planet has experienced a fiftyfold increase in the number of places experiencing dangerous or extreme heat since 1980. Human cells begin to die at only 106° to 113°F. As the global temperatures rise, we are reaching the limits of human survivability as we know it.[2] Unless we implement a fundamental change in the way we live our lives, we know where we are heading.

We Are Much More Than We Think We Are

Like Superman, who knew when it was time to take off his glasses to uncover his true identity, it's time for us to fully know ourselves as the superhumans we are, put on our red capes, activate our superpowers, and ascend through the dimensions of space, time, and limitations to move into the quantum field where all is possible.

This is required now. The days of simply moving mountains are over. We need to spring into action and tackle a climate emergency so vast that eleven thousand scientists have given us a dire warning that if we don't act now our fate is sealed.

Nikola Tesla once said, "The day science begins to study nonphysical phenomena, it will make more progress in one decade than in all the previous centuries of its existence."[3]

He, and many others, believe that humanity will not progress on a large scale until it studies nonphysical phenomena, such as linking through heart-based coherence, the power of intention setting, quantum nonlocal communication, paranormal phenomena, telepathy, clairvoyance, precognition, extrasensory perception (ESP), psychokinetic, reincarnation, remote healing and remote viewing, near-death and out-of-body experiences,[4] and communication with other intelligences as well as the living, intelligent field that connects us all, a field that we are communicating, creating, and evolving with all the time.

The study, use, and cocreative partnerships with these types of phenomena and intelligences is vital to our understanding the nature of reality, to our having the potential to shift into our next level of evolution as humanity, and quite frankly to us saving ourselves from taking a spaceship, like Superman did, to live on the yet-to-be discovered backup plan Planet B.

By linking up and stepping into a deeper relationship with our nonphysical coworkers, we are sending, and they are receiving, through the field, a clear signal that we are ready for activation. When we say, "Yes, I'm in!" to embracing and embodying the innate superpowers of the cosmos—and as we are an integral part of that cosmos, we are embracing, in essence, our innate selves—our lives will never be the same.

Using Our Powers to Heal and Harmonize

We are told that Christ traveled by teleportation, created everyday miracles, and could control the elements, including water. He was able to walk on it, calm storms, and even turn it into wine. If that was possible, surely we, twenty-first-century humans, can use such powers to reverse climate change? Why not? It's time for us to hold with inner certainty the greatest vision of what our universal selves and beloved community can be.

With the same confidence as our superheroes and miracle-makers, we will use our metaphysical energy, gifts, and techniques to reverse our course, to tip the tipping point in our favor. As cocreators of the new world, we are coded with all that is, all that was, and all that ever will be. If superheroes and miracle-makers can do it, so can we.

So, let's start creating some miracles! As any red-caped superhero knows, higher states of consciousness may be reached by many gateways and higher frequencies will activate our innate human super-capacities, but let's start with the heart. Our hearts are the portals that lift our vibrations, divine energies, qualities, and abilities upward. Through heart-based coherence techniques, like the ones our friends at the HeartMath Institute[5] advocate, we can tap into the heart's intelligence and create a direct link with each other in the field that connects us all. Our beautiful hearts will attract others that share the same mission, and together we will address our current global crises with the greatest power there is, Love, the matrix of all creation.

Silence, meditation, being in nature, expanding synergistic engagement, and heart-based conscious intention-setting opens portals to the nonlocal worlds and gives us glimpses of consciousness outside of the physical spectrum and into more expanded states of reality. Once we are plugged into the nonlocal, we are connected with higher-dimensional realities and all levels of intelligence. Here, just like we see when people spontaneously heal, we can also see a spontaneous healing of our precious planet Earth.

Experiences of deep communion and synergy with like-minded friends and colleagues can allow us to see and feel what we normally can't in our everyday lives. Years ago, the Source of Synergy Foundation presented an event called A Call to Conscious Evolution: Our Moment of Choice at UCLA. During the program, Siedah Garrett sang "Man in the Mirror," and all the members of the Evolutionary Leaders Circle who were part of the program came onstage to sing along with her, the band, and the audience. The feeling of unity in the room, all of us singing "Gonna make that change!" together was extraordinary,[6] and I saw everyone and everything in the whole auditorium as molecules of light. The harmonious vibration of our collective intention to make a change was moving matter and creating a morphic field where form became light. What a quantum moment! The oneness we were embodying must have been similar to what Superman would experience lifting off into the stratosphere and reaching an elevated frequency that transcends space, time, and matter and radiating that vibration out into a fully conscious universe ready to play in many realms of existence.

Luckily, with the World Wide Web bringing us into a global community and initiatives like the Global Coherence Initiative, Power of Eight intention groups, Earth Day, Global Oneness Day, Unity Earth, United Nations International Days for Peace, Yoga and Happiness, and many others, we are linking up and unifying with each other and the nonlocal world in more profound ways. These collective experiences of Oneness are gateways into the infinite that reveal the truth of our being. We have the superpowers of the cosmos existing within us. We don't have to be a superman, superwoman, angel, or yogi to activate them. You just have to be the awesome, invincible Super-you that you already are. So, let's take off our Clark Kent glasses, put on our red capes, and make that change.

Chapter 31 Spotlight

As Diane Marie Williams shows, in our quest to address pressing global challenges in our current climate emergency, pandemics, and worldwide human identity crisis, we can contribute to the emerging story of upshifting to the next level of human evolution by drawing upon our inherent superpowers. By shifting our perception of who we are and what we can accomplish, we come to see that we are much more than we think we are. Once we, as a global community, collectively engage and operate at the most advanced level that human beings can possess, we will cocreate a future, magnificent beyond our present imagining.

Call to Action

Did you ever experience having superpowers where you were able to do more than you ever thought possible? Take a moment to meditate on one of your experiences. What allowed you to have this experience? Was it a belief, shift in perception, being in nature, silence, compassion, wanting to feel more deeply connected, an open heart, an intention to bring about healing for another or our world, and so on? Offer gratitude for this experience. End your meditation with sending a clear signal to the field that you are ready to more fully use your superpowers in service to the greater good. Then watch the magic unfold.

32

Humanity's Change
of Heart

Claudia Welss

hen Apollo 14 astronaut and sixth man to walk on the moon, Dr. Edgar Mitchell, saw Earth from space, he had an epiphany during which he perceived the universe as an intelligent, loving, and coherent whole. His direct experience of unity included all of life, and with it came an expanded sense of himself, of humanity, and of humanity's potential for determining its future. He knew it was critical to our collective survival that we change our beliefs about the limits of our capacities as human beings. This is as true now as it's ever been.

In the Hyper-Anthropocene age debate, human behavior is likened to a force of nature, having a major negative impact on Earth's natural functioning. A traditional worldview based on mechanistic separation suggests we may now have limited choice in turning things around. But the worldview of an interconnected universe that's holographic and holonic—with the whole reflected in each part and each whole part of a greater whole—empowers us to see ourselves as not simply dependent on Earth systems but as a conscious part of Nature's organizing principles. Just in time too. In evolutionary biology, the role of crisis is to signal to an organism that incremental change will no longer suffice to transcend limitations. Humanity is being inundated with these signals. How will we choose to respond?

In his DVD *The Powers of the Universe*, cosmologist Brian Swimme advises that life has a new demand on us—the demand of synergy through conscious self-awareness.[1] Biologist and systems theorist Peter Corning calls synergy "nature's magic," because it provides for non-incremental, radical evolutionary leaps to occur by forming new whole systems that are greater than the sum of their parts.[2] In a paradigm of interconnectedness, it must be possible for humanity to consciously participate in the creation of synergy. My greatest personal discovery was the scientific evidence suggesting the coherence of my own heart is central to meeting life's new demand. We each have this creative agency.

A Synergistic Change of Heart

The quality of a connected, harmonious whole is called *coherence*. It appears everywhere, at every scale, from the atoms in our bodies to the galaxies in our universe. In biological systems, coherence indicates that the regulation of life processes is efficient and functioning optimally. The HeartMath Institute (HMI) uses the term *heart coherence* to describe when this optimal functioning and well-being is driven by the heart.[3] In this state, heart-brain interactions are facilitated, brain hemisphere activity becomes more balanced, and the body's oscillatory intelligences (such as the cardiovascular, endocrine, respiratory, and nervous systems) attune to one another. This happens because the heart is the body's master rhythm maker. When the heart's rhythms produce an ordered waveform pattern (visible in heart-rate variability biofeedback), they are sending a signal that orchestrates greater coherence in the body. HMI refers to this sine-like waveform as the physiological signature of Love at the core of the human system because it naturally emerges when we experience feelings of love, gratitude, compassion, and other regenerative emotions that bring us a sense of well-being. This psychophysiological (or mind-body) coherence is our birthright, but because of the daily stresses of life, we have to choose to reclaim it.

Cellular biologist Bruce Lipton has said that intelligence emerges when a system connects with itself. The whole becomes greater than the sum of its parts—the very definition of synergy. Similarly, heart coherence facilitates greater information flows within the body, promoting an *inner synergy* that allows for more complex functioning to emerge, such as enhanced cognition and creativity, expanded perception and intuition, and psychophysiological resilience to stressors. By contrast, stress states like fear, anxiety, and other emotions that become degenerative when chronic cause the heart's rhythms to produce a disordered waveform pattern, initiating a lessening of coherence or harmony in the human system.

Because HMI has scientifically demonstrated that we can *intentionally* increase the coherence of our heart signals through heart-focused breathing and inviting authentic regenerative emotions (a finding so significant that it was published in the *American Journal of Cardiology*), we know experiencing greater individual coherence is a choice—one, it turns out, with benefits beyond our own biology. When we're more coherent within ourselves, we become more available to cohere with others and with the world around us. Our perception expands as we take in new information due to our enlivened connection with greater wholes.

We've all experienced degrees of freedom (no matter how small) in how we choose to perceive and respond to the world, often referred to as having a "change of heart." Heart coherence increases this freedom in a self-reinforcing positive feedback loop. His Holiness the Dalai Lama advises, "When the world looks bad, look at a flower. There is another truth."[4] Even when there is no physical flower, the heart can connect us to this simultaneous truth, and that larger perception shifts our biology and our sense of reality. Our ecosystems of self, other, and world become what I call *evosystems*—ecosystems capable of evolving to meet life's new demand of synergy through the conscious cultivation of our own coherence.

By reclaiming our innate coherence, we begin to see what was previously unseen and realize what was previously unrealized. Just as our hearts orchestrate greater inner coherence, our own coherence helps orchestrate greater coherence, or harmony, in the external world.

Inner Synergy Creates Systems Synergy

Beyond shaping our perception (and therefore our attitudes and behaviors), coherence most fundamentally shapes our "vibes." As electromagnetic beings in an electromagnetic global field environment, we radiate energetic vibrations, and the heart's electromagnetic field (EMF) is the largest of the body, carrying our heart signals out into our environment, 360 degrees, 24/7—like a smartphone that's always on but without airplane mode. Whatever heart signals we're generating, we're transmitting.

Research at HMI confirmed that a person's coherent signals can be observed in the nervous systems of other people and in animals. Detectable with sensitive magnetometers, these invisible, ubiquitous fields suggest that one way heart energy transcends the personal to influence the social, and maybe even the planetary, is through resonance. This is a scientific hypothesis of the HeartMath Institute's Global Coherence Initiative—and when I learned of this possibility, it was like suddenly being able to see not just the stars in the sky but what holds the stars together.

It may be that through our own inner synergy we can choose to help meet life's new demand no matter what else we're doing in the world. This choice becomes more vital when we consider that, since Earth's EMF environment profoundly impacts human psychophysiology (with the heart being the most affected part of the body), the collective "vibe" of humanity might be impacting Earth as well. Even without our physical doings, our quality of being itself may be a vital determinant of Earth's health. And as more and more of us make the choice to claim our coherence, because of the synergistic effects, one plus one doesn't equal two. As this collective coherence reaches out into the fields around us, it may even be exponential in its power and infinite in its reach.

Other properties of coherence I've identified that seem relevant to responding to life's demand of synergy:

1. Coherent energy has power; it moves together and persists. Consider the difference between laser light (spatially coherent, capable of burning a hole through steel, and precise enough for micro-surgery) and incandescent light (spatially incoherent).

2. Coherent energy preserves information; it moves with minimum dissipation, meaning it generates minimum entropy. (Entropy is the loss of information, or order, in a system.) Through synergy, coherence may even promote the gaining of new information in a system, fostering more complex order and positive evolution.

3. In coherent systems, the part has access to the intelligence of the whole at the same time that it experiences *maximum freedom*.[5] By creating conditions that provide for maximizing the good of the part within what's good for the whole, coherence enables nature to take jumps through greater synergy.

A More Coherent Human Nature

I believe humanity is a force of nature whose nature is changing through a change of heart. As coherence moves from an occasional human state to an enduring human trait through conscious choice, humanity may evolve from being a "force" on the planet to embodying a natural power that restores wholeness.

We can choose to meet the evolutionary signals of crisis with the coherent signals of the human heart. Philosopher Ken Wilber said he believes certain patterns of invisible form will accompany the emergence of *Homo universalis* ("Universal man"), and the way humanity will know we're making the shift is through "a palpable intensification of the feeling of love."[6] The heart's coherent waveform is a response to feelings of love and is such a pattern of invisible form—one that the HeartMath Institute has demonstrated can be intentionally cultivated.

Certain theories of evolution (like those of James Mark Baldwin and Jean-Baptiste Lamarck) state that sustained changes in behavior can shape the evolution of a species.[7] In other words, *humanity can choose to shape our own evolution.* Physicists like Nobel Laureate Ilya Prigogine have demonstrated that when a complex system is far from equilibrium—as we are now—small islands of coherence can shift the entire system to a higher order. *We can choose to contribute to these islands.* Modern mystics like Thomas Hübl teach that coherence has the power to integrate fragmentation in any system as part of the self-healing mechanism of life.[8] *We can choose to be part of life's self-healing mechanism.* To paraphrase what Robert F. Kennedy once said at an election rally at the University of Kansas in 1968, the Gross Domestic Product measures everything except that which makes life worthwhile. *We can choose to measure Gross Global Coherence.* We are now experimenting with the tools to do so.

Captain Mitchell's experience of unity consciousness imbued with love was prompted by a vision of Earth from space. Considering that the sacred Hindu text, the Upanishads, is said to regard the heart as the fulcrum of the entire cosmos, the benefits of a more coherent human heart may extend well beyond Earth, creating a truly greater whole.

The choice is ours.

Chapter 32 Spotlight

How inner space connects us with outer space, through the hidden capacity of the human heart to meet the needs of our time, is masterfully explained by Claudia Welss of the Institute of Noetic Sciences. She elaborates that with human behavior acting as a force of Nature, influencing the functioning of Earth systems, we can see ourselves as not simply dependent on but a conscious part of Nature's organizing principles. This puts a new demand on us all—the demand of synergy through conscious self-awareness—with the coherence of our own hearts being central to meeting that demand. In this, we each have agency in our moment of choice.

Call to Action

Tend to the vibration of your heart. Explore cultivating greater heart coherence and notice the difference it makes in your life. Join others in creating mass coherent energy on the planet for the benefit of all life.

Circle Seven
The Big Picture

*We envision the whole to support sustainability,
prosperity, and global transformation.*

33

Evolving Our Culture: From Breakdown to Breakthrough

Justin Faerman

Despite our global standards of living reaching the highest levels in recorded history, environmental destruction, mental illness, chronic disease, and wealth disparity are simultaneously hitting peak levels and threatening to destabilize everything we've built thus far.

We are absolutely making progress toward a societal evolution—the signs of an emerging new phase of civilization are all around us—but it is largely not holistic progress, not enlightened progress. That is, it is not progress that is beneficial for all forms of life—plant, animal, human, and beyond—and that can truly support global prosperity, peace, and long-term sustainability on every level.

Ironically, the solutions to the evolutionary challenges we face are hidden in the natural environment that we are rampantly destroying— the first principles that drive the elegant, self-organizing ecosystems of our planet and, by extension, the universe at large, can be applied at scale within our societies to produce the same kind of symbiotic, highly resilient, infinitely abundant, health- and life-affirming interconnectedness that we see in untouched wilderness.

The challenge with our current predicament as a species is that our situation has become far too complex to solve with traditional practices of top-down, centrally controlled nation-state-centric legislation, due to the extreme interconnectedness of all the economic, social, and environmental systems on the planet as a result of rampant globalization over the last century. This web of increasing complexity is only being exacerbated with the rise of exponential technologies that are unleashing a Pandora's box of unforeseen ecosocial externalities that are very difficult to anticipate with our current understanding of how all the previously mentioned forces interact and play out over time.

This has created a situation where we now have an evolutionary imperative to design the next iteration of our social, economic, and governance systems so they may preemptively address unforeseen future issues through applied principles that organically sort for the greatest possible well-being of the collective, individual, and commons (that is, all life in all forms). After twenty-six years of deep inquiry, research, and study, I believe the best way to accomplish this is by individually, culturally, and collectively mirroring the pattern of decentralized, self-organizing systems that are at the heart of how nature operates and have been refined and tested over billions of years to produce life-affirming outcomes at the planetary scale.

This can be accomplished on a human scale by adopting a first-principles-driven approach to how we make decisions individually in our day-to-day lives, culturally in terms of what values we hold, and collectively in terms of how we choose what incentives to legislate and design into any new systems that are created from this point forward.

I believe the following three core principles, when adopted and applied at scale, hold the keys to not only saving us from ourselves but also birthing a truly enlightened civilization that will transform every aspect of our lives for the better—from governance, economics, science, technology, and industry to community, education, vocation, healthcare, interpersonal relationships, and far beyond.

1. Sort for Deep Self-Healing and Symbiosis at All Levels

Human behavior unequivocally follows belief, be it conscious or unconscious. Thus, our current predicaments as a species are the result of the dominant belief structures from which we are operating both individually and collectively, which have largely been driven by the idea that we are separate from each other, other living things, and perhaps most importantly, our environment. As others have noted, these erroneous beliefs have been further compounded by the conventional Darwinian maxim of "survival of the fittest" seeding a predisposition (in Western cultures especially) toward conflict and competition at scale in an attempt to dominate perceived limited resources and external threats. Virtually all existential threats we face, from climate change to the rise in chronic diseases to armed conflict, rampant polution, pandemics and everything in between, can be traced back to these fundamental misperceptions being embedded into the architecture of our current economic and social systems. This drives us away from whole-systems symbiosis and keeps us locked in psychological frames that perpetuate conflict, scarcity, and destructive attitudes toward each other, the self, and the environment.

Thus, a deep healing of the outdated Darwinian neuroses and the resulting perceptual shift toward a symbiotic view in how we see ourselves, each other, and our place in the grand scheme of things is essential if we are to avert our current destructive time line. Measuring our currently held beliefs, behaviors, and laws against how well they produce large-scale symbiosis with all life and the environment itself is a powerful rubric for determining what needs healing, how we should act, what ideas we should champion, what technologies we should value, and ultimately what incentives should be designed and legislated into our systems. Each individual choice we make has tremendous impact when magnified by the cycles of cause and effect over time. By choosing to align with principles in our day-to-day lives, immense levels of positive change can be affected in a relatively short period of time.

2. Shift from Logic to Intuitively Driven Thought and Action

Logical thinking is great for making linear progress. But we now live in an exponential world that is infinitely more complex and changing orders of magnitude faster than our rational, logical minds can keep up with. For our consciousness to keep pace with the technological and societal evolutions at hand, it must itself evolve into *superconsciousness*, which is an upshift into intuition as our primary operating system.

Groundbreaking research[1] is clearly showing us that intuition is not just unconscious processing, as previously believed. It is an integration of the conscious and unconscious, heart and mind, felt sense and thought, into an exponentially greater faculty that incorporates quantum aspects of our physiology that transcend the self.

Nature clearly has a strong bias toward equilibrium and symbiosis that is inherently expressed in all plant and animal forms into a complex ecosystem flow that produce a unified, interdependent, infinitely abundant whole. Without the need for explicit law or formal education, every species plays an essential role in maintaining the whole through a deeply intuitive orientation to reality itself.

Long before humans arrived on the scene, a clear, implicated order beyond the rationalizations of the logical mind had driven harmony at cosmological scales and expresses itself through us and all organisms via the faculty of our intuitive, felt sense. Intuition is the biologically integrated quantum operating system of nature itself, which expresses its inherent bias toward equilibrium and symbiosis through complex cellular life forms.

Thus, as we act on our intuition, we naturally do what is in the highest good of all at a level of systemic sophistication that transcends the ability of the rational mind to fully grasp. Intuitively driven thinking and action are inherently encoded for prosperity, harmony, and flow at all scales, from the individual to the collective, making them the ideal decision-making tools for navigating the ultracomplex reality we live in and by extension solving the ultracomplex challenges we face in elegant ways that are essential for us to survive and thrive through the coming decades on this planet.

Applied at scale over time, intuition-based decision-making will inevitably lead to an organic reorientation of society, our governments, our economies, and, ultimately, our technologies into a more optimal configuration for whole-systems symbiosis that naturally sorts for the highest outcomes for all forms of life.

3. Foster the Development and Expression of Purpose at Scale

Living from intuition inevitably leads to the understanding and actualization of one's purpose, as purpose is an inherent property of all things. A recent meta-analysis[2] of over fifty years of research on purpose in life has shown that when people find it, a large number of social impact metrics substantially improve, from increased health, longevity, happiness, and life satisfaction to better relationships, social cohesion, improved work performance, and far more.[3]

In other words, by failing to adequately incentivize and foster the development of purpose at its most basic levels, our current economic and social systems are burdened with extraordinary inefficiencies and negative social impacts associated with a lack of purpose and meaning in life. Studies show that only about one in five high school students and one in three college students report having a clear purpose in life and that this number drops further as one moves into adulthood. Extrapolating this to a global scale, approximately 75 percent of the people in the world (or more) likely do not have a sense of purpose in life.[4] At this scale, it becomes a hugely destabilizing force in the collective, as lack of a sense of purpose and meaning in life can lead to depression and other mental health challenges, including substance abuse and hopelessness. These stresses on society mean lost social capital and significantly reduced quality of life.

In nature, all things serve a specific and complex purpose that is essential to and intricately interwoven with the whole. Humans, as an extension of nature, are no exception. Each one of us is an important piece of the planetary ecosystem that has a meaningful role in the evolution of both our species and all life that is most fully expressed in our deep alignment with purpose. Thus, living your purpose over time has a secondary benefit: giving rise to a unique type of personal genius that is integral to the whole and serves as an important piece in supporting an evolved culture, locally and globally and contributes necessary solutions, directly or indirectly, to address the great evolutionary challenges we currently face.

Chapter 33 Spotlight

To help our global culture evolve from breakdown to breakthrough, Justin Faerman takes a highly practical approach, offering up three core principles we can apply both individually and collectively to help accelerate the birth of an enlightened civilization that will benefit all forms of life and support global prosperity, peace, and sustainability on every level.

Call to Action

Do you have a sense of your own individual purpose? How do you uniquely impact your family? Your friends? Your community? And your world? How can you live each day from this purpose? How often do you follow your intuition in your day-to-day life?

34

The Way of the
Social Artist

Jean Houston, PhD

Worldwide, societies are crying for help with the needed transformation of their citizens, organizations, and institutions. We need new ways of looking at leadership, new methods of supporting human beings to serve humanity. In the turmoil of too-rapid change, an extraordinary light has arisen.

Unique factors in human history are poised to help us become more than we thought we ever could be. We glimpse in our time the possibility of a planetary society heralding the end of ancient enmities and the birth of new ways of using our common humanity and its various cultures. In fact, we will need a gathering of the potential of the whole human race and the particular genius of every culture if we are going to survive our time. I have spent close to sixty years studying the nature of the human potential and about fifty years studying cultural potentials and harvesting them for use in education, healthcare, social welfare, personal growth, work, art, and creativity. I have found that challenges that arise in one culture can often be met by applying strategies developed in another.

This is a tremendous change, but once it is in full flower, the world will have turned a corner. In the new world that lies just ahead, all individual skills and fresh solutions will be needed to face the perils and harvest the promise of a technology- and media-driven world. People and ideas are fast becoming interconnected in ways that create a new environment—virtually a new world mind. For the first time in human history, we will harvest the genius of the human race.

As to human potential, we are coded with potentials, few of which we ever learn to use. In this time of whole-system transition, we can no longer afford to live as half-light versions of ourselves. The complexity of our time requires greater and wiser use of our capacities, a rich playing of the instrument we have been given. The world can thrive only if we can grow. We can only create this possible society if people learn to be the possible humans we are meant to be.

We exist in a time in which the world mind is taking a walk with itself. The emerging ecology of minds and psyches, our ability to dream each other's dreams and experience each other's biographies, are part of the interpenetrating wave of the current time, psyche, and memory. We are being rescaled to planetary proportions as we become resonant and intimate with our own depths. It is a world in which densely interconnected communication networks of people who cherish their communities and care deeply about life on this planet are creating something never seen before: a higher level of governance. Earth herself is becoming a vast teaching-learning community, a new order of democratic biology, as individuals and groups learn and create together a new arena for social evolution.

The Need for Social Artists

We must begin to help people, citizens and leaders alike, to bring a new mind to bear upon personal and social change. In this way, it is hoped that we can rise to the challenge of our times and ferry ourselves across the unknown abyss that separates a dying era from one being born.

The social artist is one who brings the focus, perspective, skill training, tireless dedication, and fresh vision of the artist to the social arena. Thus, the social artist's medium is the human community. They seek innovative solutions to troubling conditions, as a lifelong learner ever hungry for insights, skills, imaginative ideas, and deeper understanding of present-day issues. Above all, the social artist is always extending their capacity as well as helping others extend their human capacities in the light of social complexity.

This will involve helping cultures and organizations move from dominance by one economic culture or group to circular investedness, sharing, and partnership. It will involve putting economics back as a satellite to the soul of culture rather than having the soul of culture as a satellite to economics. It will involve deep listening and cooperative action to heal the wounds of crushed and humiliated people, those who have long been at the wrong end of the economic imbalance scale, in order to fully realize human potential. It will involve a stride of soul that will challenge the very canons of our human condition. It will require that we become evolutionary partners with each other.

The Social Artist as Contemplative Creator

The social artist participates in the art of new creation. We are called to explore the mystery of the interface between engagement with external realities and embrace of the inner journey. Creative social artistry is contemplative, with a vital synergy between inner and outer realities necessary to transform organizations, institutions, paths of possibility. It also assists visionary endeavors and, in so doing, unleashes the human spirit of those who compose the endeavor and those who are served by it. It is an activity of extraordinary balance, a tension in repose. It is a space of exquisite silence and of extraordinary service. In such a state, one has access to remarkable creative ideas, world-making patterns. Beneath the surface crust of consciousness, creative ideas and solutions are always there, ready to bloom into consciousness.

The Social Artist Is Always a New Kind of Healer

Healing involves the mystery of change, of transformation, and of the incredibly fluid nature of our bodies, minds, and psyches and, by extension, of our societies and cultures. We live in a world that is ripe for healing, and this is ultimately what motivates the social artist to take initiatives. The social artist knows that we are built for healing. The nature and process of healing, the varieties of the healing experience for people and societies seem to be the very condition of our humanity, the training ground for our social unfoldment.

The critical issue here, which distinguishes the great and inspired social artist from the ordinary, is whether they regard healing as redemptive or creative, salvational or evolutional. In our traditional medical technology and healing practice, the emphasis is almost entirely on the redemptive. All manner of fundamentalism is generally redemptive in their philosophies and liturgies. They seek to fix the old Adam, rather than understand the whole Adam. Or, if they cannot, then they assure their followers by fixing on another plane after death. This redemptive mode is carried over for jihad and defense or even preemptive strikes. They take on all manner of extreme measures to fix the fallen state.

The evolutional state works on an entirely different basis for life and for healing. There is somewhere to go; there is something to become. Even illness contains within itself the notion of deconstruction leading to a higher reconstruction, chaos leading to cosmos. Healing is making whole, the move from a limited condition felt in a most painful way through a process leading to the creation on a new level of a higher order of mind, emotions, and physical being. Something changes; the wounds in the body or of the society are experienced as doorways to higher consciousness and more evolved forms.

Social artists respect the uniqueness of each person they work with. As healers, social artists help people to ignite their potential—and do not take the credit for the ignition, to avoid continuing old dependency models. The good social artist healer is an evocator who shows people how to access their inner wisdom and knowledge without leading them like sheep. This form of healing moves us beyond the polarities of left versus right, us against them, and promotes cooperation, understanding, and networks of mutual aid. It is, above all, compassionate listening, a major training for the social artist.

In our intracultural and educational work, we try to discover the main stories, myths, legends, and teaching tales that underlie the spirit of the culture in which we are working. Then we present them as the backdrop upon which to weave our work in human development. We find that people go further as well as faster and deeper if their learning is attached to a story and, most especially, if that story is a key myth of their culture. Thus, in India we have worked with the Ramayana (a Sanskrit epic of ancient India) and the life of Gandhi; in Australia with certain Aboriginal creation myths; in England with stories of Percival, Gawain, and the other Knights of the Round Table's search for the Grail, in Bangladesh with the poetry of Tagore and other Bengali poets.

One feels instinctively when a new story is needed, when the old stories no longer speak to the current reality. And yet the old stories seem to rise again and again in fractal waves to give power and portent to the culture. What we need, then, is for stories to be remythologized and rewoven in the light of today's necessities. This has always been the job of culture, to discover again and on a deeper level, the meaning and relevancy of the once and future story—for without story, a culture becomes denatured and demoralized.

We are at that stage where the real work of humanity begins. This is the time and place where we partner with Creation in the re-creation of ourselves, in the restoration of the biosphere, and in the assuming of a new kind of culture—what we might term a culture of kindness where we live daily life in such a way as to be reconnected, charged, and made aware by the source of our reality, until our inherent inventiveness is liberated and we are fully engaged in our world and our work.

Chapter 34 Spotlight

In envisioning a planetary society heralding the birth of new ways of harnessing our common humanity, Jean Houston explains how this possible society can become a reality only if people learn to be the possible humans we are meant to be. This means understanding that social evolution needs more social artists, those who bring fresh vision to the social arena, who seek to transform all levels of society, who are contemplative creators, acting in both silence and service, and who are healers, helping people ignite their potential. We are at the stage now where this real work of humanity begins.

Call to Action

You are the *possible human*! This week, experiment with re-creating yourself as a social artist, a creative force for good in every situation that arises.

35

A Holistic Vision
of Evolution and
Consciousness

Robert Atkinson, PhD

While some people live with a consciousness that only certain things evolve, others see all things as evolving. This difference in our understanding of evolution highlights humanity's greatest opportunity today, that of transcending a prevailing, unsustainable consciousness of duality that separates us, creates hierarchies, and endangers our very survival. This crisis of consciousness distorts the way we relate to each other and the natural environment around us.

Before Charles Darwin, evolution was popularly seen as random, coincidental, and framed by separation. In 1859, Darwin's *The Origin of Species* brought biological evolution into the public discourse. His theory of evolution, which included the idea that all life comes from the same source as part of one great tree of life, opened the door to understanding all other forms of evolution, particularly social and cultural evolution.[1]

A portion of Darwin's evolutionary theory was hijacked by what became known as Social Darwinism, exacerbating the dualistic worldview, further perpetuating the illusion of separation, promoting the dominance of competition, and even justifying racism and war. When we instead understand evolution as an unfolding developmental trajectory toward an innate potential, we see the social Darwinists' view as describing a limited aspect of our nature that falls short of what is humanly possible.

The Nature of Evolution

In a holistic vision of evolution, all threats to our collective well-being are linked together, as are all solutions to our problems. The Buddha long ago said, "All things originate from one essence, develop according to one law, and are destined to one aim."[2] This worldview allows for a purposeful evolutionary trajectory to all things and sees reality as One and harmony as an abiding principle.

This perspective also sees all things going through cycles of birth, growth, maturity, decline, and renewal. Common examples of this are the cycle of the seasons and the rise and fall of civilizations, to which can be added the cycle of spiritual epochs.

Spiritual epochs have punctuated humanity's conscious evolution, bringing about a leap of human consciousness with each new cycle. A holistic vision of evolution also calls for us to consider that if all things evolve according to one law, why not the evolution of religion too?

The founders of the world's major religions—Abraham, Krishna, Moses, Zoroaster, Buddha, Christ, Muhammad, and in our time, Bahá'u'lláh—each in their own way transformed the spiritual life of the peoples of the world and even guided the course of human life over the last four thousand years. The corresponding impact on society has helped shift the focus from one social developmental level to another, from unity in the family, to the tribe, to the city-state, to the nation, and finally, to where we are now, cocreating unity on the global scale.

This latest shift can be seen emerging in the mid-1800s, when divisiveness and intolerance had reached a tipping point. Religious scholars were looking to the Holy Land and Persia as places where prophetic scripture might be fulfilled. As all prophets before him, Bahá'u'lláh then revealed spiritual teachings that focused on the need of the times ("The Earth is but one country and mankind its citizens")[3], which brought the Bahá'í faith into being in Persia, founded upon the principle of the oneness of humanity.

A century and three-quarters into this spiritual epoch, still in its springtime, a gradual but widespread increase in global consciousness appears to be undeniable, and the eventual unity of the human race inevitable. Evolution in all realms is purposeful and progressive, always leading toward an inherent potential.

The Nature of Consciousness

Something bigger appears to have been going on in the evolution of consciousness when Darwin hypothesized his theory of evolution. Prior to his famous life-changing voyage on the HMS *Beagle*, he had been a divinity student where he studied natural theology and explored the idea of divine design in nature. He could have also been inspired by the same phenomenon Jung identified some fifty years later, that "we are only at the threshold of a new spiritual epoch."[4]

To reinterpret Darwin, to understand his groundbreaking theory of evolution in the context of the evolution of consciousness, is to see it both in relation to the spiritual epoch just dawning during his lifetime and as a testament to how the power in this periodic release of spiritual energies can reinvigorate the whole of humanity.

This only makes sense when we recognize the other side of Darwin, the side we might think of as *sacred Darwinism*, which holds not only that all life is part of the same tree of life but also that evolution is purposeful, and leading to greater and greater levels of harmony, as he expressed in *The Descent of Man* in 1871:

As man advances in civilization, and small tribes are united into larger communities, the simplest reason would tell each individual that he ought to extend his social instincts and sympathies to all members of the same nation, though personally unknown to him. This point being once reached, there is only an artificial barrier to prevent his sympathies extending to the men of all nations and races.[5]

This side of Darwin aligns with the current shift in consciousness underway. His theory of social evolution itself can be seen as part of the evolutionary impulse that just started to accelerate in his own time. In laying out a developmental path for social evolution, he follows indigenous wisdom, the perennial philosophy (a holistic perspective that there is a core of shared wisdom in all the world's religious traditions), and the latest divine revelation by aligning the natural law of cooperation with the Golden Rule writ large. In Darwin's one sweeping statement, cooperation overtakes competition and is shown to be progressive, from the individual level to the global level, and collective altruism is understood as ever-expanding.

The natural law of cooperation enables transcendence from individual good to collective good to succeed. If we take this natural progression one step further, such evolutionary trajectory, though not without its ups and downs, will eventually lead to another universal spiritual principle: a future in which shared and mutual sympathies lead to peace on Earth.

Applying the law of cooperation to human communities, as Darwin intended, one's instincts and sympathies will extend to larger and larger communities until the entire global community is seen as one. We can even reinterpret Darwin's theory of social evolution as contributing to our own collective survival.

The current leap in human consciousness, which Darwin envisioned as including our "sympathies extending to . . . all nations and races," carries the principle of the Golden Rule to a global scale. Representing the leading edge of spirituality and science for their time, as contemporaries, and ultimately inspired by the same Source, Bahá'u'lláh and Darwin are not only in harmony with each other but their visions also lead to the same outcome. Consciousness is a potentiality that evolves toward wholeness and unity.

Unifying Principles to Live By

Every spiritual epoch has its own Ten Commandments, or Beatitudes, that characterize the essence of spiritual truth for that time, or the spirit of that age. As noted, the distinguishing principle, central theme, and incontrovertible truth of our time is that humanity is one.

All the world's religious and spiritual traditions share the vision of peace on Earth. Principles that can guide a universal effort toward this vision are coming into clearer focus. Across many centuries of the evolution of consciousness, we understand better today that unity, wholeness, and interdependence make up the foundation upon which this vision must be built. Also required is a framework consisting of:

- equality between women and men;

- balance between wealth and poverty;

- harmony between science and spirituality;

- freedom from all forms of prejudice;

- justice that is unitive, not punitive;

- truth that is independently discovered;

- education that is universal; and,

- nature that is protected as a divine trust.

These unifying principles are so interdependently tied together that the realization of one depends upon the realization of all the others. Each one is also a prerequisite for humanity to live as one family. When these principles are lived out in our lives, when we see all things with the eye of oneness, we will fulfill the age-old vision of peace on Earth.[6]

We can bring this vision into being, complete the process of global transformation already underway, and solve the most challenging issues of our time, all by applying the spiritual principle most closely aligned with a particular social need.

Unity of purpose is central to the evolutionary impulse; its fulfillment depends upon what is going on inside our minds. As Pierre Teilhard de Chardin reminded us, "Unity grows . . . only if it is supported by an increase of consciousness, of vision."[7] The goal is unity within the diversity that will always exist everywhere. The evolution of human consciousness will reach its fullest extent when humanity reflects the perfect unity, wholeness, and harmony that already exists in all the diversity of Creation.

Chapter 35 Spotlight

With a holistic vision of evolution and consciousness, Robert Atkinson suggests that the evolutionary impulse follows a purposeful trajectory toward an innate potential, which is as true in the realm of spirituality where cyclical epochs lead humanity toward its collective fulfillment. Approaching our age of collective maturity, principles relevant to our time—recognizing humanity's oneness; equality between women and men; balance between wealth and poverty; harmony between reason and faith; justice that is unitive; valuing all groups within the whole; seeing nature as the embodiment of the sacred; and discovering truth for ourselves—are necessary to bring about the promise of peace on Earth.

Call to Action

Practice daily seeing the interconnectedness of all things; remember to look first on all things with the eye of oneness. Breathe deeply into the perfect harmony all around you. What does it feel like to reflect this wholeness?

36

Reasoning and Experiencing Our Way to Oneness

Ervin Laszlo, PhD

The time has come to reason *and* experience our way to oneness, for they are complementary and mutually reinforcing. Oneness means realizing our connectedness to the whole web of life. Such a transformation of consciousness must be universal, and it must come from the inside. It has to be a turn that becomes a "re-turn" to the insights and intuitions that have always guided human survival at critical points.

Mounting interest in healing and spirituality signal the coming of this return, which crucially depends on the evolution of our consciousness. As this has evolved, we have inserted a more evolved consciousness in vital decision-making process in the spheres of society, business, education, health, and politics, indicating a positive, yet not widely recognized, development in regard to our common future. As we approach a critical tipping point of human existence on this planet, how we experience the world, and how we experience ourselves *in* the world, can restore or put at risk not only our species but the whole web of life itself.

Misperceiving Ourselves as Separate

A conscious species may mistakenly conceive of itself as separate from the world, a misperception called "duality." Humankind has strayed from the instinctive, intuitive oneness with which other species are embedded. But it can also rectify that mistake and recover its fundamental unity.

However, if it continues down the evolutionary trajectory of duality, oriented to fear, intolerance, and frustration, international systems will remain under the control of established dominant interests; politics will continue to cater to the interests of the group that has power without regard for others, creating growing gaps between haves and have-nots, between power-holders and marginalized populations; corporate interests will continue to drive business, making profit the purpose at the expense of "replaceable" employees and sustainable development; and feedback from the larger ecological system will be seen as disruptions to be ignored while expecting to overcome collisions and conflicts by increasing the controls and enforcing compliance with corporate directives. This path can only lead to the outcome of local crises followed by global crises, which will result in total breakdown.

Modern consciousness questions the validity of instinct and intuition; it trusts only observation and common sense. The way forward is not a return to the previous, intuitive state of oneness but a conscious recovery of that oneness. This recovery can make use of observation and reasoning, even if relevant reasoning goes beyond accepted common sense. On this path, the method of science is followed.

Using Science to Overcome Separateness

When we look at humanity's condition in the biosphere through the lens of science, we perceive the web of life as a vast, organically interconnected, and coherent system. On closer look we see that this system has become partially incoherent, harboring an element that disturbs and damages its intrinsic coherence: the human species, which some fifty or so thousand years ago evolved a higher form of consciousness.

Our species itself—*Homo sapiens*—is much older than this, with origins reaching back 5 million years or more. But the kind of consciousness that could make the mistake of separateness emerged with *Homo sapiens sapiens*, who had the capacity to distinguish the experiencer from what is experienced, creating a radical separation between them.

The modern world underscores this flawed conception with the further erroneous belief that only human beings are truly conscious beings. It is often believed other species have either a much lesser consciousness or none at all. Actions based on this belief damage the integrity of the web of life, "suboptimizing" this natural, delicately balanced and strongly interconnected system by favoring one of its elements—the human—at the expense of the others. (And within that, further favoring some humans at the expense of others.)

Science tells us that the healthy organism is coherent, with all its parts collaborating in the task of maintaining it in the dynamic, physically improbable living state. The healthy organism is not only coherent in itself, it is also coherently related to nature. This forms an all-embracing system of life on the planet that is really characterized by supercoherence, or the coherence of in-themselves-coherent systems.

Our supercoherent system has been corrupted by a factor of incoherence: the mistaken perception of duality. Such incoherence is a kind of cancer in the web of life: it is a threat to the system of life and thus also to itself.

Life Experience to Overcome Separateness

One path to recover our oneness is the realization of the urgent requirement to recover our coherence with all life on the planet. Another path is through spontaneous, lived experience that itself verifies this reality for the experiencer.

Sapiens sapiens have not lost their ability to experience coherence with the system of life on the planet and oneness with the world. Ever more people develop the sensitivity that enables them to experience this oneness. They sense that they are part of a larger whole: that they belong to nature as one of its intrinsic elements, and nature is in turn an intrinsic element of the largest reality we call cosmos. This feeling is the hallmark of the spiritual and religious experience, and it is a real experience regardless of what religious or spiritual tradition expresses it.

The scientific method and a spiritual experience can both lead to the same conclusion. The spiritual experience of sensing oneness with others can produce the same insight as reasoning, or even experimenting, through science. Through different methods, both agree on a fundamental interconnection between ourselves, other people, other forms of life, the biosphere, and ultimately, the universe.

Science and spirituality, far from being conflicting, mutually exclusive elements, are complementary partners in the search for the path that will enable humanity to recover its oneness with the world. Science demonstrates the urgent and objective need for it; spirituality testifies to its inherent value and supreme desirability.

We can reason *to* our oneness in the world, and we can experience our oneness *with* the world. Following a path of both reason and experience will take us down the evolutionary trajectory oriented to feeling, healing, and consciousness. Trends across society's realms and domains universally are leading us in this direction:

○ Social communities and new media platforms are shifting
   social structures and organization away from top-down forms
   toward decentralized networks and relations that connect
   and deeply impact people as more and more people choose
   cooperative, empathetic leaders and role models.

○ Technology is creating new opportunities for open access,
   research, and development in previously underexplored areas,
   such as farther reaches of consciousness, advances in artificial

intelligence and robotics, biotechnology, quantum computing, and smart machines that are becoming an integral part of educational, health, and security systems.

○ Interpersonal contact and communication through the emerging "media ecology" is allowing young people to experience empathy on local and global levels as they communicate their feelings, hopes, and aspirations.

○ Health and medicine trends are shifting toward alternative natural cures as people seek to live in tune with the rhythms of nature.

○ Ecologically, people's well-being is being recognized as tied to living with other species.

○ In education, new learning environments are giving learners access to peers and teachers around the world, while allowing them to be cocreators of their curriculum, resulting in greater meaning and satisfaction.

○ Economic systems are becoming a shared enterprise, with economic growth sought to offer optimum benefits to entire communities.

These trends and many more like them are moving us all further along the higher evolutionary trajectory, founded upon understanding, empathy, and cooperation. Its outcome in local, national, and global accords will create alternative social and ecological structures resulting in a flourishing world.

The challenge that faces humankind is to live up to its destiny as a conscious species. *Homo sapiens* can still create a flourishing world that is worthy of this name. We can still realize the intellectual, moral, and emotional potential present in the heart and in the mind of every human being with whom we share this planet.

Chapter 36 Spotlight

Ervin Laszlo sees the keys to global transformation, ultimately leading to sustainability and prosperity, in a vision of wholeness, or a recovery of our oneness. We move beyond the mistake of separateness either through reason, by perceiving the web of life as a vast, organically interconnected and coherent system, or by lived experience, which reminds us of the fundamental interconnection between ourselves, other people, other forms of life, the biosphere, and the universe. Both ways assist the evolution of our consciousness and enable us to make more evolved decisions as we reclaim our oneness.

Call to Action

Step out of your comfort zone today. Talk to a stranger. Walk barefoot on the grass. Experience your connectedness to the entire web of life.

37

A Synergistic
Convergence of
the Whole

Barbara Marx Hubbard

W e are at the epicenter—the "crisis of birth"—of a new humanity. Planetary evolution will either quickly spiral downward or jump to the next stage of human evolution. We can activate this natural birth process within ourselves as we all bring out our evolutionary leadership capacities together, just as the evolutionary process has worked in the past to bring us here at this precise moment of our collective development.

We can reach this next level of our conscious evolution through a synthesis of the whole, by convening people in a way that evolves us from separate beings, toward a whole system greater than the sum of our separate parts. A synergistic process to connect our own visions, dreams, and deepest desires into a new system already exists and has been used in a variety of settings, transcending win-lose systems and moving us toward a more synergistic, holistic culture.

Accessing Our Natural Rhythms of Convergence

Nature has evolved from single cells to human beings. It appears that the way nature takes jumps to higher order, at least in part, is by the power of attraction. As systems become more complex, they often increase in disorder. Meanwhile, as large systems decline, innovations in all the fields arise. In human culture we now see this happening all around us and through us as breakthroughs and innovations in health, education, justice, and relationships arise. At some point in the process, the *self-organizing system*—a sort of generic term recently developed to mean God, Spirit, Consciousness, Source, the Divine, All-That-Is, and so on—creates an invisible inner structure or process of convergence in which separate innovations are attracted to converge into a more complex whole system far greater than and different from the sum of its parts.

This convergence is more than additive or even cooperative: It is synergistic. It creates newness out of the holistic integration of the separate parts. We, humanity, are at a threshold of speeded up breakdown leading to chaos and crises while, concurrently, innovations in every field arise and converge into a new whole that is healing, unifying, and far more effective than the mere addition of any new part.

So, how can we best harness the innate natural power of this process and cultivate synergistic convergence among ourselves and our immediate connections, groups, and communities to eventually synergize the entire world?

Developing a Format to Assist Convergence

Conferencing designed for synergistic convergence was invented by John J. Whiteside and me after the lunar landing, to see how this extraordinary technological, social, and psychological process might be offered as a creative response to major issues in civil society.

At lunch one day, after John and I had suggested this idea to heads of aerospace industries and others, who had turned us down, he said, "Let's build a wheel and bring all the sectors in." We got out a paper napkin and for the first time he drew the Wheel of Co-creation with its twelve social sectors:

1. Health and wellness

2. Learning and education

3. Social justice and security

4. Spirituality and religion

5. Environment and infrastructure

6. Communications and media

7. Governance and law

8. Science and technology

9. Economics and business

10. Energy, food, and water

11. Art and culture

12. Relationships and empowerment

In 1970, John and I decided to make the first wheel a reality at Southern Illinois University (SIU). We called it SYNCON, derived from *synergistic convergence*. Visionary inventor Buckminster Fuller, whom I had also been working with, was scholar-in-residence at SIU.

The students built a large wheel-shaped environment in the gymnasium, each with separate sections for each sector. When we took the walls down between these sectors, there was an awesome pause. What made it a huge success was that something new was moving among us. It was the experience of the new social whole forming in our midst that was different from and greater than the sum of its parts.

When it was over, Bucky sent for me. "Barbara," he said, "we need women to bring this into politics. I'll create an operational plan for you." Bucky wrote a manual on how to "make the world work for all without taking it away from anyone" (through synergetics). We became partners in 1984, when I decided to bring these ideas into the political arena as a vice presidential candidate on the Democratic ticket. I did not expect to be vice president, only to make this proposal from the highest possible platform in the political world.

Now, we need to expand the use and reach of this natural process as widely as we can. The basic SYNCON process is one of getting together in small groups and asking ourselves these simple questions to identify shared goals:

1. What do we most want to create?

2. What do we most need, to create what we want?

3. What do we want to give away freely to everyone?

This can be done in one group or in many groups simultaneously. The more groups in this SYNCON process the better, as each can speak to the whole with their responses to these questions. Then there can be a well-orchestrated mingle, or exchange of findings, where groups report to the whole on what their goals, needs, and resources are. What happens in this process is exciting, even to sophisticated professionals; we all feel enthusiasm, literally filled with God or Spirit.

This is how we cultivate social synergy in our lives and work. It can be a special way of discovering the specific needs and resources of diverse members of any group. These group conversations could be videoed to share online.

After this, all groups come together as an Assembly of the Whole where the dividers between each group's focus are symbolically removed. In this assembly, each group or individual restates needs and resources, and people collectively interact to match each other's needs and resources.

In this synergistic social convergence, we work toward cooperation through attraction that fulfills our unique potentials. Nature attracts us to create more than we can possibly do alone, toward co-creation and self-evolution. This is what awakens our deepest hearts' desires, to express our own life purposes in such a way that others are joining with us to achieve their own purpose.

Our innate desire to express ourselves, coded into our hearts, gets turned on more fully. We find ourselves fulfilling our hearts' desires together—our own purposes by natural attraction, synergizing. Like nature, we fuse energies to cocreate a new synergized whole, connect what's working, and plant seedlings of new whole systems.

Nurturing Synergistic Convergence on All Levels

Such an informal synergistic process can form the basis for a social process that evolves locally, nationally, and eventually globally toward a more synergistic whole. This is not simply a good idea: it's a need for social survival.

Here's my vision for cocreating a new Earth: small group SYNCONs form worldwide from different cultures and backgrounds to express their goals, needs, and what gifts they want to give to others. These local groups avail themselves of the evolutionary leaders' (and other teachers' and philosophers') resources who can guide this process as the groups carry out their needed consultations, through online resources and public presentations. As this social synergy process unfolds in groups, amazing synthesis, synchronicities, breakthroughs, and revelations occur. This leads eventually and ultimately to a grand global synergistic convergence that synergizes the integration of our separate parts into a greater whole.

If this were to happen in the next five years, it could become a vital component of humanity's next step toward the highest point of its conscious evolution. We have to deliberately and consciously cultivate co-creation among ourselves by matching needs and resources, individually and collectively, as we come together through local SYNCONs that continue to expand and become larger in scope and inclusivity.

Chapter 37 Spotlight

In her provocative and challenging concluding piece, Barbara Marx Hubbard ties everything together, offering an inclusive vision that leads to a synergistic convergence of the whole. From separate beings, through the power of attraction, people can be brought together to create a whole system greater than the sum of our separate parts, which transcends win-lose systems and moves us toward a more holistic culture. Harnessing the innate power of this natural process, which expands and evolves locally, nationally, and eventually globally, until the dividers between all groups are removed and cooperation fulfills the potential of all, is a means of cocreating a new synergized whole, and ensuring the progress of the evolutionary impulse.

Call to Action

What do you most want to create? What do you most need to create it? What do you want to give away freely to everyone? Engage with others in this powerful process for co-creation.

Afterword

LETTER FOR THE FUTURE

Elisabet Sahtouris, PhD

Dearest Isa,

I write this letter to you, my newest and fifth great-grandchild, as a new decade is born and you, still newly on your feet, run to embrace life with open arms and bright, joy-filled, eagerly inquisitive eyes. You take me back to seeing your gram as my own baby girl, running to my open arms with the same delight. Or sometimes I leap ahead, imagining yourself at my age now, when yet another new century is already under way! I can only guess what it will be like when you look back on your own life, but I'm quite sure you will have lived through the greatest transformation in all of human history.

I see you reading this letter when you are sixteen and I would be one hundred—this '20s decade past and I no longer here. You have cross-cultural Asian, African, and European genes in your body and will naturally live your life free of prejudice as you grow up on an earth so very different from the one on which I did. I hope that by sharing some of my own experiences and lessons I've learned, before I leave, that something in them might intrigue you and feed your own dreams. I see myself among your guardian angels, following your unfolding life with loving pride, protection, and encouragement.

My faith in you is anchored in believing the reality of reincarnation—that we are all spirits or souls having a human experience and that, as souls, we all have free will to choose when and where we incarnate. And so, I am persuaded you chose to come and face this situation with both equanimity and enthusiasm for building a better world, whatever it takes.

My truly good fortune as a child was the amazing freedom and joy of being let loose in fields and forest, a beautiful stream with a waterfall and the great Hudson River's banks to explore endlessly with two brothers close in age. Our food was organic because it was locally grown and no pesticides or preservatives had been invented.

When my own children were grown, I wrote a poem called "No Grownups Watching" for an Earth Day event for kids. It tells of the valuable lessons I learned by climbing trees to see as far as possible, crossing fences that said "No Trespassing," and walking on thin river ice—my way of pointing out how much we need to see far across the world, into our future, and to break rules, as we are all "on thin ice" now, causing actual ice melt and destabilizing the fragile ecosystems that support us.

From studying Earth's history of over billions of years, I saw that in its biological evolution, species go through a youthful phase of acquisition and expansion in feisty competition. When that gets too energy-expensive, they mature into cooperation, as that proves more efficient and sustainable. Human hunter-gatherers lived a relatively simple childhood and some matured into cooperative indigenous societies, while others continued the youthful stage into empire building and capitalist growth economies. In the latter, we became arrogant, disconnected from our Earth Mother, exploiting and polluting her as if nothing could possibly be more important than our wildly inventive hi-tech lifestyle. We saw ourselves as vastly superior to nature, oblivious to the consequences of becoming a dominator species.

History has shown us that empires collapse not only from dramatic climate changes but when powerful elites create huge divides between rich and poor, then too-rigidly protect themselves when change is needed. Unlike trees that survive for thousands of years by bending with winds of change, human civilizations have all broken under such stresses. Ours is now failing on all three counts. My efforts to make people aware of this, along with many others who understood the likelihood of climate disaster and the failure of our unjust economy for up to half a century, have been ignored or disparaged as wrong till now, when it is very late. Perhaps we need the actual disasters to wake us up and to clear the way for rebuilding our way of life.

I expect your generation to feel an intense and just rage at the terribly destructive ways of those who came before you.

In the angriest time of my own life, when my nation waged a terrible, unjust war in Vietnam—the first televised war for all to see—I beat my head against the wall in anger and anguish over napalmed children and other unspeakable atrocities. Then a Bengali poet wrote me a poem with the line: *Somewhere, the tears and the agony are stored into the chest of thunder.*

I knew immediately he was telling me that energy is energy, that I could transmute my anger into useful positive action. That one line has served me well all my life since, as I learned to use every rush of anger as inspiration for some peaceful action toward making things better.

From my vantage point as an evolutionary biologist and futurist, the transmutation of energy from anger and hate to love, from war to peace, from fierce competition to caring collaboration is a matter of the maturation I described, of our growing up as a human species. From my youth to yours—a single lifetime—we humans careened from tripling our global population to having the brakes put on our reckless expansion, from reaching the heights of competitive adolescent species craziness to waking up to see we can and must shift quickly into cooperative maturity.

As I watch the ice collapsing at our poles with hair-raisingly increasing speed, not to mention the raging fires and storms, you are still a baby, rightly sheltered from disasters in your family's arms. But at sixteen, nothing can be hidden from you any longer. You see the oceans swallowing huge coastal cities in gulps, untold hordes of desperate people in flight, water wars, famine, and the spread of disease.

Yet Earth is still a gorgeous, intelligent, living planet. Fighting for its own life, it is still more suited to human life than any other in our solar system, even if we must adapt to her overall hotter climate. The catastrophes we brought upon ourselves teach us that love and respect for Earth; restoring her pure waters, rich soils, and clean air; and protecting her remaining wild forests, prairies, and living creatures as we love and care for each other is the only possible way forward. The Global Ecovillage Network (GEN), the Business Alliance for Local Living Economies (BALLE), the UN's Millennial Development Goals (MDGs), great music and art festivals such as BOOM in Europe, growing organic food and recycling even human waste, plus countless other real initiatives sprang up even before you were born, testifying to our will and creative abilities to live more harmoniously.

I thrill to what your generation will build on such foundational efforts. You have the power to carry survivors through to the light beyond this great storm. I see you bringing yourselves and your children to safe shores where you reweave the broken strands of life to build what my generation could only envision.

I do not see the universe as a downhill energy slide from a big bang to no-thing-ness nor life on Earth as doomed to endless competition in scarcity. These are both just stories scientists have told as we tried to understand the world as if it were nothing but matter. But we are not bodies with minds and spirits somehow emanating from them; we are all those at once: body-mind-spirits.

The ancient Taoists clearly knew that, as did the ancient Vedics, who saw cosmic consciousness as All-That-Is, forming matter within itself by slowing the high vibrations of soul and mind down all the way to the slowest vibrations of matter. Explore these ancient wisdoms for yourself, darling Isa, and know that the purest loving Joy is accessible to you and to anyone by going inside yourself, letting go of your outer senses till your inner senses can take over and give you access to anything you need or want as guidance for your life.

The ancient Greeks named natural science *philos-sophia*, meaning "lover of wisdom," or "one who learns from Nature." Every ancient indigenous society did that naturally, and some have survived. Recognizing this, and recalling my childhood in unspoiled nature, I was drawn to learning as much from indigenous peoples as I was studying science in universities.

Possibly the most important thing I learned from them was from a beautiful Amazon Indian whom I asked to teach me how to talk with plants and animals in the rain forest. "Oh, Elisabet," he said, "they have been in conversation as long as this forest has existed. Your job is not to talk to them, but to listen . . . to hear them."

This led me to see the difference between the languages that lead us to communicate by storytelling and the denial of our ability to communicate any other way. I came to understand deeply that all of Nature's beings, from plants and animals to the body cells we are made of, even our gut bacteria and the living molecules and atoms inside our cells, know their places through the direct transmission of information that I call *communion*, to distinguish it from *communication*, through languages. The wondrous thing about communion is that there is no need for any translation as the same system is there for all. *Nothing in Nature except humans has ever tried to get along without it!*

That is why we have strayed so far. Those who commune need no cell phones or GPS devices; they have endless help in solving problems; they work cooperatively with each other and Nature. Children do it naturally until they are told they can't. J. Allen Boone's lovely book *Kinship with All Life* explains our innate ability to commune with each other and all life forms, and in practicing it myself, I have had many amazing experiences with other species, especially with trees.

Trees may be the truest elders of Earth. According to researcher Stefano Mancuso in his book *Brilliant Green*, trees have not just our familiar five senses of sight, smell, hearing, touch, and taste but at least a dozen in *addition* to those. I hope you will one day come to love and honor and befriend trees, as I do.

Enough, sweet sister soul Isabel! Some of the other authors of this book and I belong to a "Silver Clan." In honoring the moon, we call ourselves Loominaries, and we coined the word *spinnergizing* to represent the making of the threads needed to reweave the broken fabric of Earth's systems. I hold your hand in Love and Light as you and yours spinnergize, continuing the work of navigating through crises to build caring communities for all life.

Epilogue

CONNECTING THE THREADS OF A
CALL TO COLLECTIVE ACTION

Robert Atkinson, PhD, and Kurt Johnson, PhD

W e see great hope on the horizon. Our call to conscious evolution is designed to help us all cocreate the future we envision. The very nature of the evolution of consciousness gives us an abiding hope for the future.

We have all we need to fulfill the personal visions shared throughout this book, the essential building blocks—principles, values, tools, solutions, and action steps—to assist the evolutionary impulse onward. These will all help guide us through a collective leap of consciousness that will shift us from thinking we live in multiple, divided, inequitable, and separate communities and societies to knowing that we live in one united, just, and whole global community, in which all its diverse parts are understood as vital contributors to the functioning and well-being of the whole. We are already in the midst of this great shift right now, and the light of this vision is guiding us through this fateful transitional moment to completion.

The bounty of living in an epochal period of transformation is supported by the release of spiritual and synergistic energy that will connect one with all. When we achieve this planetary consciousness, the overriding principle will be a shared sense of responsibility for the good of the whole, a recognition of our inherent unity as one human family.

We have never before seen the degree of innovation, synergy, and convergence toward interconnectedness and wholeness that we are witnessing right now. And we have the profound opportunity to participate in this critical process.

The seven thematic circles this book is built upon may appear separate. But this could only be so on the surface. When we look deeply, with an eye to wholeness, the themes, issues, and causes so eloquently and succinctly explored here are all tied together. In fact, they cannot be separated at all; they are totally interdependent.

As Pete Seeger said in 1969, speaking at South Street Seaport on the maiden voyage of the *Clearwater*,

> . . . we just won't make it unless we can talk to one another and agree on what we have to do. All of us. Young and old, black and white, rich and poor, longhair and crew cut. We hope people will say, "Gee, this river is a mess. Ought to do something about it." You see, everything in the world is tied together. You clean up a river, and soon you have to work on cleaning up society. Let's all get together and make this thing work. We can do it. Don't let anyone tell you we can't.[1]

The forty-three evolutionary leaders sharing our visions in this book, all threads of one flowing narrative, understand this well. It will take more than a handful of committed leaders to bring these visions to fruition. It will also require more than the already existing evolutionary community to act upon them and expand this field of love and healing. To generate the heart-centered future rooted in caring, respect, compassion, and cooperation that we seek, the entire human family will need to contribute all of our myriad gifts and act in a way that turns these visions into reality.

What matters most is the story we tell about ourselves, and the story we live by, as Gregg Braden so well points out in the introduction, since what we believe about our origin, our past, and our destiny defines the way we see ourselves and others. Without a story, we are bereft. In this propitious moment, our choice is either to tell, and live by, a story that has the outcome we envision—one of wholeness, harmony, and peace that all the world's sacred traditions foretell—or to tell and struggle in one that doesn't end well. This may not even be a choice, as Deepak Chopra™ notes, in his Circle Four chapter.

And from the vantage point of the future, this all comes into even sharper focus, as Elisabet Sahtouris illustrates in her letter to her great-granddaughter, who will have lived through the greatest transformation in human history by the time she reads it. Her vision includes seeing her great-grandchild's generation building on the foundational efforts of those before them, while humanity reaches maturity, leaving behind its reckless adolescent ways, and comes into its own, a time when safe shores will have been found through the building of a better world, made up of cooperative communities caring for all life.

This is our vision, and our call to action as well. The threads woven throughout the seven circles of this book—though each is critical in its own right—are all of one cloth, and all of one goal, leading us to an understanding of our unity, our inherent wholeness, not only as a species but also as part of Creation. These are all the common threads to our collective well-being. It is up to each of us to carry out our own individual call to action, which makes us all part of the collective action needed. We are all the weavers of one tapestry.

We, as evolutionary leaders, offer our solutions and resources to help guide this process of a grand, global, synergistic convergence that integrates our separate parts into a greater whole. We are here to facilitate a unified world by supporting the conscious evolution of the whole to help guide our next step toward the highest point of humanity's collective evolution.

The time has come for all of humanity to be united in purpose. We proclaim humanity's coming of age; we are approaching our collective maturity, in which every single member of the human family is here now to help usher in and cocreate a just, prosperous, and peaceful world. This is the goal all others in past ages have lived for; we are the ones to now carry it into being.

We recently had the experience of being collectively swallowed into the unknown by a pandemic. This has given us a unique opportunity to reflect even more deeply on what we want for our shared future.

We experienced, as one human family at the same time, the universal archetype of leaving the familiar behind—retreating and reassessing everything we thought we knew. This is the universe's way, through evolution's inherent process of adaptation, of ensuring that the collective transformation already underway will be successful and that the evolutionary impulse is consciously carried out.

Collectively slowing down and turning inward has shown us more than ever that

- we can feel more empathy and compassion toward others;

- we can appreciate more the things we have and give of them more freely;

- we are not only more connected than we thought, we are inseparable;

- our collective strength is dependent upon our unified action;

- we can trust—and live more by—our collective wisdom;

- we can nurture a spirit of common endeavor;

- we can place the sanctity of existence above all else; and

- we can foster a spiritual consciousness that embraces all of humanity.

This common experience can take us one step closer to the new world we envision. It has given us greater insight into our inherent interdependence. It has even shown us how all seven themes addressed within this book converge into a larger whole, one ever-evolving but unified way of knowing—and living in harmony with—the nature of reality. We have been presented with new evidence that, whether seen as providence or a natural process, at this time, confluent ascending and descending energies are in play at the most cosmic level. It is up to us all to put this knowledge into action and live remembering all things really are intricately interconnected.

To live this wholeness out in every way of every moment of our lives is how we will live into the story of our collective fulfillment. It is the commitment of the evolutionary leaders to foster the evolution of consciousness. We call upon you to cocreate with us in this most profound endeavor. Together, let us bring into being a new world of cooperation, amity, and deep relationship. Join us in our call to collective action.

Acknowledgments

*O*ur *Moment of Choice* was brought into manifestation with the support of so many gifted and visionary people.

We wish to thank, first and foremost, the Source of Synergy Foundation, the home of the Evolutionary Leaders Circle, and particularly its founder and president, Diane Williams. In 2006 she shared a vision with Deepak Chopra™ to bring leaders and organizations together to foster greater connectivity among those leading the evolution. Deepak's response was, "Great, let's do it together, and hold the first gathering at my office in New York"—and the Evolutionary Leaders Circle began its journey.

The Source of Synergy Foundation is eternally grateful to him for always believing in the vision of the Evolutionary Leaders and being a beloved source of encouragement for the past fourteen years. We also wish to thank the amazing Carolyn Rangel, president of Deepak Chopra™ LLC, for her valued support since the beginning, the Chopra Foundation for their partnership in birthing the Evolutionary Leaders Circle with the Source of Synergy Foundation, the New York Coalition for OneVoice for their passion to connect, and Barbara Fields and the Association for Global New Thought for joining us as brilliant collaborators on several West Coast gatherings.

This book would not have been birthed without the vision of Robert Atkinson, who headed the editorial team with great skill and dedication. We thank him for his extraordinary commitment to this project from proposal to publication. We marveled at how he managed to keep his good nature no matter what the challenges.

We also thank Kurt Johnson and Deborah Moldow for their light and wisdom throughout this entire process. Their vital roles in editing and formatting the overall structure of the book were carried out seamlessly. Together, the teamwork of Bob, Kurt, and Deborah has been stellar.

Deborah's gifts have not only shone brightly while working to develop this book but she has also offered her skills as a cherished Source of Synergy Foundation board member since its inception and as director of the Evolutionary Leader Project. We are so grateful to her for holding and guiding this precious community with such grace, wisdom, commitment, and care.

Kurt, a master in creating synergy, always adds his brilliant insights and commitment to connect in everything he does. We honor him for dedicating his time and creativity to this book and for all of the ways he strengthens our evolutionary leaders community with his boundless capacity to bring people, projects, and media together.

And our special thanks go to Gregg Braden, who advised the book project from the very start with his wisdom, expertise, and unwavering support. Gregg always encouraged the Evolutionary Leaders Circle to show up as a collective because it is indeed our moment of choice. We offer our infinite gratitude and appreciation to him for inspiring us, for coming up with the book's title, and for his excellent introduction to the book.

We are grateful to Claudia Welss, chair of the Institute of Noetic Sciences (IONS), for bringing this book project to the attention of Richard Cohn, president and publisher of Beyond Words. We offer our deepest gratitude to Richard for his support and commitment from the beginning and to the visionary team at Beyond Words, including Michele Ashtiani Cohn, creative director, and Chelsey Lobey, assistant to the publisher, and their partners at Atria/Simon & Schuster.

We are especially appreciative of Lindsay Easterbrooks-Brown, managing editor at Beyond Words, for her dedicated and diligent work to fast-track the publication during difficult times. We wish to also thank copy editor Jenefer Angell for her thoughtful editing. And we are grateful to our agent, Bill Gladstone of Waterside Productions, Inc., for believing in our anthology and seeing it through.

We are grateful to Sara Blum for the eye-catching book cover design and to Corrine Kalasky and Brennah Hale for all their marketing and publicity insights and efforts.

We offer our appreciation to all those who took the time and care to endorse this book and to support this collective endeavor.

We want to thank all of our forty-three brilliant contributors for the insights and inspiration they provided in their chapters, as well as others who helped along the way, including staff, consultants, advisors, donors, and board members of the Source of Synergy Foundation, especially our former board chair, Jeff Vander Clute, and our current board chair, Barbara Layton, as well as all of the members of the Evolutionary Leaders Circle who uplift and inspire us every day to serve the evolution of consciousness.

Finally, we wish to thank all our readers for joining us in this journey and for all you do in contributing to the acceleration of this shift in consciousness.

Evolutionary Leaders

This book is the collective work of forty-three members of the Evolutionary Leaders Circle, a project of the Source of Synergy Foundation, which is currently composed of 186 visionary authors, scientists, educators, and social innovators. You can find their bios at evolutionaryleaders.net/evolutionary-leaders or browse through their websites, following, for a treasure trove of information, inspiration, programs, and projects that we hope will help provide opportunities for synergistic engagement among all those committed to the evolution of consciousness.

ourmomentofchoice.com

Patricia Albere *evolutionarycollective.com*

Eben Alexander *ebenalexander.com*

Panos Anastasakis *linkmedia.org*

Robert Atkinson *robertatkinson.net*

Ciro Gabriel Avruj *gabrielavruj.com*

Cherine Badawi *thrivetrainings.com*

Pato Banton *patobanton.com*

Darius M. Barazandeh *youwealthrevolution.com*

Mindahi Bastida Muñoz *centerforearthethics.org*

Don Edward Beck *spiraldynamics.com*

Michael Bernard Beckwith *agapelive.com*

Diane Berke *1spirit.org*

Lawrence Bloom *lawrencebloom.com*

Leslie Booker *lesliebooker.com*

Joan Borysenko *joanborysenko.com*

Ben Bowler *unity.earth*

Gregg Braden *greggbraden.com*

Rinaldo Brutoco *worldbusiness.org*

Connie Buffalo *fourthfire.com*

Sandra de Castro Buffington *sandradecastrobuffington.com*

Jack Canfield *jackcanfield.com*

Scott Carlin *kdpifm.org/scottcarlin*

Jeff Carreira *jeffcarreira.com*

Deepak Chopra™ *deepakchopra.com*

John Clausen *hyfo.org*

Miranda Clendening *unify.org*

Andrew Cohen *andrewcohen.org*

Oren Cohen *geniusworks.co.za*

Roger Collis *lorian.org*

Theresa Corazon *socialightconference.com*

Bruce Cryer *brucecryer.com*

Jude Currivan *judecurrivan.com*

Téana Davis *sixpetalsretreats.com*

Panache Desai *panachedesai.com*

Stephen Dinan *theshiftnetwork.com*

Dustin DiPerna *dustindiperna.com*

Barbara Dossey *dosseydossey.com*

Larry Dossey *dosseydossey.com*

Mark Dubois *friendsoftheriver.org*

Gordon Dveirin *claritasinstitute.com*

Duane Elgin *duaneelgin.com*

Ashley Ellis *thebreathecollective.org*

Kristin Engvig *winconference.net*

Justin Faerman *flowconsciousnessinstitute.com*

Steve Farrell *humanitysteam.org*

Barbara Fields *agnt.org*

Linda Francis *seatofthesoul.com*

Hugo Francone *netspirit.com*

Ashok Gangadean *awakeningmind.org*

Marcel Gasser *akasha.space*

Alan Gegenschatz *agengenschatz.com*

David Gershon *empowermentinstitute.net*

Mark Gerzon *mediatorsfoundation.org*

Charles Gibbs *revcharlesgibbs.net*

Joshua Gorman *joshuagorman.com*

Alex Grey *cosm.org*

Allyson Grey *cosm.org*

Stanislav Grof *stanislavgrof.com*

Chris Grosso *theindiespiritualist.com*

Kazu Haga *eastpointpeace.org*

Mussie Hailu *uri.org*

Adam C. Hall *adamhall.solutions*

Antoinette "Rootsdawtah" Hall *patobanton.com/ministry*
Craig Hamilton *integralenlightenment.com*
Olivia Hansen *spirituallifetvchannel.com*
Philip Hellmich *theshiftnetwork.com*
Jarrad Hewett *jarradhewett.com*
Kristin Hoffmann *kristinhoffmann.com*
David Hofstatter *tanglelab.com*
Jean Houston *jeanhouston.com*
Jean-Louis Huard *peopletogether.com*
Thomas Hübl *thomashuebl.com*
Desiree Hurtak *futurescience.org*
J. J. Hurtak *futurescience.org*
Shamini Jain *shaminijain.com*
Shilpa Jain *yesworld.org*
Sister Jenna *americamediating.org*
Heather Johnson *whidbeyinstitute.org*
Kurt Johnson *lightonlight.us*
Anodea Judith *anodeajudith.com*
Juan Carlos Kaiten *iwg.life*
David Karchere *davidkarchere.com*
Bernardo Kastrup *bernardokastrup.com*
Tim Kelley *truepurposeinstitute.com*
Loch Kelly *lochkelly.org*
Margo King *mediatorsfoundation.org*
Audrey E. Kitagawa *parliamentofreligions.org*
Ken Kitatani *i-ceed.org*
Jackie Knechtel *flowconsciousnessinstitute.com*
Domen Kocevar *onehumanity.institute*
Kanu Kogod *leadershipalchemy.com*
Eve Konstantine *evekonstantine.com*
Emanuel Kuntzelman *emanuelkuntzelman.com*

Phil Lane Jr. *fwii.net*

Ervin Laszlo *clubofbudapest.org*

Sage Lavine *sagelavine.com*

Erik Lawyer *onebecoming.one*

George H. Lewis *georgehlewis.com*

Lori Leyden *createglobalhealing.org*

Christopher Life *onenation.party*

Bruce H. Lipton *brucelipton.com*

Lorena Llobenes *foromindfulness.com*

Kahontakwas Diane Longboat *soulofthemother.org*

Jewel Love *championsmentalhealth.com*

Carolyn Lukensmeyer *nicd.arizona.edu*

Lynnaea Lumbard *newstories.org*

Elza S. Maalouf *humanemergencemiddleeast.org*

Howard Martin *heartmath.com*

Xiuhtezcatl Martinez *earthguardians.org*

Joe Martino *collective-evolution.com*

Fred Matser *fredfoundation.org*

Peter Matthies *consciousbusinessinstitute.com*

Sarah McCrum *sarahmccrum.com*

Rod McGrew *operationhope.org*

Jennifer McLean *healingwiththemasters.com*

Lynne McTaggart *lynnemctaggart.com*

Oscar Medina *mbaproject.org*

Nipun Mehta *servicespace.org*

Nina Meyerhof *onehumanity.institute*

Oscar Miro-Quesada *heartofthehealer.org*

Devaa Haley Mitchell *devaa.com*

Sheri Mitchell *sacredinstructions.life*

Deborah Moldow *gardenoflight.org*

Anita Moorjani *anitamoorjani.com*

Karen Newell *sacredacoustics.com*

David Nicol *gaiafield.net*

Karen Noé *karennoe.com*

James O'Dea *jamesodea.com*

Rick Paine *newstories.org*

Carl Palmer *legacyworksgroup.com*

Ersin Pamuksüzer *ersinpamuksuzer.com*

Gino Pastori-Ng *youthimpacthub.unitedrootsoakland.org*

Terry Patten *terrypatten.com*

Jeanne White Eagle Pehrson *interstellarcommunityfoundation.org*

John Pehrson *mysticalnumerologyonline.com*

John Perkin *johnperkins.org*

Carter Phipps *carterphipps.com*

Anna-Mari Pieterse *school.ubuntucivicsacademy.com*

Paulette Pipe *touchingthestillness.org*

Mitchell J. Rabin *mitchellrabin.com*

Jon Ramer *sine.network*

Sommer Joy Ramer *compassiongames.org*

Carolyn Rangel *deepakchopra.com*

Ocean Robbins *foodrevolution.org*

Llyn Roberts *llynroberts.com*

Gayle S. Rose *evscorporation.com*

Peter Russell *peterrussell.com*

Derek Rydall *derekrydall.com*

Elisabet Sahtouris *sahtouris.com*

Yuka Saionji *goipeace.or.jp*

Deborah Sandella *riminstitute.com*

Denise Scotto *un.org/en/events/yogaday*

Gerard Senehi *openfutureinstitute.org*

Heather Shea *unitedpalace.org*

Vandana Shiva *navdanya.org*

Pedram Shojai *well.org*
Robert Smith *icvgroup.org*
Anneloes Smitsman *earthwisecentre.org*
Sergey Solonin *qiwi.com*
Christian Sorensen *christiansorenseninspires.com*
John Steiner *bridgealliance.us*
Alan Steinfeld *newrealities.com*
Daniel Stone *danielstone.com*
Sara Avant Stover *thewayofthehappywoman.com*
Sylvia Sumter *unityofwashingtondc.org*
Katherine Woodward Thomas *katherinewoodwardthomas.com*
Kit Thomas *circleofwisdom.org*
Lynne Twist *soulofmoney.org*
Katia Txi *t.me/katiatxilive*
Rick Ulfik *wetheworld.org*
Jeff Vander Clute *jeffvanderclute.com*
Cassandra Vieten *cassandravieten.com*
Alberto Villoldo *albertovilloldophd.com*
Anne-Marie Voorhoeve *thehaguecenter.org*
Daniel Christian Wahl *danielchristianwahl.com*
Neale Donald Walsch *nealedonaldwalsch.com*
Michael Wayne *drmichaelwayne.com*
Claudia Welss *noetic.org*
Diane Marie Williams *sourceofsynergyfoundation.org*
Mikki Willis *elevate.us*
David Sloan Wilson *evolution-institute.org*
Trina Wyatt *consciousgood.com*
Carlen Young *create.community*
Elizabeth Ashley Young *somedayfire.com*
Claire Zammit *femininepower.com*
Gary Zukav *seatofthesoul.com*

Notes

Chapter 1: The Great Map of Peace

1. James O'Dea, *Cultivating Peace: Becoming a 21st Century Peace Ambassador* (San Rafael, CA: Shift Books, 2012), 44–60.

Chapter 3: Integrating an Evolutionary Vision of the Future with "Hard" Science

1. Sheila Kinkade, "Toward a Whole World Ethic: The Role of Conscious Evolution," *Mind and Life Institute Blog*, December 9, 2019, https://www.mindandlife.org/toward-a-whole-world-ethic-the-role-of-conscious-evolution.

2. David Sloan Wilson, *Does Altruism Exist? Culture, Genes, and the Welfare of Others* (New Haven: Yale University Press, 2015).

3. David Sloan Wilson, *This View of Life: Completing the Darwinian Revolution* (New York: Pantheon/Random House, 2019); Kurt Johnson and David Ord, *The Coming Interspiritual Age* (Vancouver: Namaste, 2013).

4. Pierre Teilhard de Chardin, *The Phenomenon of Man* (New York: Harper, 1959).

5. Eva Jablonka and Marion Lamb, *Evolution in Four Dimensions: Genetic, Epigenetic, Behavioral, and Symbolic Variation in the History of Life* (Cambridge, MA: MIT Press, 2006).

6. Keven Laland, Tobias Uller, Marcus Feldman, Kim Sterelny, Gerd Müller, Armin Moczek, Eva Jablonka, and John Odling-Smee, "Proceedings B: The Extended Evolutionary Synthesis: Its Structure,

Assumptions, and Predictions," *The Royal Society Publishing* (2015): 282, https://doi.org/http://dx.doi.org/10.1098/rspb.2015.1019.

7. Ronald Giphart and Mark van Vugt, *Mismatch: How Our Stone Age Brain Deceives Us Every Day and What We Can Do about It* (London: Robinson Page, 2018).

8. Blair Witherington, "The Problem of Photo Pollution for Sea Turtles and Other Nocturnal Animals," in *Behavioral Approaches to Conservation in the Wild*, ed. by Janine Clemmons and Richard Buchholz (Cambridge, UK: Cambridge University Press, 1997), 303–28.

9. Richard Wrangham, *The Goodness Paradox: The Strange Relationship Between Virtue and Violence in Human Evolution* (New York: Pantheon, 2019).

10. James Mark Baldwin, *Development and Evolution* (Sydney, Australia: Wentworth Press, 2019).

Chapter 5: Is World Peace Possible?

1. Jill Jackson and Sy Miller, "Let There Be Peace on Earth," No. 431, *The Um Hymnal* (New York: Jan-Lee Music, 1955).

Chapter 6: Evolutionary Wisdom for a World in Great Transition

1. Luther Standing Bear, quoted in Joseph Brown, "Modes of Contemplation through Actions: North American Indians," in *Main Currents in Modern Thought: A Study of the Spiritual and Intellectual Movements of the Present Day*, Rudolf Eucken and Meyrick Booth (New York: Kessinger Publishing, 2008), 194.

2. Malcolm Margolin, *The Ohlone Way: Indian Life in the San Francisco-Monterey Bay Area* (Berkeley: Heyday Books, 1978).

3. Richard Nelson, *Make Prayers to the Raven: A Koyukon View of the Northern Forest* (Chicago: University of Chicago Press, 1983), 14.

4. Matthew Fox, *Meditations with Meister Eckhart* (Santa Fe: Bear & Company, 1983), 24.

5. Jalal al-Din Rumi, *The Essential Rumi*, trans. by Coleman Barks and John Moyne (San Francisco: Harper, 1995).

6. Daisetz Suzuki, *Zen and Japanese Culture* (Princeton: Princeton University Press, 1970), 364.

7. Sri Maharaj, *I Am That: Talks with Sri Nisargadatta Maharaj*, trans. by Maurice Frydman (Bombay, India: Chetana, 1973), 289.

8. Lao Tsu, *Tao Te Ching*, trans. by Gia-fu Feng and Jane English (New York: Vintage Books, 1972).

9. Clara Moskowitz, "What's 96 Percent of the Universe Made Of? Astronomers Don't Know," *Space.com*, May 12, 2011, https://www .space.com/11642-dark-matter-dark-energy-4-percent-universe -panek.html.

10. Eugene Roehlkepartain, Peter Benson, Peter Scales, Lisa Kimball, and Pamela, "With Their Own Voices: A Global Exploration of How Today's Young People Experience and Think about Spiritual Development," Search Institute, 2008, https://www.search-institute.org/wp-content /uploads/2018/02/with_their_own_voices_report.pdf.

11. Andrew Greeley, *Ecstasy as a Way of Knowing* (Englewood Cliffs, NJ: Prentice Hall, 1974), 57; Luis Lugo, director, Pew Forum on Religion and Public Life, "Many Americans Mix Multiple Faiths," Pew Research Center, December 9, 2009, https://www.pewforum.org/2009/12/09 /many-americans-mix-multiple-faiths/.

12. Pew Research Center, "US Public Becoming Less Religious," November 3, 2015, http://www.pewforum.org/2015/11/03/u-s-public -becoming-less-religious.

Chapter 7: Regenerating Earth and Her People

1. Michael Williams, *Deforesting the Earth: From Prehistory to Global Crisis* (Chicago: University of Chicago Press, 2002), https://rainforests .mongabay.com/general_tables.htm; World Wildlife Fund, "The Living Planet Report," October 30, 2018, https://www.wwf.org.uk/updates /living-planet-report-2018.

2. International Panel on Climate Change, "Special Report: Global Warming of 1.50C," 2018, https://www.ipcc.ch/sr15/.

3. Mary Oliver, "Wild Geese," University of New Mexico, accessed May 12, 2020, http://www.phys.unm.edu/~tw/fas/yits/archive/oliver _wildgeese.html.

4. Joanna Macy in discussion with author, March 2003, during "The Work that Reconnects" training of trainers in Madrid, Spain.

Chapter 8: One Good Person

1. Dee Brown, "War Comes to the Cheyennes," *Bury My Heart at Wounded Knee: An Indian History of the American West* (New York: Henry Holt, 2001), 86–90.

2. United States Congress, "Report of the Joint Committee on the Conduct of the War at the Second Session Thirty-Eighth Congress: Army of the Potomac. Battle of Petersburg," February 20, 1865, https://www .senate.gov/artandhistory/history/common/investigations/pdf/JCCW _Report.pdf.

3. Colorado State Archives, "John Evans," 2019, accessed March 1, 2020, https://colorado.gov/pacific/archives/john-evans.

4. Chief Seattle, "Excerpts from Chief Seattle's Famous Speech to President Franklin Pierce," 1854, Children of the Earth United, https://www .childrenoftheearth.org/chief_seattle.htm.

Chapter 9: Prophesies, Dynamic Change, and a New Global Civilization

1. White Buffalo Calf Woman, "Lakota Instructions for Living," Xavier University Jesuit Resources, accessed May 19, 2020, https://www .xavier.edu/jesuitresource/online-resources/quote-archive1/native -american1.

Chapter 11: The Dawn of a Conscious Business Movement

1. Steve Farrell, "The Dawn of a Conscious Movement," *Kosmos*, Fall/ Winter 2017, https://www.kosmosjournal.org/contributor/steve-farrell.

2. Ken Wilber, *A Brief History of Everything* (Boston: Shambhala, 2007), 499.

Chapter 12: Youth-Led Social Enterprise Projects

1. Darryl Fears, "One million species face extinction, U.N. report says. And humans will suffer as a result," *The Washington Post*, May 6, 2019 https://www.washingtonpost.com/climate-environment/2019/05/06 /one-million-species-face-extinction-un-panel-says-humans-will-suffer -result/.

Chapter 14: The Core Principles of a Business Warrior Monk

1. Pierre Teilhard de Chardin, quoted in Oprah Winfrey, *What I Know for Sure* (New York: Flatiron Books, 2014), 150.

2. Rhondalynn Korolak, *On the Shoulders of Giants: 33 New Ways to Guide Yourself to Greatness* (Australia: Imagineering Unlimited, 2008), 82.

3. Christopher Logue, "Come to the Edge," *New Numbers* (London: Jonathan Cape, 1969), 65–66.

Chapter 15: Reinventing the Planet: A Bottom-Up Grand Strategy

1. Apple, "Think Different Marketing Campaign," The Crazy Ones, the website dedicated to Apple's ad campaign, 1997, accessed May 5, 2020, http://www.thecrazyones.it/spot-en.html.

2. John Gardner, "On Potential," PBS, 1965 speech, accessed May 7, 2020, https://www.pbs.org/johngardner/sections/writings.html.

Chapter 16: Survival, Consciousness, and the One Mind

1. Larry Dossey, *One Mind: How Our Mind Is Part of a Greater Consciousness and Why It Matters* (Carlsbad, CA: Hay House, 2013), xxviii.

2. Hippocrates, quoted in *The Dreams of Dragons: An Exploration and Celebration of the Mysteries of Nature*, by Lyall Watson (Rochester, VT: Destiny Books, 1992), 27.

3. William Butler Yeats, quoted in *Irish Writing in the Twentieth Century: A Reader*, ed. David Pierce (Cork, Ireland: Cork University Press, 2000), 62.

4. Walt Whitman, "Passage to India," in *Leaves of Grass: Selected Poems* (London: Macmillan Collector's Library, 2019), 233–45.

5. Ralph Waldo Emerson and Alfred Ferguson, eds., *The Essays of Ralph Waldo Emerson* (Cambridge, MA: Harvard University Press, 1987), 160.

6. Erwin Schrödinger, *What Is Life? The Physical Aspect of the Living Cell with Mind and Matter and Autobiographical Sketches* (London: Cambridge University Press, 1969), 139, 145.

7. David Bohm, quoted in *Dialogues with Scientists and Sages: The Search for Unity*, by Renée Weber (New York: Routledge and Kegan Paul, 1986), 41.

8. Carl Jung, *Memories, Dreams, Reflections* (New York: Random House, 1965), 325.

9. Carl Jung, *Collected Works of C. G. Jung, Volume 13*, trans. by R. F. C. Hull (Princeton, NJ: Princeton University Press, 2014), 46.

10. Schrödinger, *What Is Life?*, 145.

11. Michael Grosso, *The Final Choice: Death or Transcendence?* (Hove, UK: White Crow Books, 2017), chap. 8.

12. Michael Grosso, "The Archetype of Death and Enlightenment," in *The Near-Death Experience: A Reader*, eds. Lee Bailey and Jenny Yates (New York: Routledge, 1996), 127–44.

13. Sam Parnia, quoted in Mindy Weisberger, "Are 'Flatliners' Really Conscious after Death?", *Live Science*, October 4, 2017, https://www.livescience.com/60593-flatliners-movie-death-resuscitation.html.

Chapter 17: Healing Ourselves, Our Children, and Our World

1. Kathleen K. S. Hui, Jing Liu, Ovidiu Marina, Vitaly Napadow, Christian Haselgrove, Kenneth K. Kwong, David N. Kennedy, and Nikos Makris, "The Integrated Response of the Human Cerebro-Cerebellar and Limbic Systems to Acupuncture Stimulation at ST 36 as Evidenced by fMRI," *NeuroImage* 27, no. 3 (2005): 479–96; Michael G. H. Coles, Emanuel Donchin, Stephen W. Porges, *Psychophysiology: Systems, Processes and Applications* (New York: Guilford Press, 1986).

2. Margorie. E. Maharaj, "Differential Gene Expression after Emotional Freedom Techniques (EFT) Treatment: A Novel Pilot Protocol for Salivary mRNA Assessment," *Energy Psychology Journal* 8, no. 1 (2016): 17–32.

Chapter 18: The Noble Future: Becoming Fully Human

1. Marshall McLuhan, from notes taken by the author, Gordon Dveirin, in Marshall McLuhan's graduate seminar, University of Toronto, 1972; see also, Marshall McLuhan, *The Global Village: Transformations in World*

Life and Media in the 21st Century (New York: Oxford University Press, 1989), 99–100.

2. Thomas Berry, *The Dream of the Earth* (Berkeley: University of California Press, 2006), 17.

3. Loren Eisley, *The Man Who Saw Through Time*, revised and enlarged edition of *Francis Bacon and the Modern Dilemma* (New York: Scribners, 1973), 39.

4. Kai Bird and Martin Sherwin, *American Prometheus: The Triumph and Tragedy of J. Robert Oppenheimer* (New York: Vintage Books, 2006).

5. Jamie Metzl, *Hacking Darwin: Genetic Engineering and the Future of Humanity* (Naperville, IL: Sourcebooks, 2019), loc. 165 of 6104 and loc. 219 of 6104, Kindle.

6. Yuval Noah Harari, "Why Technology Favors Tyranny," *The Atlantic*, October 2018, 70.

7. Willis Harman, "The New Copernican Revolution," *Stanford Today*, Winter 1969, 6–10.

8. The Aspen Institute: National Commission on Social, Emotional, and Academic Development, "From a Nation at Risk to a Nation at Hope," 2019, http://nationathope.org/report-from-the-nation/.

9. Jane Ellen Stevens, "Nearly 35 Million US Children Have Experienced One or More Types of Childhood Trauma," *Aces too High News*, May 13, 2013, https://acestoohigh.com/2013/05/13/nearly-35-million-u-s-children-have-experienced-one-or-more-types-of-childhood-trauma.

Chapter 19: Elevating Our Spiritual Nature: The Pathway to Healing

1. Albert Einstein quoted in "What Einstein Knows," by Elizabeth Lesser, in Andrea Joy Cohen, *A Blessing in Disguise: 39 Life Lessons from Today's Greatest Teachers* (New York: Berkley Books, 2008), 49.

2. Pierre Teilhard de Chardin quoted in Oprah Winfrey, *What I Know for Sure* (New York: Flatiron Books, 2014), 150.

Chapter 20: Conscious Evolution: A Theory We Can Thrive With

1. Kerry Grens, "Earth Experiencing Sixth Mass Extinction: Study," *The Scientist*, July 11, 2017, http://www.the-scientist.com/?articles.view /articleNo/49841/title/E.

2. Bruce Lipton, *The Biology of Belief, Tenth Anniversary Edition: Unleashing the Power of Consciousness, Matter, and Miracles* (Carlsbad, CA: Hay House, 2016), 57–81.

3. Lynn Margulis and Dorion Sagan, *Microcosmos: Four Billion Years of Microbial Evolution from Our Microbial Ancestors* (New York: Summit Books, 1986), 14–15.

4. Jean-Baptiste Lamarck, *Zoological Philosophy: An Exposition with Regard to the Natural History of Animals*, trans. by Hugh Elliot (Chicago: University of Chicago Press, 1914).

5. Bruce Lipton, "An Introduction to Conscious Evolution: A Theory We Can Thrive With," *Spanda* VII, no. 1 (2017): 183–92.

6. Lipton, *The Biology of Belief*, 57–81.

Chapter 22: The Power of Eight

1. David R. Hamilton, PhD, *Why Kindness Is Good for You* (London: Hay House UK, 2010), 108.

Chapter 23: The Current Science of Awakening

1. Zoran Josipovic, Ilan Dinstein, Jochen Weber, and David Heeger, "Influence of Meditation on Anti-correlated Networks in the Brain," *Frontiers in Human Neuroscience* (January 2012), https://www .frontiersin.org/articles/10.3389/fnhum.2011.00183.

Chapter 24: Awakening to Our Limitless Mind

1. Lynne McTaggart, *The Field: The Quest for the Secret Force of the Universe* (London: HarperCollins Publishers, 2001).

2. Elizabeth Rauscher, J. J. Hurtak, and Desiree Hurtak, *Mind Dynamics in Space and Time* (Los Gatos, CA: Academy for Future Science, 2016).

3. Zvi Ram, Chae-Young Kim, Garth A. Nicholas, and Steven Toms, "ACTR-27. Compliance and Treatment Duration Predict Survival in

a Phase 3 EF-14 Trial of Tumor Treating Fields with Temozolomide in Patients with Newly Diagnosed Glioblastoma," *Neuro-Oncology* 19, suppl. 6 (2017): vi6–vi7: https://academic.oup.com/neuro-oncology /article/19/suppl_6/vi6/4590316.

4. Pierre Teilhard de Chardin, *The Phenomenon of Man* (New York: Harper, 1959).

5. J. J. Hurtak, *The Book of Knowledge: The Keys of Enoch* (Los Gatos, CA: Academy for Future Science, 1973), 26: https://keysofenoch.org /teachings/overview/.

Chapter 26: A WholeWorld-View to Guide the Evolution of Consciousness

1. Jude Currivan, *The Cosmic Hologram: In-formation at the Center of Creation* (Rochester, VT: Inner Traditions, 2017).

2. Currivan, *The Cosmic Hologram*.

Chapter 27: Change Our Story; Change Our World

1. Gregg Braden, *Deep Truth: Igniting the Memory of Our Origin, History, Destiny and Fate* (Carlsbad, CA: Hay House, 2011), 219–22.

2. Braden, *Deep Truth*, 219–22.

3. Braden, *Deep Truth*, 139–83.

4. Braden, *Deep Truth*, 139–83.

5. Gregg Braden, *The Divine Matrix: Bridging Time, Space, Miracles, and Belief* (Carlsbad, CA: Hay House, 2007), 101–22.

6. Braden, *The Divine Matrix*, 101–22.

7. Tad Williams, *To Green Angel Tower, Part 1* (New York: DAW Books, 1993), 771.

8. George Musser, "The Climax of Humanity," *Scientific American*, special edition "Crossroads for Planet Earth" (September 2005): 44–47.

9. Musser, "The Climax of Humanity," 47.

10. Musser, "The Climax of Humanity," 47.

11. William Jennings Bryan, "America's Mission" (speech, Virginia Democratic Association banquet, Washington, DC, February 22, 1899),

https://archive.org /stream/speechesofwillia02bryauoft/speechesof
willia02bryauoft_djvu.txt.

Chapter 29: Vibrational Intelligence: Tapping into the Language of the Universe

1. James Jeans, *The Mysterious Universe* (New York: Cambridge University Press, 1930), 137.

Chapter 31: Putting on Our Red Capes, Activating Our Superpowers

1. Daniel DeNoon, "Salt-Water Fish Extinction Seen by 2048," CBS News, November 2, 2006, https://www.cbsnews.com/news/salt-water-fish -extinction-seen-by-2048/.

2. David Wallace-Wells, "The Uninhabitable Earth," *New York Magazine*, July 10, 2017, http://nymag.com/intelligencer/2017/07/climate-change -earth-too-hot-for-humans.html.

3. Cosmic Scientist, "This Is Exactly Why Nikola Tesla Told Us to Study the 'Nonphysical,'" April 27, 2016, https://cosmicscientist.com/this -is-exactly-why-nikola-tesla-told-us-to-study-the-non-physical/.

4. Cosmic Scientist, "This Is Exactly Why Nikola Tesla."

5. The HeartMath Institute (HMI) researches heart-brain communication and its relationship to managing stress, increasing coherence, and deepening our connection to self and others. HMI's scientists also explore the electrophysiology of intuition and how all things are connected. heartmath.com

6. Sung live by Siedah Garrett, lyrics written by Glenn Ballard and Siedah Garrett, recorded by Michael Jackson, "Man in the Mirror," May 1987, track 4 on *Bad*, Epic.

Chapter 32: Humanity's Change of Heart

1. Brian Swimme, *The Powers of the Universe*, directed by Dan Anderson (San Francisco: Center for the Story of the Universe, 2004), DVD.

2. Peter Corning, *Nature's Magic: Synergy in Evolution and the Fate of Humankind* (Cambridge, UK: Cambridge University Press, 2003).

3. Rollin McCraty and Maria A. Zayas, "Cardiac Coherence, Self-Regulation, Autonomic Stability, and Psychosocial Well-Being,"

Frontiers in Psychology Journal 29, September (2014): https://www
.frontiersin.org/articles/10.3389/fpsyg.2014.01090/full.

4. The Science of Mindfulness & Compassion, private conversation
attended by the author in New Delhi hosted by the Templeton
Foundation, organized by the Fetzer Institute in collaboration with
the Center for Contemplative Science and Compassion Based Ethics at
Emory University, April, 2019.

5. Mae-Wan Ho, *The Rainbow and the Worm: The Physics of Organisms*
(London: World Scientific Publishing, 2008).

6. Ken Wilber, in conversation with Barbara Marx Hubbard, Foundation
for Conscious Evolution's Agents of Conscious Evolution online course,
2011.

7. Jean Baptiste Lamarck, *Zoological Philosophy: An Exposition with Regard
to the Natural History of Animals* (London: Macmillan, 1914).

8. Julie Jordan Avritt and Thomas Hübl, "Thomas Hübl's The Pocket
Project Facilitating the Integration of Collective Trauma," *Kosmos
Journal* (Spring-Summer 2017), https://www.kosmosjournal.org/article
/thomas-hubls-the-pocket-project-facilitating-the-integration-of
-collective-trauma/.

Chapter 33: Evolving Our Culture: From Breakdown to Breakthrough

1. Marta Sinclair, ed., *Handbook of Intuition Research* (Cheltenham,
UK: Edward Elgar Publisher, 2013); Raymond Bradley, "The
Psychophysiology of Intuition: A Quantum-Holographic Theory of
Nonlocal Communication," *World Futures* 63, no. 2 (2007): 61–97;
Raymond Bradley, Murray Gillin, Rollin McCraty, and Mike Atkinson,
"Nonlocal Intuition in Entrepreneurs and Non-entrepreneurs:
Results of Two Experiments Using Electrophysiological Measures,"
International Journal of Entrepreneurship and Small Business 12, no. 3
(2011): 343–72; and Rollin McCraty, Mike Atkinson, and Raymond
Bradley, "Electrophysiological Evidence of Intuition: Part 2. A System-
wide Process?", *Journal of Alternative Complementary Medicine* 10, no. 2
(2004): 325–36.

2. Adolescent Moral Development Lab, "The Psychology of Purpose," John
Templeton Foundation: Claremont Graduate University, February 2018,

https://www.templeton.org/wp-content/uploads/2020/02
/Psychology-of-Purpose.pdf.

3. Randy Cohen, Chirag Bavishi, and Alan Rozanski, "Purpose in Life
and Its Relationship to All-Cause Mortality and Cardiovascular
Events: A Meta-Analysis," *Psychosomatic Medicine* 78, no. 2 (2015);
Patrick Hill and Nicholas Turiano, "Purpose in Life as a Predictor of
Mortality Across Adulthood," *Psychological Science* 25 (2014); and
Toshimasa Sone, Naoki Nakaya, Kaori Ohmori, Taichi Shimazu,
Mizuka Higashiguchi, Masako Kakizaki, Nobutaka Kikuchi, Shinichi
Kuriyama, and Ichiro Tsuji, "Sense of Life Worth Living (Ikigai) and
Mortality in Japan: Ohsaki Study," *Psychosomatic Medicine* 70 (2008):
709–15.

4. Adolescent Moral Development Lab, "The Psychology of Purpose," 13.

Chapter 35: A Holistic Vision of Evolution and Consciousness

1. Robert Atkinson, *The Story of Our Time: From Duality to
Interconnectedness to Oneness* (Fort Lauderdale, FL: Sacred Stories
Publishing, 2017), 116–23.

2. Paul Carus, *The Gospel of Buddha* (Chicago: Open Court Publishing,
1915), 142.

3. Bahá'u'lláh, *Gleanings from the Writings of Baha'u'llah* (Wilmette, IL:
Bahá'í Publishing Trust, 1983), 250.

4. C. G. Jung, *Modern Man in Search of a Soul* (New York: Harcourt, 1933),
217.

5. Charles Darwin, *The Descent of Man* (New York: Penguin Classics,
2004), 147.

6. Atkinson, *The Story of Our Time*, 103–8.

7. Pierre Teilhard de Chardin, *The Human Phenomenon* (New York:
Perennial, 1976), 3.

Epilogue: Connecting the Threads of a Call to Collective Action

1. Robert Atkinson, *Year of Living Deeply: A Memoir of 1969* (Wilmette, IL:
One Voice Press, 2019), 16–17.

About the
Contributors

In alphabetical order.

Eben Alexander III, MD, was an academic neurosurgeon for over twenty-five years, including fifteen years at the Brigham and Women's Hospital, Children's Hospital, and Harvard Medical School in Boston. He has a passionate interest in physics and cosmology. He authored the *New York Times* #1 bestsellers *Proof of Heaven* and *The Map of Heaven* and coauthored *Living in a Mindful Universe* with Karen Newell. ebenalexander.com

Reverend Michael Bernard Beckwith is the founder and spiritual director of the Agape International Spiritual Center in Los Angeles and a cofounder of the Association for Global New Thought. A sought-after speaker, he is also an author; three of his most recent books—*Life Visioning, Spiritual Liberation,* and *TranscenDance Expanded*—received the prestigious Nautilus Award. He is renowned as a harbinger of the world's quest for peace. agapelive.com

Joan Borysenko, PhD, is a world-renowned expert in the mind-body connection. A licensed psychologist and Harvard Medical School–trained cell biologist, she synthesizes cutting-edge science with deep humanity. A *New York Times* bestselling author of seventeen books, she has work that has also appeared in the *Washington Post* and the *Wall Street Journal* and on public television and numerous websites. She is president of Mind-Body Health Sciences, LLC, in Santa Fe, New Mexico.

joanborysenko.com

Gregg Braden is internationally renowned as a pioneer in bridging science and spirituality. He is a five-time *New York Times* bestselling author with books including *The God Code*, *The Divine Matrix*, and *Deep Truth*. His scientific expertise led to successful problem-solving careers as a computer geologist during the 1970s energy crisis, a senior liaison with the US Air Force Space Command during the 1980s Cold War, and a technical operations manager with Cisco Systems during the first Gulf War.

greggbraden.com

Rinaldo S. Brutoco is the founding president and CEO of the Santa Barbara–based World Business Academy and a cofounder of JUST Capital, which ranks America's most just companies. He is a serial entrepreneur, executive, author, radio host, and futurist who's published for over thirty-five years on the role of business in relation to pressing moral, environmental, and social concerns. He serves on the board of Omega Point Institute, JUST Capital, and numerous other for-profit and nonprofit enterprises.
worldbusiness.org

Constance Buffalo, a tribal member of the Red Cliff Band of Chippewa, gained valuable experience from her corporate positions as president and CEO of Intelagard, a chemical warfare decontamination company, and as director of promotion and advertising with CBS television network. Her Chippewa heritage, which created for her a canvas upon which all life is seamlessly woven in sacred patterns, drives her commitment to a deep relationship with all of life.
fourthfire.com

Deepak Chopra™ MD, FACP, founder of The Chopra Foundation, a non-profit entity for research on well-being and humanitarianism, and Chopra Global, a modern-day health company at the intersection of science and spirituality, is a world-renowned pioneer in integrative medicine and personal transformation. He is a Clinical Professor of Family Medicine and Public Health at the University of California, San Diego and author of over 90 books—translated into over forty-three languages—including *Metahuman* and numerous *New York Times* bestsellers. *Time* magazine has described Dr. Chopra as "one of the top 100 heroes and icons of the century."
deepakchopra.com

Jude Currivan, PhD, is a cosmologist, planetary healer, futurist, author of *The Cosmic Hologram*, Nautilus Silver Award winner, and former senior international businesswoman. Integrating leading-edge science, consciousness research, and universal wisdom teachings in a paradigm of unified reality, she cofounded WholeWorld-View.org. She holds a PhD in archaeology and an MA in physics from Oxford University, specializing in cosmology and quantum physics.
judecurrivan.org

Barbara Dossey, PhD, RN, is an internationally recognized integrative, holistic nursing pioneer and nurse theorist. She is director of the International Nurse Coach Association (INCA), international codirector of the Nightingale Initiative for Global Health, and core faculty of the Integrative Nurse Coach Certificate Program (INCCP), Miami, Florida. She has authored or coauthored twenty-five books, including *Holistic Nursing* and *Nurse Coaching*. dosseydossey.com

Larry Dossey, MD, a physician of internal medicine, was a cofounder of the Dallas Diagnostic Association. He served as a field battalion surgeon in Vietnam in 1968 to 1969, where he was decorated for valor. He is the author of thirteen books, including *Space, Time & Medicine, Recovering the Soul, Healing Words, Reinventing Medicine, The Power of Premonitions,* and *One Mind.* larrydosseymd.com

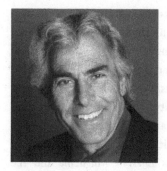

Gordon Dveirin, EdD, approaches organizational, social, and cultural change as "learning our way into the future" together; he described this in his doctoral dissertation, *From Manpower to Mindfulness: The High-Tech Culture of Emergence and Its Implications for Education.* He assisted Rachael Kessler in founding the PassageWorks Institute, a leading catalyst in humanizing education. With his wife, Joan Borysenko, he codeveloped the Claritas Institute for Interspiritual Inquiry and coauthored *Your Soul's Compass.* claritasinstitute.com

Duane Elgin, MBA, MA, is an internationally recognized author, speaker, educator, and citizen-voice activist. His books include: *The Living Universe, Promise Ahead, Voluntary Simplicity,* and *Awakening Earth.* He received Japan's Goi Peace Award in Tokyo in 2006 in recognition of his contribution to a global "vision, consciousness, and lifestyle" that fosters a "more sustainable and spiritual culture." duaneelgin.com

Justin Faerman is a visionary change-agent, international speaker, serial entrepreneur, and consciousness researcher dedicated to evolving global consciousness, bridging science and spirituality, and spreading enlightened ideas on both an individual and societal level. He is the cofounder of *Conscious Lifestyle Magazine* and the Flow Consciousness Institute. He is a sought-after teacher known for his pioneering work in the area of flow and the mechanics of consciousness. justinfaerman.com

Steve Farrell is the president and executive director of Humanity's Team, a global grassroots spiritual movement with over 650,000 friends in over 150 countries. Humanity's Team focuses on awakening and embodying Oneness so humanity may enjoy a sustainable world of peace, harmony, and happiness. Their projects include Global Oneness Day (created in response to visiting the United Nations in 2010), a Oneness Declaration, and a year-round Living in Oneness summit. humanitysteam.org

David Gershon, cofounder and CEO of Empowerment Institute, applies his visionary leadership and social change expertise to designing second-order change solutions for cities and countries that enable the seemingly impossible to become possible. Author of twelve books, including the award-winning *Social Change 2.0* and the bestselling *Empowerment*, he has dedicated his life to empowering humanity to believe we can create the world of our dreams and designing strategies and tools to help make this a reality.

reinventing.earth

Jean Houston, PhD, is a scholar and researcher in human capacities. For the past forty years (with her husband Dr. Robert Masters until his death), she codirected the Foundation for Mind Research in New York City and Ashland, Oregon, focusing on understanding latent human abilities. The author of some twenty-six books, she is also a senior United Nations consultant in human development and the founder of a program of cross-cultural mythic and spiritual studies dedicated to empowering change agents.

jeanhouston.com

Barbara Marx Hubbard (1929–2019) was a futurist, evolutionary educator, author, public speaker, and cofounder and president of the Foundation for Conscious Evolution. She authored seven books on social and planetary evolution, including *Conscious Evolution: Awakening the Power of Our Social Potential*, and she is the subject of the documentary *American Visionary*. She is known for the concepts of the Synergy Engine, SYNCON (Synergistic Convergence), the Peace Room, the Wheel of Co-creation, and the "birthing" of humanity. Barbara's chapter was one of her last writings, offered to this book just before she passed.

Desiree Hurtak, PhD, MSSc, a social scientist, futurist, and environmentalist, is president of the Foundation for Future Science, which assists communities and individuals in many developing countries, and is also the vice president and cofounder of the Academy for Future Science. She is an author of several books, including *Overself Awakening*, coauthored with her husband, J. J. Hurtak, which seeks to bring insights and understanding of our true potential in life.
futurescience.org

J. J. Hurtak, PhD, PhD, a social scientist and futurist, cofounded the Academy for Future Science (AFFS), an international NGO, to foster cooperation between science and consciousness through social projects and dialogue. He is the author of numerous books showing how science and religion need not be mutually exclusive, as well as *The Book of Knowledge*. He holds two PhDs, one from the University of California and a second from the University of Minnesota. futurescience.org

Shilpa Jain is the executive director of YES!, where she works with social changemakers to cocreate a thriving, just, and balanced world for all. She has written numerous books and articles; facilitated workshops on topics such as globalization, creative expressions, ecology, democratic living, innovative learning and unlearning; and facilitated transformative leadership gatherings with hundreds of leaders from over fifty countries. yesworld.org

Loch Kelly, MDiv, LCSW, is an educator, author, meditation teacher, psychotherapist, recognized leader in the field of consciousness and awakening, and the founder of the nonprofit Open-Hearted Awareness Institute. His work is to help people access awakening as the next natural stage of human development. He is the author of the award-winning books *Shift into Freedom* and *The Way of Effortless Mindfulness.*
lochkelly.org

Eve Konstantine, MPH, is a thought leader with a gift for seeing the arch of evolutionary patterns and revealing a perspective on their implications, having committed her entire life to raising consciousness on the planet. An international speaker and contributor to journals and books, during her two decades in Washington, DC, she coached leaders of international organizations and executives on Wall Street, was executive chairperson of the International Monetary Fund's Family Association, and was a Clinton White House volunteer.
evekonstantine.com

Hereditary Chief Phil Lane Jr. is an enrolled member of the Ihanktonwan Dakota and Chickasaw Nations and an internationally recognized leader in human, community, and economic development. For fifty years, he has worked with indigenous peoples from the Americas, Micronesia, Southeast Asia, China, India, Hawaii, and Africa. He was an associate professor of education at the University of Lethbridge, Alberta, Canada. In 1982 he founded the Four Worlds International Institute, dedicated to unifying the human family through the Fourth Way.
FWII.net

Ervin Laszlo, PhD, author or editor of more than seventy books, has published in excess of four hundred articles and research papers, including six volumes of piano recordings. Generally recognized as the founder of systems philosophy and general evolution theory, he was twice nominated for the Nobel Peace Prize. He serves as the founder and president of the Club of Budapest and was past president of the International Society for the Systems Sciences.
ervinlaszlo.com

Lori Leyden, PhD, MBA, is an internationally known trauma healing professional, transformational leader, and spiritual mentor. She is the developer of the Grace Process, the founder of the nonprofits Create Global Healing and Project LIGHT, as well as the producer of the award-winning documentary *When I Was Young I Said I Would Be Happy,* chronicling the transformation of Rwandan genocide survivors and how they paid forward their healing to hundreds, from Rwanda to Newtown, Connecticut.
createglobalhealing.org

Bruce H. Lipton, PhD, scientist and lecturer, is an internationally recognized leader in bridging science and spirit. He is the bestselling author of *The Biology of Belief, Spontaneous Evolution,* and *The Honeymoon Effect.* He is the recipient of the 2009 Goi Peace Award and formerly served as associate professor of anatomy in the School of Medicine at the University of Wisconsin, participating in the medical curriculum as a lecturer in cell biology, histology, and embryology.
brucelipton.com

Sarah McCrum is an author and teacher whose work explores how people can transform their relationship with money so they can experience abundance, fulfillment, and a life of generosity. She trained with Chinese masters for twenty-two years, learning traditional and modern teachings about energy applied to all areas of life, including healing, relationships, and business. Receiving a series of messages from the energy of money, she wrote the book *Love Money, Money Loves You*. sarahmccrum.com

Lynne McTaggart is one of the preeminent spokespersons on consciousness, the new physics, and the science of spirituality. She is the award-winning journalist and author of seven books, including the worldwide bestsellers *The Field*, *The Intention Experiment*, and *The Power of Eight*. She is cofounder of the international magazine *What Doctors Don't Tell You* (wddty.com) and the health expo Get Well (getwell .solutions). She is also the architect of the Intention Experiments, a web-based global laboratory to test the power of intention to heal the world. lynnemctaggart.com

Nina Meyerhof, EdD, is cofounder of One Humanity Institute, a "City of Hope" adjacent to the Auschwitz Museum, and president and founder of Children of the Earth, a renowned worldwide organization for young people to know their leadership potential. She coauthored the book *Conscious Education*. Her work focuses on peace through recognizing our interwoven unity and advocating for all people to go beyond differences and strive for altruistic ethics. coeworld.org

Karen Newell has spent a lifetime seeking wisdom through esoteric teachings and firsthand experience exploring realms of consciousness. She empowers others by demonstrating how to connect to inner guidance, achieve inspiration, improve wellness, and develop intuition. She is cofounder of Sacred Acoustics, which offers brainwave entrainment audio recordings designed to reduce anxiety and inspire creativity. She coauthored *Living in a Mindful Universe* with Eben Alexander. sacredacoustics.com

James O'Dea is author of *The Conscious Activist, Cultivating Peace, Soul Awakening Practice*, and other acclaimed works. He is a former president of the Institute of Noetic Sciences, Washington office director of Amnesty International, and CEO of the Seva Foundation. He has taught peace-building to over a thousand students in thirty countries. He has also conducted frontline social healing dialogues around the world. jamesodea.com

Gino Pastori-Ng is a tree-hugging hip-hop artist born and raised in Oakland, California, and educated at University of California, Santa Cruz, where walks through the forest cultivated a passion for environmental stewardship. After travels to Europe, South America, and Asia, he cofounded Youth SEED (Youth Social Entrepreneurship for Equitable Development) and then Youth Impact Hub, Oakland, to support youth in low-income communities in launching their own social enterprise projects. youthimpacthub.unitedrootsoakland.org

John Perkins is an author and activist whose books, including *Confessions of an Economic Hit Man* and *Touching the Jaguar*, have sold millions of copies and are translated in over thirty-five languages. A leading authority on shamanism, he is a founder of the Pachamama Alliance and Dream Change, nonprofits partnering with indigenous people to protect environments and build sustainable economies. He is also advisor to the World Bank, United Nations, International Monetary Fund, and Fortune 500 corporations.
johnperkins.org

Elisabet Sahtouris, PhD, is an internationally known evolution biologist and futurist. She taught at MIT and the University of Massachusetts and is currently a professor of business at Chaminade University in Honolulu. Her books include *EarthDance*, *A Walk through Time*, and *Gaia's Dance*. She has an honorary chair at the World Business Academy and cofounded the Worldwide Indigenous Science Network.
sahtouris.com

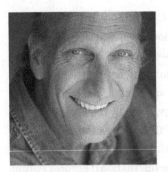

Reverend Christian Sorensen, DD, a renowned contemporary new-thought leader, is the spiritual leader of the Seaside Center for Spiritual Living in Encinitas, California. At twenty-two, he became one of the youngest new-thought ministers in its 150-year history. He served as a member of the Leadership Council for the Association for Global New Thought and is the author of ten books, including *Living from the Mountaintop* and *Be the Mystic You Were Born to Be,* and he coauthored *Joyous Abundance Journal.* Watch his Sunday livesteam at seasidecenter.org.

christiansorenseninspires.com

Reverend Sylvia Sumter has served as the senior minister at Unity of Washington, DC, since 1991 and prior to this served as the chairperson of the Communication Studies and Skills Department for the Unity School of Religious Studies, in Unity Village, Missouri. A graduate of the Unity School of Christianity, she was ordained as a Unity minister in 1987 and holds an MEd and a BA in psychology. She is called to inspire people to transform their lives by gaining awareness of their innate Divine potential. For more information about Stand Up For Humanity, visit unityofwashingtondc.org/standup.

Daniel Christian Wahl, PhD, works internationally in the fertile intersection between education, transformative innovation, futures practice, activism, and culture change. His background is in biology, zoology, and holistic science, with a PhD in design for sustainability (University of Dundee). He is a member of the International Futures Forum, a fellow of the Findhorn Foundation and the Royal Society of the Arts, on the advisory council of the Ojai Foundation, and the author of *Designing Regenerative Cultures.*
danielchristianwahl.com

Claudia Welss is chairman of the Institute of Noetic Sciences (IONS) and with the Global Coherence Initiative. She invited HeartMath to coach corporate executives while director of executive programs at the University of California, Berkeley, Haas School of Business, and to join the Digital Earth/ Digital Mind initiative for the International Symposium for Digital Earth. She is also on the board of Space for Humanity and is Chair of the Invest In Yourself Working Group at NEXUS Global Network.
noetic.org

Diane Marie Williams is the founder and president of the Source of Synergy Foundation. She was the co-initiator with Deepak Chopra™ of one of its main projects, the Evolutionary Leaders Circle. She served as founding chair of the NGO Committee on Spirituality, Values, and Global Concerns at the United Nations in New York and is a recipient of the Spirit of the United Nations, the Golden Rule and the PEMAC Peace Awards.

sourceofsynergyfoundation.org

David Sloan Wilson, PhD, is SUNY Distinguished Professor of Biology and Anthropology at Binghamton University and president of the Evolution Institute. He has made fundamental contributions to evolutionary theory, including the books *This View of Life, Does Altruism Exist?, Evolution for Everyone,* and *Darwin's Cathedral.*

evolution-institute.org

About the
Editors

Robert Atkinson, PhD, author, educator, and developmental psychologist, is a 2017 Nautilus Book Award winner for *The Story of Our Time*. He is also the author of eight other books, including *Year of Living Deeply: A Memoir of 1969, Mystic Journey,* and *The Gift of Stories.* With a PhD in cross-cultural human development from the University of Pennsylvania and a postdoctoral fellowship at the University of Chicago, he is professor emeritus at the University of Southern Maine, director of Story Commons, and founder of the Piscataqua Peace Forum, as well as an internationally recognized authority on life-story interviewing, a pioneer in the techniques of personal myth-making and soul-making, and deeply committed to assisting the evolutionary impulse toward wholeness and unity.

robertatkinson.net

Kurt Johnson, PhD, has worked in professional science and comparative religion for more than forty years. A prominent figure on international committees, particularly at the United Nations, he is coauthor of the influential book *The Coming Interspiritual Age* and two award-winning books on science, *Nabokov's Blues* and *Fine Lines*. Long associated with New York City's Interfaith Seminary and the American Museum of Natural History, he codirects the Convergence radio series on *VoiceAmerica* and the *Convergence, Light on Light,* and *Conscious Business* e-magazines. With a PhD in evolution and ecology, he has authored more than two hundred technical scientific publications. A cofounder of the Interspiritual Dialogue with interspiritual pioneer Brother Wayne Teasdale, Kurt is a member of the Evolutionary Leaders, the UNITY EARTH network, and many other organizations.
lightonlight.us

Reverend Deborah Moldow is an ordained interfaith minister committed to assisting in the transformation of human consciousness to a culture of peace through her ministry, international peace work, interfaith efforts, speaking, and writing. She is the founder of the Garden of Light, a platform for the emerging global spirituality. She is director of the Evolutionary Leaders, a project of the Source of Synergy Foundation, which brings together visionaries committed to the acceleration of the conscious evolution of humanity in these critical times. She served for more than twenty years as the representative to the United Nations of May Peace Prevail on Earth International and has traveled the globe for peace. She leads a Spirit Salon at her home in San Miguel de Allende, Mexico.

gardenoflight.org